Creating Uncommon Worship

Richard Giles received degrees from Newcastle University in both town planning and theology, and trained for ordination at Cuddesdon. He served in a number of parishes before becoming Canon Theologian in the Diocese of Wakefield, and in 1999 was appointed Dean of Philadelphia in the Diocese of Pennsylvania. He is the author of the best selling *Re-Pitching the Tent*, now in its third edition.

Also by the same author

Re-Pitching the Tent
– the definitive guide to re-ordering your church

'a very important and well-documented argument for a radically new kind of church architecture designed to serve and inspire a new sort of Christian community'

Alison Lurie,
New York Review of Books

'Richard Giles has done the church a great service'
Ministry

'most impressive'   *Worship*

'a bold and innovative attempt to challenge, encourage and inform the church to make our buildings meet the needs of mission'

Ecclesiastical Architects and Surveyors Association Journal

Over 15,000 copies sold.

Available from the Canterbury Press in the UK and from the Liturgical Press in North America.

CREATING UNCOMMON WORSHIP

*Transforming the Liturgy
of the Eucharist*

Richard Giles

Liturgical Press
Collegeville, Minnesota
www.litpress.org

© Richard Giles 2004
Photographs by Henry Carnes and Jason DeCesare

First published in 2004 by the Canterbury Press Norwich
(a publishing imprint of Hymns Ancient & Modern Limited,
a registered charity)
St Mary's Works, St Mary's Plain,
Norwich, Norfolk, NR3 3BH

www.scm-canterburypress.co.uk

Published in the United States of America and in Canada by
the Liturgical Press, Collegeville, Minnesota 56321.

British Library Cataloguing in Publication data

A catalogue record for this book is available
from the British Library

ISBN 0-8146-1518-X

Typeset by Regent Typesetting, London
Printed and bound in the United Kingdom

CONTENTS

For Simone,
most uncommon of daughters

ACKNOWLEDGEMENTS

This book could not have been written without the
  encouragement and enthusiasm of Christine Smith at Canterbury Press
  adventurous and fun cathedral community at Philadelphia
  patience and support of my colleagues, and
  technical expertise of Jason DeCesare.

–

INTRODUCTION

The liturgy is and remains the centre of the life of the church. If this can successfully be renewed, won't that also have effects on all the areas of church activity?

(Küng, 2002, p. 285)

Chef re-interprets traditional American food. It sounds familiar, but often it's not like anything you've had before. We're a small place with limited storage and a fierce commitment to freshness.

(Menu card, Colorado Kitchen, Washington, DC)

The Sunday Liturgy at the Cathedral in Philadelphia is not all that uncommon, certainly not to us who participate in it, but it is uncommon enough to raise a few eyebrows if not hackles. It tends to be loved or hated, rather than leave one unmoved.

Our Liturgy aims at noble simplicity, and has about it a monastic feel arising from a Cistercian minimalism in vesture, symbol and movement.

Our Liturgy is theologically demanding, seeking always to give clear expression of who we are and why we are doing the things we do.

Our Liturgy is highly participatory, emphasizing at every step that it is the assembly – the 'chosen race, royal priesthood and holy nation' of 1 Peter 2.9 – that is the minister of the eucharistic action.

Our Liturgy aims to integrate the sensory and spiritual dimensions of worship to create an all-embracing experience of beauty.

Our Liturgy takes place within a liturgical space that in 2002 was stripped of its furnishings and remodelled on the pattern of a fifth-century Christian basilica, facilitating free-flowing movement for the assembly between font, ambo and altar table. Around the perimeter is a stone bench – symbolic seat of the community of the baptized – which at the east end becomes the semi-circular *presbyterium*, familiar to us from the earliest known Christian buildings, at the centre of which is the bishop's *cathedra*.

These characteristics together produce a liturgy which can have a profound effect on those who join with us to offer the eucharist, and they are often moved and exhilarated by what they have taken part in and have helped to fashion.

All this requires of course a great deal of hard work and dedication on the part of many, but liturgy at its best is deceiving in this regard: it gives few clues as to the enormous amounts of time, creativity and attention to detail that have been poured into it. The artist Andy Goldsworthy, who uses only natural materials to create structures of breathtaking beauty in the landscape, spoke of his process of creation as 'All that effort – to produce something that appears effortless'.[1]

A frequent response from our visitors is: 'This is truly wonderful, but of course . . .'. The 'but of course' refers to the apparent impossibility of doing such things in the community of faith from which they have come and to which they will return, reinvigorated for the work of liturgical renewal but perhaps also with a growing sense of frustration. They are telling us, in effect, 'but of course you could never do this where I come from'.

This book is therefore a 'but of course . . .' book. It attempts to encourage all who long for the renewal of the liturgy to take heart and to know that it is indeed possible to do good liturgy anywhere and everywhere. That being said, we really have to mean business and not just play at it. So then, turning on its head the 'but of course' lament of many of our visitors, this book offers a step-by-step procedure by which a liturgy like ours can be replicated, and indeed improved, in any parish in the world. 'But of course it can be done!'[2]

Richard Giles
Philadelphia, February 2004

Notes

1 Film: *Rivers and Tides: Goldsworthy Working with Time*, Thomas Riedelsheimer, 2003.
2 A cathedral, by definition, straddles that middle ground between upholding the norm and breaking new ground, between reassurance and adventure. The views expressed in this book therefore are not necessarily those of our bishop or diocese but of a cathedral community called to live at the edge, between the familiar and the yet-to-be-discovered. As you read this book, we invite you to enter with us into that creative tension, to bear with the inevitable loose ends and unresolved issues, and to stay faithful to the journey. For more information about the worship and life of our community, visit the cathedral website: www.philadelphiacathedral.org

PART 1 PRINCIPLES

1 PRELIMINARIES

1 Purpose

This book is offered as a practical guide to those who yearn to do something about liturgy in the local church, those who wish to create liturgies with the power to engage, inspire and transform. It is for local communities of faith that wish to emerge from long centuries of liturgical captivity to embrace liturgy as a fully participatory experience for the whole assembly.

Those of us in the main liturgical traditions of Christianity today have beautiful texts, ancient of provenance but contemporary in language, but we are not always sure how best to use them. We are not certain where to start and how far to go, in the task of bringing to life the words on the page in such a way that lives will be changed and communities empowered. What follows is a suggested approach to how such 'uncommon worship' might be accomplished.

A few things need to be said at the outset:

1 This is a book for practitioners rather than scholars. Although the attempt is made always to base practice on sound theological principle and shared liturgical experience, of prime concern throughout this book is the criterion 'Does this *mean* anything? Does this *work*?'

Once upon a time I thought that a liturgist was a clever academic with very thick glasses who spent all day in a library stack amid dusty tomes. That certainly discouraged me from thinking very much about liturgy for some time after seminary. As the pastor of a parish I felt grateful for the academic labours of others, for the end products of the liturgists in the shape of new prayer books and missals, honed in the seminar and the committee, and sent down to us hedge priests in the outback.

Now I have come to see things differently. Liturgists I now realize are the people who get things changed on the ground floor; artists, dreamers, musicians, choreographers, craftspeople and pastors who wrestle with the fascinating and fun problem of translating theory into practice on the parish front line. Gregory Dix, as usual, said it best:

> when the revisers and the bishops and the liturgists have all done their best for our rite, there would still have to be the work of the church upon it, not only to improve it, but to *use* it and pray it and give it meaning in its own life. (Dix, 1964, p. 732)

This book tells the story of the attempts made in one corner of the vineyard to use, to pray, and to give meaning in its life, to the eucharistic rite of the Church. It is a work of 'applied liturgy' rather than 'pure liturgy'. It is about what happens when a community of faith embarks on liturgical exploration understood as a journey into transformation.

A liturgist is in fact someone who weaves together these texts, and resources, and music, and images and symbols to help a community of faith become itself for the first time and to step out with joy and boldness into God's calling. The 'end product' is not therefore a prayer book or a missal, but a liberated, transformed and imagination-filled community of faith living in peace and love with God and with all those who seek God.

A new prayer book is just the beginning. Like a new house, a new prayer book needs a family to take hold of it, make it their own, and fill it with activity and affection, laughter and tears. Otherwise it will stand for ever empty and forlorn.

2 This book emerges from the particular experience of two local communities of faith – separated by the Atlantic Ocean – which for some years have striven to make liturgy a work of the whole people of God (which is of course exactly the meaning of the original Greek word λειτουργία from λεώς 'people' and ἔργον 'work').

These two faith communities – St Thomas', Huddersfield, and Philadelphia Cathedral – could not have been more different in character; one an inner-city parish in a textile town in Northern England, and one a cathedral in America's fifth largest city, located on the edge of the campus of America's oldest university. Despite their strikingly different locations and socio-religious cultural settings, they share a common experience of developing uncommon worship which has changed their lives.

This suggests that the bulk of the insights and suggestions that follow will work pretty well anywhere. A few may depend on the particular circumstances pertaining to these two locations, but my guess is that on the whole, 'where there is a will, there is a way' remains true in the vast majority of cases. As far as possible, attention will be drawn to difficulties that may arise for those facing different circumstances, and suggestions given to meet those challenges.

In any event, you will find that in this book, adaptation to local circumstances and opportunities is held to be a virtue, not a vice, and that such adaptation adds to the fun of the whole process. After all, we are here trying to *create* uncommon worship, not mimic it.

3 In the case of both of these faith communities, this book speaks about the experience of the people of God working at its worship in the local church, which is not necessarily identical in every detail to the official stance of bishops or liturgical commissions, or to the written formularies of the Church.

By definition, worship that is uncommon is a little different, and communities that labour at it tend to live life at the edge, pushing the envelope (and sometimes the patience of diocesan authorities) as far as they dare. So don't shoot the pianist, or the bishop; just the author.

The liturgical experience that forms the basis of this book is that of the local community of faith 'at home' on a regular Sunday, rather than 'on parade' for some special celebratory occasion when all the world and his dog shows up.

4 Although written from an Anglican perspective, this book is designed for all those who would know more of the risk-taking adventure which liturgy can become, irrespective of allegiance or label. This mirrors the approach of Philadelphia Cathedral which, although *domkirche* of the Episcopal Diocese of Pennsylvania, aims to be a home for pilgrims and adventurers from all kinds of religious backgrounds and none.

Nevertheless, the particular frame of reference for this book is the ordo of the Western Church and the liturgical life and experience of the Anglican, Lutheran and Roman Communions which continue to shape it. Those from other traditions, many of which are experiencing something of a liturgical explosion themselves, will I hope also find something useful here, and applicable to their own situations. We all have so much to learn from one another, and this is one of the strongest pointers that we are on the right track as we share excitedly the different insights each of us has glimpsed at each turning of the path on this glorious breathtaking journey.

2 Background

The last fifty years have seen an extraordinary transformation of liturgical life in the mainstream Western Church. All three major liturgical traditions – Roman, Anglican and Lutheran – have given their liturgical documents a complete and major overhaul, providing radically renewed eucharistic rites that now bear a striking resemblance to one another's liturgical practice. As Dan Stevick[1] often reminds us, these new resources across our three traditions have more in common with each other than with the books they replaced. That is some leap forward.

To attend an act of liturgical worship in the mainstream Church today is an experience totally transformed from the same activity fifty years ago. Language, form, layout, music and vesture have all changed, in some cases beyond recognition, and the common theme everywhere is that the liturgical action is now the work of the whole people of God, not just the clergy. We have taken ownership of who we are and what we are doing. Here is a revolution indeed.

These events, flowing to a large extent from the reforms of the Second Vatican Council in the early 1960s, and from parallel initiatives in the other communions, are the fruit of the Liturgical Movement of the early 1900s. They have brought about a wholesale change, not just in the way liturgy is *experienced* by the faithful Sunday by Sunday in the local church, but more significantly in the way it is *understood*.

The theological themes of baptismal covenant, the church as a community of shared ministry, and the priesthood as a calling shared by the whole community of faith assembled for worship, are all clearly expressed in the liturgical texts that now enrich the Church's life.

Furthermore, creative and inspired leadership has ensured that in all three traditions these liturgical texts have not been allowed to lie dormant in missals and prayer books, as jewels of academic scholarship, but have been released into the bloodstream of the Church. They have been given vocal and sensory expression in the local church with great vitality, beauty and joy. They have been enriched with new music, new vesture and art, and have brought about a total reappraisal of the spaces we need to allow liturgy to be celebrated effectively and freely. As the Church strives to do justice to the liturgies it has created, old spaces have been reordered and new ones created, allowing the people of God to awaken fully to the wonder of who they are.

3 Present situation

Despite this immense leap forward, problems remain. All too often we imagine that the introduction of a new eucharistic text is all there is to liturgical renewal. We say we've been there and done that, and if we haven't quite got the T-shirt, at least it's in the mail.

In reality, liturgical renewal involves the creation of a whole new way of doing liturgy, a process of transformation whereby the community of faith arrives at a place where it sees and understands everything it says and does in a totally new light. No text, however poetic or inspired, can carry the weight of this task by itself.

New texts demand creative liturgical leadership, new music, new vesture and new furniture, and a reappraisal of the space in which the assembly gathers. We know only too well that it is possible to celebrate new texts in precisely the same way as the old, so that the process of renewal is sabotaged, although this is more the case with Anglicans and Lutherans, who have lacked the wholesale approach of their Roman cousins.

The texts cannot do the job that is rightly ours. 'Accumulation of facts doesn't set one free, what one does with, how one experiences, those facts is what sets one's heart dancing in freedom' (Fowler, 1995, p. 131). What George Fowler writes about theological study is equally true of liturgy.

It is far too easy for us to introduce the new rite and leave it at that. Timidity or inertia can result in delay in initiating the demanding parish programme of exploration and learning that must accompany the texts. In avoiding the upheaval of inaugurating new music, or the confrontation of moving the furniture, we end up with the worst of both worlds. The traditionalists are irritated by the new rites, while the progressives are frustrated by the mere recitation of these rites without fervour or imagination, in ways which rob them of their potential to transform. No one is satisfied, and 'liturgical renewal' is reduced to just another movement which came and went in the life of the Church, and which now can be quietly forgotten.

Although the Roman Communion – coming late to worship in the vernacular and to the reformation of the Church which Vatican II represented – has enjoyed a more thorough and comprehensive experience of renewed liturgy in which everything was of a piece, even there the winds of change have been getting chilly. In recent years Rome has been exhibiting tensions inseparable from any headlong dash into a new era, especially in an organization so centralized and controlled. In many quarters liturgical renewal is seen as exemplifying all that is wrong with a church that has made too many concessions to a changing world.

The malaise in the liturgical life of the Church is particularly evident in the United States, where both the Roman and Anglican Communions are experiencing stagnation, even retrenchment, where liturgy is concerned. For too many faith communities, 'good liturgy' is seen to consist of doing exceptionally well that which has always been done: in liturgical matters they are creationists rather than evolutionists.

Roman Catholics in the USA are experiencing something of a quiet but determined turning back of the clock. After fifty heady and dazzling years of bold and adventurous exploration in the wake of the Second Vatican Council, the voices of conservatism and restraint are not just holding the line, but undoing some of the reforms. The replacement in 2000 of *Art and Environment in Catholic Worship* – a publication that enriched the life of every liturgical church in the world – by *Built of Living Stones*, a new set of guidelines revised in a more conservative direction, was a development of grave significance for those who wish to continue the journey instead of staying put or turning back.

In his intervention in the Second Vatican Council on 22 October 1962, Giovanni Montini (later Paul VI) identified 'simplification' and 'comprehensibility' as the two crucial marks of liturgical renewal (Hebblethwaite, 1993, p. 309). It would now seem that these characteristics are losing their lustre. The progressive Catholics, who rode the crest of a wave organizing such events as the life-changing 'Form/Reform' conference on liturgical space, now experience a trough in their energy and influence. Reforms of a liberalizing nature, such as the admission of girls as servers at the altar, are introduced only to be withdrawn, subjecting the progressives to further demoralization.

The Episcopal Church, having produced in 1979 a new *Book of Common Prayer* which led the way for the whole Anglican Communion and which in particular brought the Baptismal Covenant to the theological and liturgical centre stage, now seems thoroughly exhausted by the process. Of course it has had other things to contend with, not least having bishops from the Third World on its back for suggesting that, when it comes to moral theology, scientific knowledge of the human condition should be given at least some consideration alongside an obscure text from the Book of Leviticus, but that's another story. For whatever reason, there is today little fire in the belly of American liturgists, and despite a few glorious exceptions, the regular diet of Sunday worship for most Episcopalians is a case of burying one's nose in the *Book of Common Prayer* (1979) and working one's way steadily and stolidly from page 355 to page 366.

In England the comparatively more varied resources of *Common Worship* (2000) and the many alternatives it provides also has its pitfalls. Fumbling of books and flicking of pages – at the altar no less than in the pew – distract mightily and noisily from good liturgy, and the reason why so many presiding ministers feel it necessary to interrupt the flow with proclamations about eucharistic prayers and page numbers is a mystery second only to the eucharist itself.

Whatever our liturgical tradition, therefore, we have reached something of a plateau on our journey onwards and upwards, with something of a stalemate between those who view things from different perspectives.

This is no place for us to think about liturgy. We can take heart, however, from the many and various voices, from all kinds of different points of view, who remind us of what liturgy *can* be like, once we have a taste for travel.

4 Some fresh starting points

Kathleen Norris, in *The Cloister Walk*, an appreciation of monastic life from a Protestant's point of view, has a wonderful story of her New York City gay hairdresser with whom she got into conversation about monks and nuns. The hairdresser, having been ostracized by his home church for being gay, had given up on religion until he found his way to the Trappist Abbey at Spencer, Massachusetts. The rest must be told in his own words:

> 'Boy, did I love that,' he said, 'just sitting in that church, the way they let you come to church with them. They don't preach at you, they let you experience it for yourself.'
>
> He stilled the scissors for a moment and said, 'You know, I've never felt so close to God before or since. It blew me the *@!! away.' (Norris, 1996, p. 70)

Getting blown away by God is a theme taken up by Annie Dillard, who writes powerfully on liturgical space as a danger zone:

> On the whole, I do not find Christians, outside of the catacombs, sufficiently sensible of conditions. Does anyone have the foggiest idea what sort of power we so blithely invoke? Or, as I suspect, does no one believe a word of it?
>
> The churches are children, playing on the floor with their chemistry sets, mixing up a batch of TNT to kill a Sunday morning.
>
> It is madness to wear ladies' straw hats and velvet hats to church; we should all be wearing crash helmets. Ushers should issue life preservers and signal flares; they should lash us to our pews.
>
> For the sleeping God may wake someday and take offense, or the waking God may draw us out to where we can never return. (Dillard, 1982, p. 52–3)

The common thread to all such insights is the transformative power of worship at its best. A worship service, says the religious sociologist Keith Hadaway, should be like 'a raft ride down a mountain river, with exciting passages that leave us breathless and calm places where we sit and contemplate – with bends and curves where we cannot see where we are going' (Hadaway, 2001, p. 82).

Although eager to see churches grow, Hadaway is convinced that 'programs for growth' will not work. Instead, growth is a natural by-product of a community of faith which, centred on God and at peace with itself, enters into a journey towards transformation.

The sad truth is that, even in communities of faith belonging to so-called 'liturgical churches', there is precious little excitement, practically no silence, and zero unpredictability.

The overriding purpose of a community of faith is not growth, or worship, or education or social action, or any such activity in itself. 'The business of a church is to change people,' says Hadaway, quoting Peter Drucker (p. 11). We need liberation 'into a new state of seeing and being' (p. 87), and our liturgies should be like the parables of Jesus which were, according to Norman Perrin, 'the bearers of the reality' (p. 88).

If we are committed to the process of transformation, unafraid to go forward in the discomforting company of Jesus of Nazareth, then we too can proclaim liberation, 'giving people new images that react violently with the notions, beliefs and habits that keep them in bondage' (p. 86).

Talk of imagery leads us back to Kathleen Norris, who quotes Bishop John V. Taylor who once wrote that 'imagination and faith are the same thing, giving substance to our hopes and reality to the unseen' (Norris, 1996, p. 65). She goes on to liken the process of growing into faith to that of writing a poem, an insight that again can be equally applied to liturgy:

> It takes time, patience, discipline, a listening heart. There is precious little certainty, and often great struggling, but also joy in our discoveries. (p. 61)

> To make the poem of our faith, we must learn not to settle for a false certitude but to embrace ambiguity and mystery. (p. 62)

These insights, which call on us to engage our imaginations in faith and in worship which is more metaphor than cold hard fact, will not suit those for whom liturgy is primarily a matter of textual accuracy and rubrical precision. Our encounter with God in the liturgy will always elude such things: God is always waiting for us around the next corner.

A third voice we may bring to bear on this topic is that of Enzo Bianchi, founder of the ecumenical monastic community of men and women at Bose in northern Italy. From a small beginning of a handful of pioneers in the late 1960s, Bose now numbers 70 members with houses in Jerusalem, Assisi and Bari. Although based on the Rule of St Benedict, it is a new foundation which has thought new thoughts and dreamt new dreams about how this great Rule might be reinterpreted today with fresh vigour.

Enzo Bianchi wrote that 'Liturgy is the wellspring of the life of the community' (Bianchi, 2002, p. 13), and all who stumble on this community are taken by surprise by the power and beauty of the worship of the community, which, like everything else

The community of Bose singing the Divine Office

about the place, has been rethought from basic principles. The Daily Office is three-fold – morning, midday and evening – and the eucharist celebrated on Sundays and Holy Days only. The community is overwhelmingly lay, and is made up of roughly equal numbers of men and women, whose antiphonal singing, women on one side, men on the other, revolutionizes our understanding of monastic music.

Enzo Bianchi speaks and writes with great effectiveness on all aspects of the spiritual life, but one which is pertinent to our discussion of liturgy is his emphasis on the communal life.

In many a parish, the term 'community' remains a nice idea or an unattainable ideal. Bianchi explains that community isn't for real until it causes us to experience what he calls 'the crisis of our self-image', that 'painful but necessary beginning of conversion in which our unreal, idealized "I" . . . is shattered' (Bianchi, 2002, p. 2). This is a tough call in the context of 'the current cultural myth of spontaneity and permanent adolescence', but we can take heart. In the midst of this struggle to die to self in order to be reborn, our spiritual experience is 'above all the experience of *being preceded*: it is God who goes before us, searches for us, calls us'. It is also the experience of '*discovering that we are children of God*'.

This experience then, of dying to self, of being reborn, of knowing ourselves to be children of God, is what worship in community should open up to us. 'Faith', says Bianchi, 'leads us to a *"genuine experience"* of God' (Bianchi, 2002, p. 1). Moreover, doctrinal correctness is not the issue here. Our liturgies should lead us into a real encounter with God, not just into a thinking and praying session with a departed presence: 'Anyone who believes in God also needs to experience God – correct ideas about God are not enough.' Such encounter is what our liturgy must engender within us, or it is pointless.

It is instructive to apply these criteria of liberation, transformation, the kindling of imagination and a genuine experience of God to the regular worship of the community of faith to which we ourselves belong. How does it begin to shape up? Are our liturgies controlled and contained, or do they threaten to leap off the page and bite us?

Our communities of faith will need to develop the theological and imaginative skills to realize what these texts are actually *saying*, about God and about God's people, and will allow themselves to be shaped and reformed by their subversive message. Far from being a method of control (not unknown in the history of the Church), the liturgy will become an uncontrollable force for renewal and transformation, and not just in the Church but in the world too. But what we need are risk-takers, and, up until now, 'risk' and 'liturgy' have not been thought of as two words which have any connection.

Writing in 1995, William Seth Adams spoke enthusiastically of the 'permissive rubrics of the [American] Prayer Book' that 'invite the shaman's touch and imagination, for the sake of the health of the community'. Adams' only wrong note was an incurable optimism, for the liturgical shaman has proved to be an elusive creature, pushed to the edge of extinction by the swarms of the priestly gatekeepers of the ritual mystery who, clutching prayer book in one hand and canons in the other, seek to stifle creativity and eradicate all traces of local life and colour.

One of the tragedies of the Episcopal Church today is that its liturgical formulation emasculates the laity. At our cathedral in Philadelphia new faces appear at the Sunday Liturgy every week, many of them in their twenties. As they emerge from the liturgy, many will bear that anxious, haunted look of someone who hasn't found a prayer book or hymnal in the pew, indeed hasn't even found a pew. If afterwards over coffee, when asked about their background, they answer 'cradle Episcopalian', then I know we are doomed. In most cases their liturgical training, so heavily dependent on rigid notions of place, text and music, disables them from participation in liturgy which enfolds, energizes and transforms. Worship is seen as beginning on one page and ending on another, something to be got through with the minimum of inconvenience and on the strict understanding that nothing will change. They have been sold cheap liturgy and have become hooked on it.

The notion of being caught up into the eucharistic action of the ordo of the Mass, common to the whole Western Church, and into the fun and adventure of re-expressing its timeless message with new voices and fresh images, is totally lost on them. Of course we are blessed with members of our own tradition who discover creative liturgy and lap it up, as thirsty desert travellers at a green oasis, but those from different traditions or none are just as likely, if not more so, to find their home with us.

Those who arrive at our doors as good honest heathens are better able to enter into the mysteries of Christ, because they bring with them no baggage, and have eyes to see and ears to hear, and imaginations to be stirred. What does that say about all our liturgical toil in conventions, revision committees and seminaries?

Herein lies the problem. Splendid resources and rich contemporary texts seem to be no match for those determined to reduce liturgy to the mindless recitation of words on a page, preferably in a book at least decades, if not centuries, out of date.

If Adams' optimism is to be well founded, the Church will need:

- Ordained leaders retrained in presiding in the assembly, able to articulate the theological basis of all that the assembly is and does, to draw forth the gifts of the community, and to imbue the proceedings with dignity, style and grace.
- Assemblies hungry for spiritual maturity and theological understanding, unafraid to let go, and eager to explore new territory in the journey of faith.
- Eucharistic rites which give framework rather than formula,[2] providing merely the building blocks of the ordo of the Western Rite, leaving the community of faith elbow room to do some fine brick-laying and joinery to clad the basic structure with skill and flair.
- Resource materials from mainstream liturgical churches across the world, collected and classified to enable those who plan and preside to quarry material from a variety of sources to enrich the worship of their faith community.

It should not be supposed for one minute that good liturgy is of significance only to those aesthetes interested in that kind of thing. The way the church does liturgy, the work of the people of God, will exert an enormous impact on both our understanding of God and on our ability to be and to share good news.

Teaching the faith

Archbishop Thomas Cranmer, the driving force behind the English liturgical renewal in the sixteenth century, was well aware that the ferment of new ideas from Continental Europe would go nowhere if they remained the preserve of theologians and philosophers. They had to be released into the bloodstream of the Church, and this demanded their expression in the regular Sunday worship of the ordinary parish, and in the space in which that worship was celebrated. As well as providing new texts therefore, Cranmer gave instructions as to how the parish churches of England were to be adapted to make sense of, and to bring to life, the words on the page. Text and space were inextricably bound.

Meeting in Dublin in 1995, the Fifth International Anglican Liturgical Consultation reinforced this connection:

> Whatever their form, buildings shape the experience of worship. For this reason they inevitably express an ecclesiology, and, for good or ill, that easily becomes the self-understanding of the congregation.
>
> Appropriately ordered, buildings express an understanding of the church as a community which shares in the celebration of a foretaste of the kingdom. Such an understanding emerges when the worship space or spaces enable people to relate fruitfully to God and to one another.[3]

Cranmer was before his time in this regard, being well aware how human nature works. He knew it wouldn't be enough to talk about the eucharist as a communal meal, nor even to translate and rewrite the Mass in the vernacular. No, he knew full well that he must lay hands on the space and on the liturgical furniture. So he took the revolutionary step of requiring the altar table, hitherto firmly stuck at the east end of the church building, to be brought down into the chancel and turned through 90 degrees. This enabled the congregation to gather around the table, to see and feel how it looked, to begin to understand who they were and what they were doing together as God's people. The renewal of the Church which the Reformers were striving to bring about was no longer a treatise, or an intellectual concept, but that which 'we have seen with our eyes, what we have looked at and touched with our hands' (1 John 1.1). The ideas of the Reformation were enfleshed and made real through the physical changes to the actual experience of Sunday worship in the local church.

Exactly the same experience was shared by the Roman Communion following the Second Vatican Council. The Council enriched the whole Christian Church with its Spirit-filled theology and the beautiful, poetic language of its new liturgical texts, but the bishops knew full well that unless these new gifts and insights were worked through in terms of physical space, the faithful would remain largely untouched. Hence the insistence that overnight the altars were brought forward, that the priest stood behind facing the people, and that the tabernacle housing the Blessed Sacrament was relocated in a less conspicuous place.[4]

The fact that now, forty years on, there are attempts in some quarters to put the clock back is proof enough that the Bishops of the Council were onto something. The arrangement of our liturgical furniture, rather than a theological position paper or academic treatise, is the *real* indicator of how we feel about God and our fellow worshippers.

Sharing good news

The evangelistic impact of good worship cannot be ignored by mainstream churches, which in the Western world are perishing on the vine. Churches in the de-Christianized culture of Western Europe have learned that in designing worship appropriate for urban mission areas it is necessary 'to bring together "Him who is totally other" and that "which is genuinely local"; to integrate with "universality of form" that which is "informal and flexible"' (Saxbee, 1994, p. 70).

> The only way to engage the cycle of transformation into a new way of seeing and being is by disrupting our hardened, taken-for-granted understanding of reality. That is exactly what Jesus did. The purposes of Jesus' proverbs and parables were disruption, not instruction. They challenge the hearer, not to radical obedience, but to radical questioning. They were verbal 'hand grenades' thrown by Jesus to blow up our settled, taken-for-granted worlds – our comfortable prisons. (Hadaway, 2001, p. 88)

If we can imagine a *whole liturgy* – not just a homily – that disrupts as much as it consoles, that offers us alternative images, that reshapes the way we imagine, that enables us to react violently against the forces, internal and external, that enslave us, then we shall be on the way to a new state of seeing and being. Perhaps also we shall no longer need to ask questions about why the Church has lost its way and speaks no longer to the young.

The secular press continues to be fascinated by the burgeoning expressions of how young people are finding new ways to become church. 'Hip New Churches Pray to a Different Drummer' was a headline which made it to the front page of *The New York Times* in February 2004, and described various emerging or postmodern churches across the United States, each of which draw hundreds of seekers, and which together represent a new wave of growth in the current development of Christianity.

These new churches are base communities for the wealthy, which set a premium on shared meals, on working things out together, on non-hierarchical structures, and on the revival of pre-Enlightenment mystical and liturgical practices. The details hardly matter; the point is that the emerging churches capture the loyalty of a significant proportion of under thirties who have found wanting both the liturgy of the Church and the highly polished 'performances' of the mega-churches.

These young people embrace new untried ecclesial formations because they see in them a form of worship which draws them into communion with God and with each other. One such seeker, a 26-year-old graphic designer who had given up mainstream religion after high school, is quoted as saying, 'There is no question what we're doing. We're talking about Jesus. We're taking communion. We're just doing it together, as a journey.'

5 Terminology

In what I hope will prove to be an ecumenical-friendly book, not all the terminology all the time will be familiar, and I have tried to use terms which are most widely used or which make the most sense. Some are listed here:

Assembly is used to describe the body of worshippers offering the eucharist. This is well established in Roman usage, and seems more theologically positive than 'congregation', which somehow suggests a gathering of individuals rather than of a community of faith. The General Notes of *Common Worship* (2000) state clearly that 'Holy Communion is celebrated by the whole people of God gathered for worship' (p. 158), and the Vatican II document *Instruction on the Worship of the Eucharistic Mystery* speaks of the need to 'explain the doctrine of the royal priesthood to which the faithful are consecrated by rebirth and the anointing of the Holy Spirit' (in Flannery (ed.), 1996, I.11).

Presiding minister is used to describe the ordained person presiding over the celebration of the eucharist. As an Anglican caught between the 'president' (UK) and the 'presider' (USA), and looking in vain for help from the Roman Missal which refers only to 'priest' or 'celebrant', I have gone for the Lutheran 'presiding minister'.

Although the Vatican II Document *Instruction on the Worship of the Eucharistic Mystery* speaks freely of those exercising ministerial priesthood as 'ministers', and refers to the assembly as exercising the 'common priesthood of the faithful', rubrics of the Roman Missal slip back into old usage by consistently referring to the presiding minister as 'priest'. The text of the Missal refers to 'celebrant', but that is not much help in that all members of the assembly gathered to make eucharist should be understood as celebrants. Perhaps we could use 'chief celebrant', but that has a more hierarchical ring to it than 'presiding minister', as well as being associated with the practice of concelebration by presbyters.

Presbyter is used to describe the second order of the ordained ministry. 'Presbyter' is derived from the Greek word meaning 'elder' and thus has New Testament authenticity, whereas 'priest' in the New Testament is used to refer to Jesus himself or to the whole community of faith, never to an individual minister or believer. The word 'priest' came into use in the medieval period, and although it is derived etymologically from 'presbyter' rather than from Greek or Latin terms for priest, it is too narrow a definition, and too redolent of clericalism, to be appropriate in an era when the priesthood is being reclaimed by the community of faith.

Interestingly (and unhelpfully) Anglicans and some Lutherans retained at the Reformation the word 'priest' for the second order of ministry, despite its lack of New Testament credentials and its overtones of sacerdotalism. Although Anglicans in the UK have yet to grasp this nettle (for some, 'presbyter' is tainted by its proposed use in abortive reunion schemes with other ecclesial bodies), American Anglicans have been bolder, restoring the use of 'presbyter' in the *Book of Common Prayer* (1979), albeit interchangeably with 'priest', with the latter gaining the upper hand. Still, half a loaf is better than none, and in other provinces of the Anglican Communion it is used more widely.

Pastor is used as the generic for the ordained minister with responsibility for a parish or church. This is by far the most ecumenical term as it is used by all traditions in the United States, including Rome but excluding the Episcopal Church, which likes to retain those quaint old English terms like 'rector' and occasionally 'vicar'. Interestingly, 'parish priest' is the norm across Roman–Anglican boundaries in England, where the use of 'pastor' is restricted to the Protestant or Evangelical churches. 'Parish priest' would however be difficult for the majority of Lutherans, as well as associating priesthood with a person rather than a community, so 'pastor' it is.

Eucharist is used always to describe the central act of Christian worship which has so many other names, depending on our tradition: Mass, Holy Communion, Lord's Supper, etc. Here we have gone with the Greek original which now seems to have won general acceptance in all liturgical churches. Although rather cryptic, and unhelpful to the newcomer, it seems to have stuck.

Liturgical space is used to describe the area in which worship takes place, and *church building* is used to denote the building that houses the liturgical space. Both these terms are used in an attempt to drag us away (albeit kicking and screaming) from the use of the word 'church' to describe anything other than the community that inhabits this space and this building.

Ambo is used to describe the single piece of furniture at which the Scriptures are both read and interpreted. In the early Church its use was universal, but it was gradually replaced by the dual symbols of lectern and pulpit, probably as a result of increasing clericalism. The ambo is now making a comeback in many liturgical reordering projects.

Altar table is used to describe the central piece of furniture in the liturgical space, both parts of the term necessary to do justice to the many faceted meanings of this focus of both sacred meal and sacrificial worship.

Notes

1 Dan Stevick was Professor of Liturgics and Homiletics, Episcopal Divinity School, Cambridge, Mass., from 1974 to 1990. He is the author of *Baptismal Moments, Baptismal Meanings* (New York: Church Publishing, 1987).
2 For example, 'Rite Three' of the Book of Common Prayer (1979).
3 'The Dublin Report: Renewing the Anglican Eucharist' in Rosenthal and Currie, 1997.
4 'Historians will someday conclude that the decision to "turn the altar around", so that the priest would face the congregation during Mass, did more to unglue Roman Catholicism than the Protestant Reformation' (Day, 1998, p. 132).

2 COMPONENTS OF LITURGICAL ASSEMBLY

When the assembly of God's faithful converge on a particular building to offer worship, a number of things happen at once. All need to be acknowledged, and accommodated, or channelled, or in some cases even relegated, for the common good. Where different needs or activities conflict, a decision must be made about priorities. What are these different components of assembly?

1 Gathering

Gathering is in itself a mark of the counter-culture which is Christianity. Our Western culture has long emphasized the virtues of individualism. We should 'do our own thing', we should express our thoughts, be ourselves, live life to the full, just 'go for it', come what may and at whatever cost to wider society.

This is the age when our hard-won liberty is defined in terms of the freedom to concrete over green fields, to guzzle gas with macho vehicles that should be jeered off our streets, to water the driveway as well as the lawn, to keep our swimming pool full in a drought. In this culture of self, the simple act of riding a train to work is seen as a monstrous inconvenience instead of an act of sharing resources with the rest of humankind. We have lost the larger view.

The very act of gathering, of getting together, puts us immediately in a direction in life which is diametrically opposed to the prevailing mores of our society. That's a good start, and reconnects us immediately to the first Christian communities which were perceived as such a shocking, and exhilarating, new departure to the people of their day. These early Christian groups were deeply counter-cultural.

Elaine Pagels ponders the attraction of these early communities of faith linked to Jesus of Nazareth: 'From the beginning, what attracted outsiders who walked into a gathering of Christians . . . was the presence of a group joined by a spiritual power into an extended family' (Pagels, 2003, p. 6). By simply gathering on the Lord's day, as Christians have done from the first days, by forming a genuine community not just in word but in deed, the assembly bucks the trend of society. In so doing we are allowing ourselves to be shaped by God, and thereby place ourselves in a position to offer humankind fresh hope. In gathering for liturgy we are putting ourselves on the line, placing ourselves at risk by this spiritual surrender: 'participation in liturgy', says Don Saliers, 'requires our humanity at full stretch' (Saliers, 1994, p. 28).

It is far from being a question of grim sacrifice and sweaty toil, however. Gathering for worship releases the gifts within us and enables us to rise towards our full human potential. It is a thing of beauty which brings out the best in us: 'Christian liturgy forms us in certain characteristic ways of being human . . . The very act of gathering is a slow, inexorable dance in which we assemble in the name of and by invitation of Jesus' (Saliers, 1994, p. 28).

2 Worship

We gather because we want to worship God. Gathering for worship is a God-centred activity which takes us beyond ourselves into the realm of God's presence and sovereignty. This too is a deeply counter-cultural activity. Made aware by God's grace that the human being is not, to everyone's surprise, the centre of the universe around which the planets fly in orbit, we come gratefully, joyously, not believing our good fortune, to encounter God, the originator and sustainer of all that is held in being. We want to shout and we just want to gaze; we want to dance and we just want to be still; we want the world to sing with us, and we want to be alone. When we worship we become like people in love, with God.

In worship too there is the strange paradox of the role of the community around us. Our fellow-worshippers are at the same time essential but irrelevant. Because we are caught up in something so much bigger than ourselves, like a crowd at a football match, those alongside us, around us, are not the centre of attention, even though we desperately need them to be with us. When a goal is about to be scored, people jump to their feet, straining to see, intent only on the goal mouth, oblivious to who and what is going on immediately around them, yet fully aware they are but one individual in a mighty roaring crowd. In worship that engenders a true experience of God, we too will be caught up in moments that leave us breathless before the wonder of God, moments in which we shall have become oblivious of those around us, yet fully aware of our being just one among a countless host.

This of course in no way excuses what we in the Anglican tradition might call the '8 o'clock syndrome' of those who attend worship in order to avoid other people. In liturgy that is full and rewarding our need to interact with the fellow members of our community is absolute, non-negotiable, while at the same time we shall, in a mature community of faith, be aware that in gathering for worship we look beyond each other to God in our midst.

3 Building community

The assembly comes together because we want to 'be church'. Gathering is a social activity. We want to be with fellow Christians, to be strengthened and inspired by their companionship. We want to see each other, to bask in the warmth, to dream dreams with each other of what might be achieved in the power of God, 'receiving ourselves and one another as gifts' (Saliers, 1994, p. 32).

Enzo Bianchi (2002) identifies the distinctive Christian spirit as bearing 'an attitude of communion and not consumerism' (p. 14). This too is a counter-cultural activity, in which our primary concern always is the other person, a spiritual endeavour which in 1975 Paul VI recognized as the building of what he named a 'Civilization of Love'.

The recurring theme of the apostle Paul's attempts to set his fledgling churches on the road to strength and maturity was his appeal that they determine the value of things, including all spiritual gifts, on the basis of whether or not they helped to build up the body. Paul favoured prophets over those who spoke in tongues, for example, for the simple reason that 'those who prophesy build up the church' (1 Cor. 14.4). Every other consideration was secondary. He likens his own role to that of 'a skilled master builder' (1 Cor. 3.10), precisely because he saw 'building up' as the most urgent need within the infant Christian Church, and the primary task of those with oversight.

This task of building a community of faith which appeared to its surrounding culture as startlingly new and powerful was the secret of the success and influence for the tiny embattled Church of the first century. Two things stand out among the characteristics of the first Christians: their generosity, even towards those for whom they had no responsibility except under Christ's law of love; and their chaste way of life amid a culture of excess and depravity:

> For the people called Christians . . . contempt of death is obvious to us every day, and also their self-control in sexual matters . . . they also include people who, in self-discipline . . . in matters of food and drink, and in their keen pursuit of justice, have attained a level not inferior to that of genuine philosophers.[1]

There is no shortage of opportunities in today's culture for the Christian community of faith to develop a simple, generous, disciplined and sacrificial way of life which would take our society by storm. Our gathering as an assembly is the primary time each week when we are reminded of, and equipped for, this new (and truly scandalous) way of living.

4 Journey

In a contemporary culture where individuals in pursuit of success spend so much of their time giving the impression that they have 'arrived', it is a beautiful thing that the Church should exult in its conviction that we are a community that never arrives. At the end of our brief span on earth the Christian comes to realize that he/she has just begun. This conviction that the community of faith is always on a journey is a refreshing tonic to a jaded world. In this way it is able to give flavour to the society in which it is set, fulfilling its calling to be 'salt of the earth' (Matt. 5.13).

The whole Judaeo-Christian story is a traveller's tale. Moreover, it is a cautionary tale which warns that coming to a halt, settling down and building bigger barns is usually a sign that decline and fall is imminent.

The Israelites as portrayed in the Pentateuch of the Hebrew Scriptures were people on a journey who encountered God on the move. They were a nomadic tribe who had wandered around the Middle East, settling for a time wherever pasture or food was available, in a ceaseless search that eventually led them to Egypt, where one day they woke up to find themselves no longer honoured guests, but slaves.

The Jewish, Christian and Islamic traditions are united in their devotion to Abraham the 'wandering Aramean' (Deut. 26.5) as spiritual father and ancestor, and indeed share a common classification as 'Abrahamic faiths'. The fundamental insight into our common heritage can be glimpsed in a single word from the first verse of Genesis 12: 'go'.

> Now the Lord said to Abram [later to be called Abraham] 'Go from your country and your kindred and your father's house to the land that I shall show you. I will make of you a great nation, and I will bless you, and make your name great, so that you will be a blessing.' (Gen. 12.1–2)

Ever since, those faithful to any of these three traditions have been called to be people on the move, people without a place to call their own, people journeying in response to God's call. The wonder of Abraham's response to God's call is that 'he set out, not knowing where he was to go' (Heb. 11.8). There was no question here of a relocation package with full removal expenses, but of a journey into the unknown; we too in our generation are called to this perilous but rewarding adventure.

The Israelites' escape from captivity in Egypt led only to a further punishing journey, lasting 40 years, through the desert of the Sinai peninsula. Throughout this period, however, the vision of a people of God faithful in their journeying flickered on, and was never extinguished. They saw in nature and in the events of each day the hand of God leading them forward:

> The Lord went in front of them in a pillar of cloud by day, to lead them along the way, and in a pillar of fire by night, to give them light, so that they might travel by day and by night. Neither the pillar of cloud by day nor the pillar of fire by night left its place in front of the people. (Ex. 13.21–22)

Their transformation from tent people into Temple people, with a state, a monarch and a capital city, was a long time coming and, though it gave them stability and security, robbed them of their essential nature as God's spiritual nomads. They became static and centralized, a prey to all the neuroses that come with territorial possession, more anxious about giving an inch of ground than about honouring the God who had called them into being as chosen and special.

Their rediscovery of their nomadic roots, following the later destruction of the Temple, and the Exile, although catastrophic, enabled the Jews to re-invent themselves as a people of the home and of the synagogue, dispersed throughout the world. Today, however, we can see how the reoccupation of the territory understood as theirs by divine right brings with it a recurrence of those neuroses of territorialism that in the end bring down every earthly empire, denying us spiritual authenticity in the process.

The teaching and practice of Jesus of Nazareth, who told stories about the foolishness of building more barns, who urged his listeners to take no thought for the morrow, and who ordered his followers 'to take nothing for their journey' (Mark 6.8), revived the ancient tradition of travelling light through this world, but ever since the concordat with the Emperor Constantine in AD 312, the Christian Church has for the most part spent the last two thousand years trying to ignore the teaching and example of Jesus in this regard.

It has seemed to fully enjoy every minute of privilege and power that subsequently came its way, and has built temples with great gusto. Never mind what the New Testament says; we like temples, sanctuaries, altars and priests, and we like staying in the same place, doing what we've always done.

Every now and then a Francis of Assisi or a Charles de Foucauld will inspire or shame us into recapturing something of our spiritual heritage as people of the road, but we are a generation of associates rather than members, oblates rather than professed, and prefer our religion at arm's length. Here it is slightly more controllable and slightly less disruptive of our cherished notions and our ordered routine.

This is precisely why our Sunday Liturgy may be the only place where we can be recalled to our essential nature as people on a journey: tired, a little afraid, not sure when or where the next stop will be, but exulting in the call of God to go forward, and in the 'glorious company' and 'goodly fellowship' (in the words of the Te Deum) whom God gives us as companions on the way.

The first description applied to the followers of Jesus, as recorded in the Acts of the Apostles, was that of those 'who belonged to the Way' (Acts 9.2), and in the account of Paul's defence before Felix the Governor, Paul refers to himself as a follower of 'the Way' (Acts 24.14), and we are further told that Felix himself was 'rather well informed about the Way' (Acts 24.22).

Only in Antioch (subsequent to the first description of 'the Way') were the disciples 'first called Christians' (Acts 11.26), and it is interesting to speculate how differently Christian history might have unfolded had the original designation prevailed.

Had the designation 'the Way' survived, we would perhaps have had a faith that was more humble and dependent upon God, and have been less certain that the dogmatic definitions of the fourth century, with all its violent upheaval and religio-political intrigues, gave us the final and incontrovertible revelation as to the mystery of who Jesus is.

We should have been more likely to have understood revelation as a gradual process, and definitive truth for ever elusive, as we concentrated on Jesus' commands to love God and neighbour, rather than on doctrinal purity or ecclesiological pedigree.

Equally important, the body of followers of Jesus would have continued to rejoice in a name which identified us as people of the road, people on a journey, followers of the itinerant teacher, the 'Son of Man who had nowhere to lay his head' (Matt. 8.20).

The life of the Christian community was, in its formative period, as was the life of the Hebrew community originally, a life of journey and pilgrimage, of encountering God on the road. Now as then, temple-building has been found to be a practice which gradually drains a faith tradition of its energy, as it settles down to a static lifestyle and begins to worry about roof repairs, attendance figures and giving levels.

Just as there had been a time when the children of Israel lived in tents, from which they vanquished all before them, so there was a time when the followers of Jesus the Christ met in catacombs and private houses, and from there conquered the mighty Roman Empire.

We have, however, lost our way on the road, taken a turning on the path that has led us to create and adorn a temple in every town and village of the world, buildings that now threaten to consume the energy and resources of many Christian communities. No matter how glorious or inspirational they can be, we pay a heavy price for our sacred buildings. In many of them, the lack of 'living stones' has become an irrelevance beside the new-found craze to 'preserve' at all costs these dead stones redolent of a God who has (apparently) departed.

Robert Louis Stevenson, in *Travels with a Donkey*, wrote: 'For my part, I travel not to go anywhere, but to go. I travel for travel's sake. The great affair is to move.' That says it perfectly. This too has long been the insight of the Judaeo-Christian tradition, an insight that history teaches us is all too easily buried beneath stability, success and worldly influence. What is to be done?

We can start by doing everything in our power to revive 'the Way' as the first and best description of what we are about, and in so doing we would rediscover much common ground, not only with the Jewish community, but also with the Sufi mystical tradition within Islam.[2] For both these traditions, the concept of 'the Way' is central to their spirituality.

Integral to this concept of the Way is the realization that 'we ourselves are "unfinished"' (Bianchi, 2002, p. 24), that we ourselves are a work in progress, a project that could still go either way.

In response, in terms of creating worship that honours God and does justice to all that we are becoming, we can ensure that every time our assembly gathers for worship we don't just *talk* about journey, but within our liturgy we actually *make* a journey by getting on the move through our liturgical space. How this can be done is examined in Part 3.

5 Listening

To hear the word 'go', Abraham first had to be listening (Gen. 12.1). Had he been totally preoccupied with himself, he would never have heard the command which led to his being named a blessing. Because he listened, he heard, and was sufficiently attuned to the voice of God to be able to embark on the adventure of faith. The journey began.

Worship in the Church of the twenty-first century is all too often preoccupied with self, or at least with the concerns of our own little ecclesiastical tribe. Our liturgies are sometimes a ceaseless torrent of words which, although addressed primarily to God, succeed in keeping God out. There is no moment in which to be still and to hear what the Spirit is saying to the churches. We have lost the ability to listen.

All the more reason then to ensure that within our liturgies we dam the torrent of words from time to time, creating pools of silence in which we are able to immerse ourselves in the presence of God.

Christian prayer, says Bianchi, is 'essentially an act of listening', and furthermore, listening 'generates us as believers' (Bianchi, 2002, p. 56). Listening in attentiveness and anticipation should be the frame of mind of the assembly at worship, an attitude of spiritual awareness and openness which in the Buddhist tradition is called mindfulness. Such awareness or mindfulness requires stillness, and stillness silence.

In his poem 'The Habit of Perfection', Gerard Manley Hopkins exalts in the sharpening of the awareness of God that comes from the ascetic practice of taming and channelling our senses: sound, speech, sight, taste, smell and touch will all be the more acute and delightful in so far as we harness them to serve our spiritual needs. Above all, to choose silence is to choose to hear the music of God's voice:

Elected Silence, sing to me
And beat upon my whorled ear,
Pipe me to pastures still and be
The music that I long to hear.[3]

Silence in worship frees us to hear God's music. Because it tends to get pushed out of most liturgical traditions, or reduced to a perfunctory nod to the notion, silence in liturgy needs to be worked at and established slowly but surely. It needs to become an accepted part of the Sunday Liturgy, the thing we do in the assembly at worship, naturally, without embarrassment, and without sneaking a look at our watches.

In the silence, in listening, we are enabled to enter the stream of God's being, and discover our deepest selves. In the context of the liturgy, this means that this discovery is set in motion, not just individually, but corporately, so that the community of faith is enabled to 'taste and see that the Lord is good' (Ps. 34.8) and in so doing to find its core being and direction within the life of God.

6 Finding God

Worship is a God-centred activity, in which God is made real to us, is enfleshed among us. Far too often Christians have been under the mistaken impression that when we assemble in the church building, we are the only people showing up for worship, whereas the mystery and the wonder is that God shows up too. 'Liturgy is a self-giving of God to us, an encounter whereby grace and glory find human forms' (Saliers, 1994, p. 22). Moreover this is not merely a passive presence to console us, but an active presence to jolt us, what Saliers calls 'the power of God to break in upon us'.

Worship can therefore present enormous problems for self-centred humanity.

Worship in the midst of the assembly is the time each week when our attention is fixed on God, as opposed to every other waking moment of the week when it tends to be fixed on ourselves. When the Victorians inscribed over the chancel arch (as they were prone to do) Jacob's exclamation of praise and wonder after his encounter with God at Bethel while on the run, they were onto a good thing: 'How awesome is this place! This is none other than the house of God, and this is the gate of heaven' (Gen. 28.17).

All we need do today is to redirect our focus somewhat; away from a particular building or its furnishings, to fix instead on the assembly itself as the 'holy place', in the midst of which, wherever it is gathered, God is made known. In our liturgy we share Jacob's sense of utter astonishment at God's visitation to him, the cheat, the scoundrel, who is told by God, 'all the families of the earth shall be blessed in you and in your offspring' (Gen. 28.14). We are lost in awe and wonder at the immensity of God's love. For a moment, we forget even ourselves.

If the liturgy is indeed a holy place where the primacy of God reigns, then this means that we must never attempt to reduce it to a political pawn in some game we wish to play. Those of us who are involved in any way with shaping the form our liturgy takes, or the words and ceremonies it contains, have constantly to be on our guard.

It is frighteningly easy to come out of the liturgy with a checklist of all the things 'they didn't do right', and to find that, in our busyness critiquing the liturgy, we rendered ourselves unable to worship. We missed God when he came to call. We also missed the truth that because God is ridiculously generous, he somehow fixes it so that, however cluttered the building, however incorrect the language, however atrocious the music, there will be a little gem hidden there for us. A germ of an idea, a helpful practice or perhaps just a glorious human smile, in which God is revealed.

7 Finding self

'Finding oneself' or 'finding peace' can sound a self-centred, rather escapist kind of activity, but for the Christian a good definition of a well-rounded mature person of faith is someone who is at peace with God and with themselves. If we have ever tried to 'escape' into the country or to a monastic house for a time of retreat, and have taken our troubles or our obsessions with us, we will know what a waste of time it was.

So then finding peace is about finding God and finding ourselves at the same time, to arrive at that state of mind, that inner place, where 'the peace of God that surpasses all understanding' (Phil. 4.7) will guard our hearts and minds in Christ Jesus. The

Buddhist teacher Thich Nhat Hanh says that our ability to be at peace with the world and with our neighbour 'depends very much on our capacity to make peace with ourselves' (Nhat Hanh, 1995, p. 10).

The place to do this is not 'away from it all' (although retreats are blessings too) but rather 'in the middle of it all'. That was the secret the first communities were required to learn, as they waited for the footfall of the secret police: it was a journey inwards. In the depths of our need and nakedness, as we painfully learn to let go of everything that would cheat us of God, we are clothed again in glory.

The gathering of the assembly for worship is the place where the journey to God, and the journey inwards to God's peace, is entered into week by week. We gather because we seek meaning in a puzzling and frightening world. Gathering is a spiritual activity. We seek peace because we find none elsewhere; we seek the journey inwards away from the treadmill of frantic activity.

8 Getting wet

Getting wet is a necessary and unavoidable part of the experience of baptism, and of the baptismal life that follows, in which we are constantly recalling, and being recalled to by the Church, most especially in the Easter Vigil, the significance of water in the Judaeo-Christian salvation story. From the waters of creation, through the stories of Noah's flood and the parting of the Red Sea, to the ministry of John the Baptist on the banks of the Jordan, and the early use of water in the initiation rites of the Christian community, water is an ever-present reality and potent symbol of both death and new life.

Getting wet, like getting our hands dirty, means that we have entered fully into the enterprise set before us. It signifies that we are not content simply to loll around at the edge of the pool, our swimming gear remaining dry and in pristine condition, but instead we dive in. Furthermore 'getting wet' for those who cannot swim has fearful overtones of sadistic PE teachers throwing one in at the deep end, and other variations on the theme of water torture. Water can spell death as well as life and fun:

> The water is not tame. Never far from our imagination is the sense that, rising, it could drown us, wash away our place, destroy the signs of our centred cities. Just as with the bread, our very need for water means that in its symbolic meanings, death is never far away. (Lathrop, 1993, p. 94)

When we come to the liturgy, getting wet (and I speak as a non-swimmer) is absolutely essential, and should be made unavoidable. It speaks louder than many words about getting involved, getting off our poolside recliner and diving in, refusing merely to watch any longer, and instead to become immersed in what is going on.

Getting wet in our liturgical space therefore requires more than the shallow 'bird bath' or covered font isolated in a corner of the church building. It requires more than the large salad bowl stuck on a tripod in the middle of the nave. Although this may have to suffice for a (preferably) limited period, such a temporary expedient sets up a duality between visual and actual foci which is confusing and destabilizing.

No, what is needed is a proper baptismal font located in the appropriate spot in relation to the liturgical life of the assembly, sufficiently prominent as a single symbol of baptismal covenant, sufficiently large to allow for copious amounts of water speaking of God's reckless generosity. As Gordon Lathrop reminds us:

> In the places where the people have begun to fill the basin again, perhaps to enlarge it to a flowing pool, perhaps to place it near the entrance of the assembly room in its own strong space, the water may be seen as a symbol already . . . we may see in it a birthing place, a watery sipapu, a magic pool, or our connection to mountains and streams away from here, our hopes for a cleaner and more cared-for earth. If bread and wine are at the center of the assembly, water is at its edge, marking its boundary, slaking its thirst, holding its life and its death. (Lathrop, 1993, p. 95)

See photograph in colour section: 'Sufficiently prominent . . . sufficiently large'

If this means relocating the existing font, and losing its heavy wooden lid, then so be it. No congregation that asserts a theology of baptismal covenant should tolerate a font that is badly sited or inadequate in scale.

The 1979 Prayer Book of ECUSA was notable above all for its overriding emphasis on the Baptismal Covenant as the supreme event and process by which the whole Christian assembly is defined: 'Holy Baptism is the full initiation by water and the Holy Spirit into Christ's Body the Church. The bond which God establishes in Baptism is indissoluble' (*Book of Common Prayer* (1979), p. 298).

More significant than its language, however, is the prominence given by the *Book of Common Prayer* (1979) to 'Proper Liturgies for Special Days', which consist of the liturgies of Lent, Holy Week and Easter, culminating in what is described as 'The Great Vigil of Easter'. These are placed before the order for Baptism or the Holy Eucharist, or any other sacramental rite. Within the Great Vigil of Easter, the 'Renewal of Baptismal Vows', comprising the Apostles' Creed in question-and-answer form followed by supplementary questions (p. 292), is a fine piece of work used often at other times of the year. This was a breakthrough of mammoth proportions when one considers prayer books from other parts of the Anglican Communion of that period, for example the *Alternative Service Book 1980*, in which the renewal of baptismal vows was tucked away in the Baptism section, with no provision for the full ceremonies of the Easter Vigil.

How tragic therefore that, 25 years on, a baptismal pool in an Episcopal Church is harder to find than a buffalo on the Great Plains. The same is true in England perhaps, but the excellence of the American texts in this regard makes the lack of transition from theory into practice the more surprising and disappointing. The fine words make the let-down all the bigger.

The Baptismal Covenant has been interiorized, stripped of its tactile, sacramental impact on our worship week by week, suggesting that we can proclaim each Sunday the theory of a dynamic relationship with God in baptism, and talk of the waters welling up to eternal life out of the empty bird bath in the corner, covered with a lid, which we presume to call a font.

In his book *Moving the Furniture*, William Seth Adams writes of the Episcopal Church in the USA that 'what we claim about the importance of initiation is *not* supported by the physical, observable evidence. The failure to support discredits our claims.' Citing a recent systematic tour of church buildings across the United States, Adams discovered 'how subject to disregard the font [was]. I was thereby taught that the theological claims made for baptism were seriously challenged, even undermined by the subtle and persistent disjuncture between our claims and the physical evidence' (Adams, 1999, p. 111). This disconnection speaks volumes about the extent to which this particular part of the Church universal has lost its way liturgically. Furthermore, we have lost touch with the very sacramentalism which defines our tradition. Sacraments are not head things, but heart and hands things. We need to experience and handle them, not think about them.

This is one very good reason why sprinkling the assembly from the waters of the font is so helpful in the process of making our symbols real. First, it makes the bird bath appear more and more silly, inadequate and unusable. Second, it means that every Sunday we get wet.

9 Showing hospitality

When the assembly gathers, we learn together to recapture the gift of hospitality so powerfully set before us by Jesus himself, for whom unconditional table fellowship was a central motif in his ministry. He loved to sit down to eat a meal with all and sundry, he fed the thousands, he broke bread in an upper room, and on beaches at breakfast time, and in a wayside house after a long day on a dusty road. In all these things Jesus mirrors the lavish hospitality of God, who not only shares with us the stewardship of his creation, but (incredibly) in the eucharist invites us to share God's board.

There is a beautiful verse in the Letter to the Hebrews, exhorting us to mutual love and generous hospitality to strangers, in which the writer reminds us that 'by doing that some have entertained angels without knowing it' (Heb. 13.2).

When Abraham was suddenly confronted by the Lord, appearing as three men before his tent, his first instinct was to offer hospitality. The passage in Genesis describes in detail the exertions made by himself and by Sarah his wife, to honour their guests, and how 'he took curds and milk and the calf that he had prepared, and set it before them; and he stood by them under the tree while they ate' (Gen. 18.8). This charming scene of God – one yet three – sitting in the shade of a tree outside Abraham's tent, immortalized for Christians in the icon by Rublev, is a further dimension of the eucharistic feast. At the table that we prepare, hopefully with the same anxiety to please that Abraham showed, God deigns to sup with us. The modern eucharistic hymn by Robert J. Stamp[4] has a refrain that says it well: 'God and man at table are sat down.'

Hospitality is therefore an essential component of liturgical assembly, first because we are ourselves put at ease in the presence of the saints of God, 'living and departed in the Lord Jesus' (*Alternative Service Book 1980*, p. 315), and are thereby enabled to participate fully in the offering of the liturgy without hesitation or embarrassment. 'As common prayer and ecclesial experience, liturgy flourishes in a climate of hospitality: a situation in which people are comfortable with one another.'[5]

Second, hospitality is essential because at the same time it enables us to look beyond ourselves to those around us. At the heart of our hospitality at this table lies the desire to say to others the words Jesus said to those who asked where he lived: 'Come and see' was his invitation (John 1.39). If we are concerned to share good news, this is our invitation too. An invitation, not to discuss ideas or to expound proof texts, but to sit at God's table and eat and drink with him. Gathering for worship is an evangelistic activity, for the sacred meal is not for us alone, but for all God's people. As we are told when guests are expected: 'family holds back'.

In conclusion, there are those who would see also social action as a component of liturgy, although the view taken here is that social action is a stimulant to and a fruit of our worship, rather than a component. Our compassion for the world should inform our praying and worshipping, sometimes colouring its mood, and our encounter with the crucified risen Lord in the liturgy should inspire and mobilize us to translate compassion into action.

These then are just some facets of the assembly gathering to make eucharist. As a community of faith our aim should be to attempt to do justice to them all.

Notes

1 From Galen's (lost) summary of Plato's *Republic*, quoted in Pagels (2003), p. 9.
2 An example of the Sufi use of the concept of 'following the Way' can be found in Appendix A.
3 Gerard Manley Hopkins, 'The Habit of Perfection', *The Centuries' Poetry*, Vol. 5 (Penguin, 1954).
4 'Welcome all ye noble saints of old' in *Celebration Hymnal for Everyone* (McCrimmons, 1994).
5 *Environment and Art in Catholic Worship* (US Conference of Catholic Bishops, 1978), p. 11.

PART 2 PRACTICE

3 BASIC STEPS IN THE MANAGEMENT OF CHANGE

1 Renewing liturgy in the parish

Once it is established in our parish community that we share (at least on the part of the leadership team at the outset) an earnest desire to rethink liturgy from basic principles and to transform it into a genuine experience of God, where does one begin?

This book is a sequel to *Re-Pitching the Tent* (Giles, 1999), which dealt with the possibilities and problems of reshaping and reordering liturgical space to facilitate and encourage liturgy that is all we long for it to be.

The question as to which comes first, however – redesigned space or renewed worship – is a classic chicken-and-egg situation. A redesigned space will make possible all those things we used to read about in books but never thought realistic. A renewed liturgy will cause a community of faith to become frustrated by the restrictions of an outdated liturgical space and hungry to reorder or rebuild.

Just because *Re-Pitching the Tent* appeared first, it should not be thought that the reordering of the worship space is the first step or prerequisite of liturgical renewal. It rarely is, and if we waited for a new liturgical space before starting on the work of liturgical renewal, most of us would never begin.

So what really is first? Why some parishes are centres of renewal while others are not is of course a mystery, but perhaps we can draw the parallel with what makes a good place of learning, for example a sixth-form college in the UK or a magnet school in the USA, where students are expected to be full participants in the process.

The reasons why some educational institutions flourish and some slide downhill will be made up of an amalgam of factors. Chief among them will be the character of the principal: has he/she just arrived, burning with zeal for education and with new ideas by the truckload, or has he/she been there twenty years and is just hanging on until retirement? Is the principal wonderful on theory but hopeless on communication? Is the school a tight ship or a shambles?

The principal will not be the only factor by any means. The quality and morale of the staff is of tremendous importance, as is the rate of turnover among them. A good team of dedicated teachers can *almost* neutralize the effect of a poor principal, but never quite. In the end, the best teachers become frustrated and demoralized, and look elsewhere.

Then there are the students themselves. Do they come from supportive homes, happy to be where they are, eager to learn? Or are they in school just to hang out with their friends until free to leave, reluctant to show interest, resistant to participation?

So it is in the parish looking to renew its liturgy. The role of the pastor continues to be the biggest single make-or-break factor, for without the pastor's enthusiastic backing there is very little that is going to get done or survive as a long-term project. This is especially true in the field of liturgy, where the most well-informed and enthusiastic community in the world can do little to renew a liturgy in which the central figure of the pastor continues to drag his/her feet.

The pastor, however, can never be the whole story or deciding factor. The pastor will remain ineffectual unless he/she is able to gather and to energize a small team of supportive and open-minded individuals to form his/her 'staff'. This team may include one or two other ordained ministers, but most will be ministers simply by virtue of their membership of the assembly.

And both pastor and staff team remain powerless without a faith community open to the Spirit of God. As with schools, some parishes appear charmed, while others bear a marked resemblance to the 'congregation from hell'. What can be done about that will be looked at a little later.

Given the indefinable nature of communities of faith and their capacity for liturgical renewal, it will be useful to try and determine a few common denominators.

2 The pastor

Any parish desiring to study and explore the renewal of liturgy will need a pastor who actively supports and engages wholeheartedly in this process. In exceptional circumstances, the main thrust of the process might be led by another member of the support team, but this is difficult to envisage precisely because eucharistic liturgy is so bound up with its presiding minister. In those situations where someone other than the pastor carries the burden, the clear and total support of the pastor will need to be shown at every stage, if one leader is not to be played off against another.

The pastor will need to be well read and knowledgeable on the subject of liturgy, in order to open the eyes of the assembly to the possibilities before them, and to lead them gently but firmly along the right path.

It is surprising to find how, at clergy gatherings, many pastors will speak despairingly of their parishes as if they were places in relation to which the pastor was but a helpless bystander. Nothing can be done, they will say, because it is not in their power to make things different. This attitude arises from many factors, ranging from a training and an expectation geared to a ministry of maintenance, to the avoidance of conflict and (especially in the US) a fear of setting in motion a chain of events that could eventually lead to dismissal. Over and above these there is plain lack of interest or, more commonly, a failure to make any connection between liturgical theory and the experience of Sunday worship. None of these factors bear scrutiny as solid reasons.

The role of the pastor is that of teacher and enabler; the person who is aware of the wider horizon and can envision the assembly to look beyond what they have always known to what they might discover, and what they might become. The pastor is the person who spies out the land of the wider Church and returns to motivate the community of faith by infecting them with his/her own sense of excitement. The pastor's teaching role is not one that can be abdicated or set aside.

In this process, academic prowess will not be the main criterion. The supreme quality necessary in a pastor is a passion about liturgy that arises from having seen it done superbly well and having experienced its power to transform communities of faith. The pastor will also need to possess an acute eye for detail, and have a well-developed aesthetic sense. These gifts will be more important than an arcane knowledge of the anaphora of Addai and Mari.

In seeking to combine these skills, the pastor will grow into a role in which he/she serves as both teacher and designer, learning resource and inspirer, prophet and poet. In all these ways the pastor is truly the artist of community.

3 Liturgical models

To a certain degree, the qualities described above are gifts we are born with, or not, as the case may be, but fortunately that is not the end of the story. There is an awful lot we can do, either by way of honing skills we already possess, or developing them, putting ourselves in the way of them, if we do not.

It is instructive to look back and ask what got us interested in liturgy in the first place. Was it a parish, or a person, or a book, or a one-off unforgettable experience of worship that caught us up into heaven? Each of us will have a different experience, a different model of liturgy at its best that will keep alive our liturgical spirit, and serve to continually deepen and extend our formation in liturgical life. Here I can but share my own liturgical model, which consisted very simply of hanging around monasteries and picking up a few things here and there.

Kathleen Norris found this to be true in her own spiritual journey as she discovered the power of communal worship at St John's Abbey, Minnesota:

> Good liturgy can act like a window into a world in which our concepts of space, time, and even stone are pleasurably bent out of shape. Good liturgy is a living poem, and ceremony is the key.
>
> Any outsider writing about monastic life runs the risk of romanticizing it. I've simply described what I experienced one Sunday morning at St John's. I'm assuming, hoping even, that some of the monks were wondering what was for dinner, or thinking dark thoughts about a confrere who had annoyed them at breakfast, or regretting a sharp remark they'd made over the pool table the night before. Good ceremony makes room for all the dimensions of human experience in the hope that, together, we will discover something that transforms us. This is why I suspect that individuals can't create true ceremony for themselves alone. Ceremony requires that we work with others in the humbling give-and-take of communal existence. (Norris, 1996, p. 266)

My own introduction to this wondrous world of monastic formation came in 1965 when Donald Allchin appeared at Cuddesdon to tell us seminarians about the outpouring of the theology of Vatican II in the liturgical life of the monasteries of France. He had just returned from a period of time spent at the Benedictine Abbey of En Calcat in southern France and his descriptions of the wondrous liturgies to behold there made me determined to go there myself. Although I had little interest in liturgy as an academic subject – I was always getting mixed up between the first English Prayer Books – I was fascinated by it as an experience.

When I duly arrived at En Calcat during my next seminary vacation, I found it an intoxicating experience. I realized I was witnessing a re-formation in progress, being worked out in the ways we prayed, and moved, and talked, and sang and dressed in the presence of God. It was in its way no less significant than the Reformation of the sixteenth century; Rome's own reformation that would spill over into the experience and worship of all mainstream churches.

I still remember my first sight of around one hundred concelebrants, all (in those days) in matching chasubles, processing in at the beginning of the conventual mass, the gathering of the whole community around the altar table moved into the centre of the choir, and the bus-loads of pilgrims who every Sunday crowded the galleries of the great abbey church to catch the fire of this revolution in our understanding of God and one another. In some ways the details matter less than the conviction that here was the 'Spirit speaking to the churches' and one's knees shook.

Equally powerful were the encounters that flowed from En Calcat by one of those wonderful chains of human interconnection whereby one introduction led to another. There were the Dominican Sisters at Prouihle, in a convent on the same site where St Dominic founded his first community of enclosed nuns to pray for his mission to southern France, beautifully chanting the new French psalm settings, accompanied on a zither; the Benedictine sisters at La Barre in Anjou who had converted an ancient granary into their chapel and in its midst had erected an altar in the pattern of a prehistoric stone monument or *menhir*; the Little Brothers of Jesus,

St Dominic's village of Fanjeaux, Aude, seen from Prouihle

inspired by Charles de Foucauld, who contrived to create, amidst the poverty they embraced, tiny prayer rooms of exquisite beauty, in the tower of an ancient church or in a hut in the corner of a field, containing just the Blessed Sacrament, a lamp and perhaps the twisted branch of a tree or driftwood – God's own sculpture free of charge.

Later came a group visit to the incredible seminary of the Mission de France at Pontigny, in the shadow of that matchless abbey church, the largest Cistercian building still in use. There I found a community of very tough and happy-go-lucky young men, who might just as well have been recruits to the Foreign Legion, but were in fact in training for the ministerial priesthood to serve in situations in de-Christianized France where other priests feared to tread. Their education was probably only basic (probably no English theological college would have looked at them), but they were the salt of the earth.

What struck me most at Pontigny, however, given its General Patton approach to most things, was the simple, unaffected way in which this new breed of seminarian could celebrate the liturgy as I had never seen it. These macho seminarians remained exactly who they were, but were able to offer the eucharist with unaffected joy, and a beauty born, once again, of noble simplicity. There was no assuming of a 'religious' mien for worship, no speaking with a 'plum in the mouth' (as English Anglicans are prone to affect), but neither was there casualness or carelessness. There was an attention to detail but with a complete absence of the fussiness and prissiness that is so familiar from 'High Church' worship on a bad day.

I hope you will excuse my little diversion down the side roads of France, but that part of the story explains much of what follows in this book, and gives the *feel* of the kind of liturgy I attempt to describe. France in the late 1960s was my own particular catching of the vision, but each of us will find an equivalent road to a place where we might stumble upon liturgy that transforms.

The monastic model is of course but one of many, and there are many others, some of which may have greater appeal. Monastic communities, however, have been at this a long time, are by and large stable places able to work at liturgy consistently over a long period, are not subject to machinations of parish councils, and are wonderfully hospitable. In any country of the world there will be a monastic community where we can glimpse the glory, catch the bug, of worship. Not that any old monastery will do, for each will have its stance and its priority, but seek diligently and you shall find.

In England, go to Worth Abbey or to Mirfield, in the States to Gethsemani, Kentucky, or the monastery of St John the Evangelist, Cambridge, or St Meinrad, Indiana, or Christ in the Desert, New Mexico. Above all, when you go to these monastic houses where we can learn so much, go not just to gaze or listen. Go and learn to be a *smuggler*. Pester those in charge of the music for a copy of the piece you can't get out of your head, ask to talk to the sacristan about what you have observed, go with your cheque book to the gift store and carry off an icon, or some incense, for home. Learn everything you can, pick up new ideas, new music, new gestures, new ways. Return home determined that your time away is going to make a difference; that things back home will never be the same again.

In addition to monastic communities, there will of course be parish communities within a sabbath day's journey where much can be learnt. Seek them out in the same way, and do not be put off simply because they may have a different label on the noticeboard outside. We need to gather liturgical rosebuds as we may, and where we may.

In every diocese there are likely to be at least one or two parishes where the flame has caught and liturgical renewal is high on the agenda. Listen out for them, knowing that the first reports you hear are likely to be uncomplimentary. If the clergy are being catty about a parish doing 'weird things' then that's a sure sign things are moving there, and very probably in the right direction.

It only takes a small group of dedicated men and women to make a difference, and parishes now spoken about in hushed tones as leaders in their field all started off looking very much like yours or mine. St Gregory of Nyssa, San Francisco, is a prime example. Begun in a borrowed church basement by two presbyters with a vision, Rick Fabian and Donald Schell, it is now a byword for exciting exploratory liturgy matched by radical theological thinking. Not a huge parish by any means, it is internationally known, a place of pilgrimage for liturgists from all over the world. Even if you don't live in San Francisco, you will be able to find, if you look hard enough, a parish community which is faithfully putting into place some small building blocks as a foundation for liturgical renewal. Ask around, go on the net; the parishes are there.

4 Forming the team

The fact that I set about writing this book, and the fact that you have been moved to read it, are both signs of the times. There is an aching hunger out there among the people of God for liturgy that takes hold of one's imagination and of one's life.

One of the ministries at our cathedral is to those people visiting relatives and friends in the many teaching hospitals that are within a few blocks of our building. One woman who came to our midday eucharist was visiting her sick husband, and when he was well again they joined us for our Sunday Liturgy. Their joy in having discovered our community was overshadowed by what they knew they would face liturgically when they went back home to their parish in a neighbouring diocese: a pastor and a parish council who were determined that 'nothing must change'. These two delightful people – let's call them Gloria and Bill – have been in correspondence ever since, seeking help on how they might 'do their bit' towards renewing the liturgy in their small corner.

So in every parish in the land it is my conviction that there lurk people just like Gloria and Bill, awaiting the revolution. They may even represent in many places the silent majority, feeling powerless before the vociferous minority who apparently hold the pastor in their thrall. What can be done to identify them and give them new hope?

The first step for any pastor wishing to renew the worshipping life of a parish seems to be the same everywhere: to gather around him/her a small group of kindred spirits. By this I do not mean people who already subscribe to *Worship*[1] or have been on weekends organized by *Praxis*[2] (hopefully that will come later), but simply people who are open,[3] and who by their nature will tend to say 'yes' rather than 'no', and who have the potential to see the big picture and to bring along others with them.

The means of identifying this group is again relatively simple. The pastor needs to address the question of liturgical renewal at the principal Sunday Liturgy or some other appropriate occasion when the majority of the community is gathered together. In so doing, the pastor is making a 'declaration of intent', not describing some hobby or pastime which he/she would like to pursue depending on how things work out.

This needs to stir people's imagination by sketching out a picture of how things might be in the future, and be given with conviction, seriousness and with a fair degree of passion. Humour will also be necessary, of course, to lighten the pudding and to make the point that this is not going to be a grim struggle in which everyone will become polarized or distressed: it is going to be an adventure, in which people will have fun.

However it is put (and afterwards we will always wish we had put it differently), the assembly needs to get the message that the pastor means business on this one, and will take some deflecting from his/her course.

The vital nature of the pastor's role in this initial stage cannot be overestimated. The pastor has really to communicate that what is being set before the assembly is not some vague wish-list of things to dream about, but an actual programme of liturgical formation that will be instrumental in transforming the parish. The pastor must not only communicate it, he/she must *believe* it, and not just believe it, but *know* it in the gut.

It is at this point that the eyes of many clergy glaze over, and they drag out that well-worn phrase about this not being a ditch they are willing to die in. The problem is, this response often signifies that they have no intention of making a stand at any ditch on any issue. They just stroke the congregation and wait for better days. If so, neither this book, nor any other on liturgical renewal, is going to be of much use to them. Some dying has to happen somewhere if we are to experience rebirth, and it is as well to recognize that before we begin.

Having thrown into the gathering this little hand grenade, the pastor then simply waits and sees. There may be some immediate expressions of opposition, but this is by no means always the case, as the majority probably view it as 'the pastor's little thing' and take the view that if they ignore it, it will go away. At the other end of the spectrum there are likely to be one or two who will come up later and quietly voice interest and support. The pastor can always nudge the assembly in the right direction by inviting responses to his/her address and by talking openly of forming a small working group to study the subject. If all else fails, promising individuals will have to be approached directly and their good nature prevailed upon.

From this initiative will come the nucleus of the small team who will in time be the 'bearers of the reality' and the people who will infect the whole body with the 'virus' of liturgical renewal.

First of all they themselves have to get excited, and to do that they need to see for themselves. 'Come and see' were Jesus' most telling words on the subject of evangelism. Whatever it is that is being put before us as an exciting new idea, we all need to 'see' it: to have it carefully described and explained, and then to be taken to see it; handle it, experience it for ourselves.

So then, the pastor's main task in the initial period of formation is not to give lectures or organize discussion groups on the hypothetical topic of liturgical renewal, for they will be talking about something that is not in their experience. Instead, the pastor needs to pile the group into a few cars and go off on a day's outing, or better still an overnight visit, to a place of stunning liturgy. This is where those monasteries come in so handy. Above all, these houses of prayer speak for themselves. As Kathleen Norris's hairdresser said, 'They don't preach at you; they let you experience it for yourself.'

On the way home, and at a debriefing session later, the pastor can unpack things a little, explain something of the history and development of what the group experienced, and tease out from the group some of the differences between what they have witnessed and what has been their previous experience. The pastor can also help the group identify the ways in which the liturgy they saw disturbed or challenged them.

The next stage in this formation period is to get the group into a pattern of regular meetings at which they can study liturgical sources, begin to share questions and ideas, and most importantly of all, actually *do* some liturgy in an informal domestic setting: liturgy which they themselves have helped create and in which they will participate. This is an eye-opener to most people and can be an exciting dawning of a whole new experience of God's presence.

5 Establishing the pattern

Once the liturgical working group or think-tank, or whatever people want to call it, is up and running, then the group can become a testing ground for ideas for enhancing the regular Sunday Liturgy of the parish.

I say 'regular Sunday Liturgy' quite deliberately because one of the culs-de-sac available to the pastor and the enthusiasts is the 'special service'. The good news about such a special event is that here you can be as experimental as you like, but the bad news is that none of the people who need to be there will come to it, and having stayed away they will dismiss it as peripheral to the life of the parish. Furthermore, the pastor will also be in danger of cultivating a new breed of Christian reared on the 'milk' of the special service alone, who will never be weaned off it onto the 'solid food' of regular worship (1 Cor. 3.2). Meanwhile the worship experience of the main parish community is left untouched and unreformed. The special service may look an attractive option but as a means of transforming the parish liturgy it is a dead end, and can have many damaging repercussions on parish life. Remember, a liturgical bird in the hand at the principal eucharist is worth two or even twenty in the bush at a special service.

Special services do have a place if all the cards are placed on the table from the outset. For example, it can be set up as an interim solution within a fixed time frame, after which, on a date already known, the special service and the principal eucharist will be amalgamated, preferably at an hour every Sunday that will be new to both groups, and require some readjustment on everyone's part.

Special services are also necessary if we are reaching out to a largely unchurched sector of the population. At Philadelphia Cathedral we have experimented with services of Night Prayer at 9 p.m. on Sundays, encouraged by the experience of St Mark's Cathedral, Seattle, which has encountered a real hunger for spirituality among those disenchanted with organized religion. Services such as these have liturgical components but are primarily sensory experiences. We might find the Kyrie from the *Missa de Angelis* cheek by jowl with the recorded voice of Joni Mitchell singing *A case of you* echoing through the darkness, or a chant from Iona or Taizé leading into silence, concluding with the sprinkling of the assembly to the sound of Bar Scott singing *Where the angels sing*. Such events are where we must begin again with those who have given up on us.

So then, back to our 'ditch': the principal eucharist of the parish. Even this holds a catch, as 'principal' suggests other secondary eucharists, a notion which needs to be challenged. This is a peculiarly Anglican problem, but cannot be passed over.

When, in the 1950s, the Parish Communion Movement achieved a remarkable success in replacing Matins with the Eucharist in the vast majority of English parishes, it made only one mistake. It failed to kill off the 8 o'clock Holy Communion. This early service was necessary in the bad old days when it was the only opportunity to receive the Sacrament, later services being either Matins or non-communicating High Mass. When the Sung Eucharist became the principal liturgy of the day, the early service was rendered superfluous.

It survived this crisis, however, and has now developed a new lease of life as a 'special service' at the other end of the spectrum: for those who wish to take no part in the principal liturgy of the parish, nor in anything that anyone else is doing. To misquote Dr Johnson, the 8 o'clock is the last refuge of the liturgical scoundrel.

The 8 o'clock needs to be discontinued wherever possible, and where it is not, needs to be brought into the same liturgical framework as the principal eucharist(s), so that there is no safe haven from the message of liturgical renewal. Introducing a homily, a little music and a change in venue or seating plan will soon thin out the ranks.

Turning now to the principal eucharist, the aim of the pastor and his/her support team is to identify certain priorities for change of a foundational nature – more to do with the skeleton than the flesh. Here they will resemble the Tractarians rather than the Ritualists of the Anglican Catholic Revival of the nineteenth century. The Tractarians were concerned with fundamental principles; it took the Ritualists a few decades to dress those principles in a new suit of liturgical clothes.

A few suggestions might help illustrate the point, any two or three of which will make a difference:

- *Journey*. Let it be constantly said, in written and spoken word, that the liturgy, like life, is a journey. Make provision for some element of journey to be experienced every Sunday. This may involve a procession involving the whole assembly, a gathering round the font, or beginning the liturgy in the parish hall. Any journey will do, the thing is just to get the assembly used to *moving*. This was discussed in Chapter 2 and its practical application will be examined in Part 3.
- *Change*. Let it be constantly said, in written and spoken word, that the Christian gospel engages all followers of Jesus Christ in a life of *metanoia*: of constant upheaval and change. Follow this up by arranging each week for there to be something different about the space, and about the liturgy. They may be little things, but they will make the point that from now on this community of faith is exploring, not resting. To be effective, the changes will need to be gently pointed out with a word of explanation, rather than be left unmentioned, to be missed or to be chuntered over.
- *Music*. A broad variety of musical styles from a variety of sources is foundational to good liturgy. It is also controversial, with a higher irritation factor than any other liturgical component. This is where the demand for a 'special service' rears its head, in the hope that all the crazy people will go away and leave us in peace with our hymnals. From this it is evident that *from the beginning* of any process of liturgical renewal, the assembly needs to get used to the idea that at its gatherings there will always from now on be something for everyone, and that, wherever possible, music will be provided by a variety of singers and musicians. My colleague Robert Ridgell has provided invaluable material in Appendix M, written from a professional musician's point of view, on the issues involved and the resources available.

  New music will also be *within* the liturgy, not just tacked onto it in the form of a warm-up session beforehand, which can so easily be avoided by the grumpy at heart.
- *Silence*. Most of the liturgies encountered in the regular parish setting are impoverished by a complete lack of silence. They rush headlong from one thing to the next. The introduction of silence – such a simple and incontrovertible

improvement – can make a dramatic change to the feel of our worship. By this is meant silence not in the sense of a brief accidental gap between one component and the next, but as an intentional period of silence, begun and ended by a clearly understood signal, silence into which the assembly settles purposefully.

Two places where a period of silence is particularly appropriate are following the homily and following communion. In each case we ponder what we have broken open and received.

- *Vesture*. The breathless pace of some of our liturgies is mirrored by the fussiness in which the liturgy is dressed up. Even though it may take some time to arrive at a wholesale parish policy covering who is vested and in what, the presiding minister from day one can make a difference by wearing vestments which signal a new direction (this is one area at least which remains his/her prerogative). This question is dealt with in more detail in Chapter 4, but is here identified as a key indicator of a new approach which should be addressed early in any process of liturgical renewal.

- *Orders of service*. The written material we give into the hands of worshippers is a question of high importance in encouraging good posture and engagement in the liturgy. The sooner we can get the assembly's nose out of its books, the sooner we shall renew the liturgy. Very early in the process, prayer books, hymn books and supplements should all be replaced by a single order of service printed on the parish copying machine. These can change every Sunday, or every season. In the latter case, a small selection of hymns and songs can be provided for each part of the liturgy where music is needed, with the psalm refrain printed on the news bulletin for the particular week. In addition to their practical advantages, orders of service are invaluable to the pastor by way of the explanatory notes that can be included.

- *Leading the assembly in prayer*. A good example of our being book-bound is the issue of the prayers of the people. Although the assembly may well be used to a lay person leading the prayers of the people, it is probable that their experience is limited to the reading out of set prayers, the leader's creativity restricted to the insertion of names at appropriate places.

The simple step of discarding the set prayers and training a small team of people to lead these prayers in their own way is a revelation to many, and can be liberating, as well as moving.

It will be noted that none of these suggestions affect in any way the *text* of the liturgy. The assembly can go on using the rite it is used to, but approaching it in a different way, appreciating it for the first time. These suggested changes reaffirm the truth that in liturgy, as in much of life, it's not so much a question of what we do, but how we do it.

These changes do not require resolutions of committees or consent of bishops, but are all things which should be seen as within the pastor's purview. Neither do any of these suggestions cost money, except perhaps for the issue of musical balance, where some new resource books may need to be purchased, and of orders of service, where some staff time may have to be reallocated.

All these suggestions can be implemented from day one, or very soon after, in this preliminary period of establishing basic patterns and approaches. Not in every parish would one necessarily choose to implement all of them at one go, but it will be evident that such simple steps together send a powerful signal to any community of faith. They are the 'writing on the wall' that change is already happening and that transformation is already on the way.

Such signals are important to send, not only because we need at all times to be honest and open, but also because it enables individual members of the community of faith to make their own adjustments and to decide where they stand. In any programme of liturgical renewal, some losses will be inevitable. It is best to face that fact early on, and to let it be known in the parish that such an outcome has been carefully weighed and that, should it occur, it would be considered a regrettable but necessary price to pay for the renewal of the parish's life and worship. It is important for this to be said early, so as to pre-empt the inevitable threats and attempts at blackmail that are sometimes voiced by those who consider themselves indispensable.

6 Teaching the assembly

Once these basic patterns and approaches have been established, and the writing clearly discerned upon the wall (hopefully not in the parish cloakroom), a process of parish education can begin.

This may seem back to front to some people, but in my experience education in these matters is a case of 'show and tell'. We need to show what we mean, to illustrate some of the theory, before we can as a parish community have anything to talk about. Otherwise a discussion on liturgy degenerates into the desperate defence of our particular liturgical trench, from the limited standpoint of what we have 'always done'.

The purpose of the period in which basic patterns are established is to arrive at a position where, without having changed the shape of the liturgy or its text, we shall be able to discuss it in an informed way. We shall have something to bite on and chew over. The liturgy has been shown in a new light, and fresh possibilities await us, possibilities which we are now beginning to glimpse for ourselves and understand.

It is at this point that a liturgical study and discussion programme can move into top gear, with the pioneers of the pastor's working group coming into their own as enthusiastic enablers and caring ministers of reassurance. No, the world is not going to fall apart if we . . .

The many resources available from liturgical institutes and other agencies of renewal (see Appendix O) can now be brought into play, and every effort made to include the maximum number of community members in the process. For example, Sunday mornings could be redesigned to incorporate this study time in the regular programme involving all ages, even within the liturgy itself, though this could be off-putting to visitors.

There is no need for the process to go on for ever, but it needs a beginning and an end which are clear from the outset. The period of Lent, or a month in the autumn, might well be appropriate. Arrangements should be made to offer the whole community a chance to see for themselves some of the places visited and liturgies experienced by the pathfinders in the original working group. All should be encouraged to enter into the chase and catch the bug.

It is at this point that some of the issues and options available to a community, as it rethinks how it does liturgy, can be examined in a group setting. This should be done, however, in such a way that the assembly is not misled into thinking that designing liturgy is a democratic process in which all is decided by a show of hands. Here the leadership team is bringing the assembly on board the process insofar as it has already developed, and taking soundings of concerns, interests and ideas.

In this process, the community of faith is not involved in determining solutions to the detailed decisions outlined in Part 3 which follows, for these remain the responsibility of the pastor and his/her team. Instead, members of the community are being encouraged and equipped to engage, probably for the first time in their lives, with the theological principles that undergird the changes they are beginning to see in the Sunday Liturgy. In broad brush strokes these are such concepts as:

1 the assembly as the minister of the eucharist, in which all participate
2 priesthood as residing in the community rather than the person
3 the role of the presbyter as convenor and conductor of the orchestra
4 the evangelistic dimension of the eucharist
5 'real presence' in the community rather than an object.

If creatively prepared and facilitated, such topics should keep a parish community buzzing long into the night, and these ideas need to be thrashed out if people are ever to grasp why liturgical renewal holds the key not just to Sunday mornings but to our whole spiritual lives.

This process is not a matter only of specially arranged courses. In every parish newsletter, in every homily, these themes will be woven through every project, every season, every eucharist. Consistent and holistic and unrelenting teaching by the ministerial team will be the primary tool in communicating this new dawn of theological understanding and liturgical expression.

The design of liturgy is an art, and can never be reduced to a set of tables or rules. For that reason final responsibility for liturgical matters needs to remain in the hands of the parish pastor. That being said, not even the most gifted pastor can go it alone, and it is essential that he/she continues to keep in good running order the small team with whom leadership in liturgy can be shared. These are the people who have exhibited skill and sensitivity in liturgical matters and have built up with the pastor an atmosphere of mutual trust. Liturgy cannot be designed in an atmosphere of mutual suspicion or in a group whose members are uneasy with one another, unable to express their views and feelings without pre-wrapping them.

This group won't be identical to the original working team; some will have dropped out, while others in the assembly will have shown eagerness to join once they saw what was going on in the parish. It remains, however, an informal group, called together by the parish pastor, and he/she will be wise to keep it as transparent as possible and always on the lookout for new talent. (The membership of this group will not be subject to voting at an annual meeting, otherwise we can imagine the fun that could be had, packing the meeting with people clutching copies of the Latin Missal or the 1928 Prayer Book.) The pastor will be wise, however, to ensure that the team operates in a very open manner, showing itself always appreciative of feedback and new ideas, and delighted to welcome those with something to bring to the table.

In the relaxed atmosphere of the worship team, new ideas and practices seen or read of elsewhere can be tested, subjected to a reality-check, kicked around and occasionally laughed out of court.

7 Formalizing change

Depending on the tradition to which we belong, the 'big day' when a whole new way of doing liturgy is inaugurated can take on a host of different appearances. In some traditions it might be thought to require a public meeting, in others a long session with the bishop, or in others a waiting upon consensus.

I would venture to suggest, however, that in most cases, provided that the previous stages outlined above have been worked through, the final 'big day' will be something of an anticlimax, going almost unnoticed, because we will have been slipping into these new ways and patterns imperceptibly over a period of time.

Ecclesiastical authority expends much energy on jealously guarding the liturgical *texts* of our liturgies, surrounding them with ramparts of rubrics, as if it was unaware that texts are secondary to ceremonial in the impact of liturgy upon us. Apart from a few additions which might enrich the liturgical action, and a little tweaking here and there, it will be seen from the chapters that follow that the vast majority of ways of doing things differently are concerned with matters other than texts. Rather they concern gesture, posture, ceremonial and movement. This means that for the most part, the kind of changes worked through in our local community will not require official sanction or consultation. The bishop can sleep easier at night.

Changes in texts may require ten years of purgatory on committees and commissions, and yet go unnoticed after an initial period in which they retained novelty value. Changes in ceremonial may be nobody's business but the local assembly's, and yet can change for ever people's perception of our being and our doing as we make eucharist.

So the 'big day' may be just an appropriate Sunday of the year – the First Sunday of Advent, let us say, or the community's dedication festival – when a fresh start is particularly appropriate. By this time a lot of what will be formalized has already been experienced, but on this day the various consistent parts will perhaps be brought together for the first time into a cohesive whole. It will be worth making a big splash for the occasion, and throwing a party afterwards. It's not every day that a parish community can celebrate a bold step forward of such magnitude and consequence.

Notes

1 *Worship* is a bi-monthly journal of liturgical renewal, published by the monks of St John's Abbey, Collegeville, Minnesota 56321.
2 *Praxis* is a magazine of liturgical renewal in the UK. Contact address: 20 Great Peter Street, London SW1P 3BU. Telephone: +44 (0) 20 7222 3704. E-mail address: praxis@stmw.globalnet.co.uk
3 'Theologians and pastors were described in this period not as conservatives or liberals but either as *fermé* or *ouvert*, closed or open' (Hebblethwaite, 1993, p. 274).

4 SETTING THE SCENE

Before we can begin to think about the liturgical action itself, it is necessary to consider a host of physical factors that will impinge upon our worship. Ignoring these factors, or dismissing them as of marginal importance, has led to the kind of liturgy we are all too familiar with, in which a size 14 liturgy is shoved painfully into a size 10 setting. The physical constraints, if not addressed, lead us into celebrating new rites in very old ways: all those liturgical scholars and revision committees could have saved themselves a whole lot of trouble.

1 Separation of zones of activity

The tensions inherent in housing the different components of worship outlined in Chapter 2 above suggest that we need to separate out into two distinct physical spaces the complementary but conflicting components of gathering. Distinct zones of activity are needed if we are to do justice to the full and diverse nature of assembly. The problem with buildings for worship inherited from previous generations is that they offer only one zone – the main worship space itself – in which various, and often conflicting, activities must be accommodated.

To do justice to the multi-faceted process of assembly, two separate zones are needed:

- *The outer zone*: a space separate from the worship area itself in which the welcome of newcomers and the greeting of one another can take place without intruding upon the special character of a space set apart for prayer and worship, or disrupting the prayerful silence appropriate to preparation for worship.

    This outer zone is traditionally called a narthex. It fulfils the same function as the reception area in a hotel, library or office complex. It serves as a buffer between two worlds, between the hurly-burly of the street and the focused activities of the space within. It is a decompression chamber in which we change pace and adjust

Narthex: meeting and greeting

our lens and take a breath. It's also the place where we need to find the cloakrooms. The outer zone facilitates gathering as arrival.

- *The inner zone*: the worship space, a demarcated space identified in the shared experience of the assembly as our 'holy ground', the place of encounter with God who is Other and yet, in Christ, God-with-us. Traditionally this space has been known as 'the church', an unfortunate term highly destructive of our sense of vocation to *become* church, that is, living building blocks for God to assemble and knock into shape. We desperately need a new term to describe this inner zone. 'Worship space' is hardly sexy, while 'sanctuary' is too redolent of Levitical notions of the sacerdotal elite.

  The inner zone is in effect 'God's landing strip', the place where we wait in a clearing in the jungle for the arrival of vital supplies and rescue. Those religious traditions which require us on entry to remove our shoes can teach us a lot about the inner zone.

If only we have eyes to see, we come to recognize that when we assemble for worship

Liturgical space: preparing for worship

we are realizing our full potential as 'a royal priesthood, a holy nation', and that we stand on holy ground. The inner zone, therefore, facilitates gathering as beginning.

2 Clearing the space

The phrase 'liturgical space' can be highly misleading if used to describe the interior of the typical church building which members of most mainstream churches experience as the norm. In these places, 'space' is the very last word that springs to mind, as they are usually cluttered from end to end with fixed furniture. No cat need ever fear being swung in them. There just isn't any room, for cat swinging or for anything else.

In the typical interior derived from the traditional gothic floor plan of nave and chancel, the impossibility of moving around, or of moving the furniture, or of deviating from the given norm of a rigid seating configuration facing in one direction, is all part of the conspiracy to deprive the people of God of their liturgical birthright.

Full participation in the liturgical action by the whole people of God was the norm at the beginning, and at the various periods of re-formation and renewal in Christian history, but it is a freedom constantly being eroded by subsequent generations who crave repetition and regularity, who like to know what comes next, and who, rather than exercise a shared priesthood, would prefer to pay a priest to do things on their behalf.

The one thing that the liturgical status quo abhors and fears above all other is space. Once you have open *space* in a church building, anything can happen, and all kinds of unstoppable forces can be unleashed. If we are intent on facilitating liturgical renewal, therefore, an essential first step is to clear some space.

This process of clearing the space is not always done in one go, and the most pressing need in a conventional floor plan is usually for the removal of pews at the front of the nave, or of choir stalls from the chancel, to provide a fitting space for the altar table. In both cases we are addressing the need for some form of liturgical platform.

Talk of 'liturgical platforms' requires a word about the difficulties that can be encountered in clearing the space. First we have the educational phase, the lengthy consultation process and the meetings late into the night, necessary to get the assembly sufficiently excited about its own liberation from the bondage of the pew. Aidan Kavanagh, in his classic book *Elements of Rite*, says it all so well that every word must be quoted:

> Pews, which entered liturgical place only recently, nail the assembly down, proclaiming that the liturgy is not a common action but a preachment perpetrated upon the seated, an ecclesiastical opera done by virtuosi for a paying audience. Pews distance the congregation, disenfranchise the faithful, and rend the assembly. (Kavanagh, 1990, p. 21)

Is there any more to be said on this subject, any conceivable defence of the indefensible?

The pews need to go! No community of faith can pretend to mean business about liturgical renewal if it leaves its members enchained in rigid pew formation. Pews are an inexcusable anachronism in today's Church.

Second, even after all the meetings and the extra doses of valium, there remains the problem of the construction of the floor we inherit. At this moment we may stumble on a booby trap or two. Church floors are rarely what they seem. Rarely is it a matter of taking up the pews to reveal a level, usable floorspace.

First, pews were often constructed on wooden platforms raised above the level of the aisles alongside. Furthermore, such platforms (in Victorian England at least) were most often not built on the floor but above open cavities perhaps several feet deep. All very strange, but there we are. Nothing worthwhile is achieved without a struggle.

3 Seating the assembly

Seating configuration

Of supreme importance in the renewal of the liturgy today is the rediscovery of the assembly as the minister of the eucharist, and indeed of the divine office and other forms of worship too. This is a reversal of the top-to-bottom process perceived as the norm throughout the medieval period and up to the twentieth century. Dom Gregory Dix spoke powerfully in *The Shape of the Liturgy* of the '*plebs sancta Dei* – the holy people of God' (Dix, 1964, p. 744), but it is highly significant that, in that pre-Vatican II era, Dix could still speak of the holy community being 'made' by faithful pastors.

Today we would speak of the process of sanctification and commissioning as being the other way round: the assembly making holy its members, including those members called to preside over it. The priesthood resides in the assembly, not in the person (1 Pet. 2.9) and the ordained members of the assembly have a special calling to call forth and give expression to that which already inheres in the whole assembly. The liturgical shoe is on the other foot.

Gabe Huck's *Liturgy with Style and Grace*, which turned so many liturgical heads in the 1980s, remains a masterpiece of its genre, and says this about the liturgical movement at the root of which was:

> the renewal of the assembly's right and privilege and obligation to celebrate eucharist actively . . . participation meant more than keeping the assembly busy with singing and making responses. Active participation meant and still means that no one is a spectator. Everyone, by virtue of baptism, actively offers the one sacrifice of thanksgiving; everyone is a celebrant, though there is only one presider. (Huck, 1998, p. 45)

Although all of us tend to begin a process of liturgical reordering with thoughts of the primary foci of font, ambo and altar – how they should look and where they should be placed – it becomes more and more obvious as time goes by that when we do this we are starting at the wrong end.

A far higher priority and pressing need is to get the assembly seated in a configuration that suggests that not only are its members speaking to each other, but that on the whole they are mighty glad to be here in the Body of Christ. Nothing can be of greater importance, for from the assembly's sense of its own sacred character and calling everything else will flow. We need to ensure, therefore, as we set the scene for the liturgy to begin, that the assembly is seated in a configuration that does justice to, and clearly identifies and communicates, the assembly's holy priestly calling. In other words, the assembly needs to be seated, no longer as an 'audience', but as full participants; and not just as participants but as co-celebrants.

If we take the seating of the assembly as our starting place then we shall also find that the education process is speeded up quite naturally. If we deflect attention away from things to people, away from the altar given by a certain benefactor to the assembly itself in its need to be appropriately and comfortably seated in a manner which speaks of sacred character and purpose rather than 'bums on pews', then we are in with a fighting chance that people will see the point. The New Testament has much to say about the calling of God's holy people; not much to say about altar design.

No seating plan is neutral. The way we sit in relationship to one another is critical in any sphere of life, and often jealously guarded. The seating plan of any liturgical assembly will have the same power to spell out, to first-timer and regular alike, exactly what is going on in this room. As Christians, our attempts to model the kingdom in our assemblies will be either helped or hindered by the seating arrangement we adopt.

Thomas Day rightly points out that in an era of liturgical reform, we can all too easily rubbish the past by the use of misleading simplifications couched in emotive language. He makes a good job of defending the old practices:

The liturgical experts work themselves into a state of fury when they remind everyone that, in the old days, the priest used to say Mass 'with his back to the congregation'. But that is a modern interpretation. For centuries priest and people, offering the Mass together, thought they were facing the same direction; symbolically, they were pointing themselves and their prayers toward an unseen God. (Day, 1998, p. 132)

He is right in asserting that to place an altar table in the middle of an open liturgical space is to oversimplify primitive practice in which a baldachino, or canopy, would always surmount the altar.

But for good or ill, the toothpaste is out of the tube, and there is no forcing it back. While future generations may come to see things differently in a century or two, we can but be faithful to God-in-our-time. Today there is an unstoppable movement of the Spirit which demands of us a liturgical sense of corporate responsibility, shared involvement and a repudiation of status and privilege.

The seating plan needs therefore to enhance this sense of the inter-dependence of the community and awareness of one another. A worship space that retains an east-facing pew formation will emphasize individual as opposed to corporate prayer, and in this configuration worshippers are often thinly scattered across a considerable acreage of pitch pine.

The central liturgical axis

A worship space that places worshippers in a square, circular or oval configuration will emphasize corporate as opposed to individual prayer, by requiring awareness of one another as members of a single body.

A configuration with much to commend it, especially in buildings of a rectangular rather than square plan, is the antiphonal or choir formation, with parallel rows of chairs, on an east–west axis, facing one another across a central aisle. In this configuration, familiar to us from many different kinds of assembly, from the British House of Commons to the seating for the Second Vatican Council in St Peter's, Rome, the central aisle becomes the liturgical axis of the whole space. On this central axis can be placed font, ambo, altar table and chair, in a dynamic relationship which engages the whole assembly.

4 Liberating the assembly

Like a new nation emerging from a long period of totalitarian rule into a participatory democracy, the liturgical assembly at this juncture in Christian history is just now finding its voice and its feet. After centuries of conformity to a fairly static pattern of ritual behaviour, embodied in the rigid seating plans of most church buildings, the restrictions on movement have been removed, or at least vastly reduced.

Our liturgies need to exhibit this new-found freedom. The assembly need no longer stand still while others process, but can itself 'form a procession with branches up to the horns of the altar' (Ps. 118.27). The assembly need no longer be confined to pews while it observes others engage in a ritualized sharing of the Peace, but can move freely about the liturgical space to 'greet one another with a holy kiss', a practice to which the New Testament exhorts us no less than five times (e.g. Rom. 16.16).

The assembly need not gaze longingly from afar at the altar table half hidden behind screens and rails, but can itself gather around the table to take its rightful place at the feast, laying claim to every aspect of being God's holy nation and royal priesthood, rejoicing in 'what we have heard, what we have seen with our eyes, what we have looked at and touched with our hands' (1 John 1.1).

See photograph in colour section: 'The assembly on the move'

When we consider the needs of the community of faith gathered for its Sunday Liturgy, and we find that it is not possible for the assembly to move easily from its seats, or to gather around font or altar table, then somehow it must be *made* possible.

It is incumbent on the leadership of every community of faith to engage the assembly, with enthusiasm and determination, in the task of 'knocking the building into shape' in a theological way. Bringing into play the hearts, minds and practical skills of the community of faith to examine together the limitations and possibilities of the liturgical space is a task in which the 'presidency' of the pastor is really tested. In this process the pastor will need to use the same skills and sensitivity necessary to bring forth a beautiful and powerful liturgy, but even more so.

Of supreme importance in this question of free movement through the liturgical space is the issue of the assembly's access to the altar table. Other restrictions might have to be lived with, but the single most potent symbol of liturgical renewal is the deregulation of the altar table. No longer the centrepiece of the holy of holies, hedged about with steps and fences, no longer the sole possession of the priestly caste, the altar table once again belongs to the holy community, and it must be seen to be so.

5 Presidency of the assembly

Closely related to the question of the seating plan for the faithful is the seating for the presiding minister. This should never be a mere afterthought, as this detail also will speak volumes about how the presiding minister understands his/her role, and how the assembly understands itself in relation to that role. Gabe Huck quotes Eugene Walsh on the role of the presiding minister: 'to minister does not mean "do things for" people, but rather "to be with" them. To minister, at its deepest level, is to "be present" to others' (Huck, 1998, p. 42). The seating of the presiding minister needs to reflect this relationship; leadership that is open, enabling and alongside.

When the bishop presides, the answer is straightforward, for

The cathedra *of the Bishop of Pennsylvania*

he/she should always sit at the east end of the liturgical space – at the head of the table – facing west, presiding over all that takes place. It is the bishop's chair, not any 'high altar', that is the appropriate liturgical focus for this primary visual location. All reordering projects therefore which leave in place a high altar at the east end have dodged the issue of liturgical reform. The fact that such altars are no longer used is no argument for the defence, for they remain monumental and potent symbols of the cucumber fields of Egypt which the people of God long ago left behind (Num. 11.5).

When the bishop is not present, however, it would be inappropriate for the pastor to occupy the bishop's chair, for the bishop's seat should always be kept vacant in his/her absence, as in those communities whose tradition it is to keep at the table an empty chair, for Christ, or for Elijah, or for the guest who may yet arrive.

In this case, the seating of the presiding minister should spell out his/her relationship to the assembly. This requires a careful balancing act, for the presiding minister (in the absence of the bishop) is at the same time both a member of the assembly and yet also the bishop's representative, and convener of, and presider over, its worship.

The custom of bringing out of retirement a heavy ornate chair from the sanctuary (usually one of several) to serve as a presider's chair is not a solution. Even if not the bishop's chair, it will look as though it is, and give the wrong message.

At the other end of the spectrum, for the presiding minister to occupy a seat in the front row of the assembly, in a chair indistinguishable from any other, is an attractive notion as a corrective to many centuries of clerical domination, and as a means of celebrating the fact that leadership of the assembly emerges from within it. This custom too, however, fails to keep the balance, or reflect the paradox, inherent in the presiding minister's role. The task of presiding over the assembly's worship is a significant ministry that should be honoured in a way which is visually evident and self-explanatory.

The *via media* therefore is to have made a presider's chair which is different from, but only slightly, the chairs occupied by the rest of the assembly. It might, for example, be identical in design, but have arms. There is no need for a chair covered in symbols, or for embroidered cushions, or for any other symbols of primacy. The distinction should be evident, but understated.

The presider's chair can be placed in a number of positions within that part of the liturgical space reserved for the liturgy of the word (there being no need for the presiding minister to be seated near the

The presiding minister's chair

altar table). This might be in one of the front rows of the antiphonal seating of the assembly, or in a west-facing position 'closing the square', or placed diagonally to one side. It is probably wise to avoid getting dug into a rut on this question, but to ring the changes for different liturgical seasons, or simply when the presiding minister feels like it.

Wherever the presiding minister sits, the position should reflect his/her role and ministry in relation to the ministry of the whole assembly, who *together* offer the liturgy.

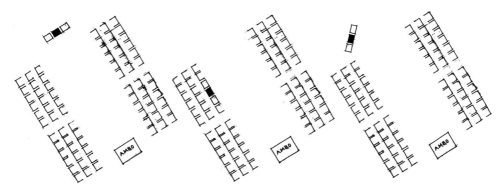

Some alternative locations for the presiding minister's chair

6 Centring the community

Now that the assembly is seated, and its freedom of movement assured, what is the proper focus of its attention?

Through the ages of Christian history, different answers will have been given to this question. During England's eighteenth-century Evangelical Revival, for example, the pulpit displaced the altar as the centrepiece of the parish church, reflecting the dominance of word over sacrament which then prevailed. At other times and in other places, church builders might have thrown their energies into any one of a number of liturgical foci vying for attention: baptistry, ambo (or pulpit), altar or (in cathedrals) the bishop's throne.

a Sign

At the end of the day, however, what sets Christianity apart from other major faith traditions is not our reverence for the word, for the veneration of sacred Scripture is also the mark of the other Abrahamic traditions, and many others too. No, the startling feature of Christianity is that at its heart stands a table.

This table symbolizes the ministry and person of Jesus of Nazareth in more ways than can be chronicled. It stands for his outrageous table fellowship with social outcasts, his unconditional hospitality to the untouchables of this world, his *joie de vivre*, his heart-rending farewell meal with his friends, his breakfasts and suppers reunited with his followers as risen Lord, and the heavenly banquet promised to his followers.

Furthermore, given the priorities of our Lord's own ministry, this is a table not just for us, but for those on the edge, standing in the doorway looking in. For this reason this section is titled 'centring the community', for it is more than the assembly itself that is being centred when the altar table stands in our midst.

In the early Church the eucharist quickly became the definitive liturgical act by which the Christian community was recognized and shaped. The focus of their gathering was a table which was also an altar insofar as it gave expression to the vision that the whole community of believers was now called to share in the priesthood of Jesus the Christ. The famous verse found in 1 Peter 2, naming the community of faith as 'a royal priesthood' (verses 5 and 9) is in the *plural* form, addressed to the *whole community*, not an individual. Not so much therefore a 'priesthood of all believers', but rather the priesthood of the gathered community.

The wonder of the New Covenant is the replacement of the old sacrificial system centred on the Temple in Jerusalem by the person of Jesus Christ who becomes for us a 'one-man temple system'; he himself becoming for us priest, victim and even altar.

b Location

One of the tragedies of the evolution of Christian thought, expressed in its architecture, has been the gradual erosion over two millennia of this foundational New Testament insight, and our drift back to the cosy and convenient world of a sacrificing priesthood conducting mysterious rites on our behalf behind chancel screens in our own version of the holy of holies.

In the Anglican tradition, which led the way liturgically five hundred years ago with the rediscovery of the primitive Church's emphasis on the holy community of faith, it is bizarre that one of our liturgical specialities, prevalent in far too many churches, continues to be the ceremonial slamming shut of the gates of the altar rail as the eucharistic prayer begins. In this way the people of God are cheated of their birthright. Essentially, this is a travesty of all that we stand for, a betrayal of the cause for which our ancestors shed blood. So let's get busy 'on all your carved work with hatchets and hammers' (Ps. 74.5).

At the centre of our liturgical space, therefore, we need to place a table; we have no choice.

'The holy table', says Kavanagh, 'is the physical focal point of every eucharistic place . . . the main architectural symbol of Christ's abiding presence' (Kavanagh, 1990, p. 70). 'For us,' says Philippart, 'the Living God's altar has become a dining table, our sacrifice the lifting up of our hearts, the sharing of Christ's paschal meal' (Philippart, 1996, p. 4).

Such is the importance of the altar table in our liturgical life that we should pay great attention to both its design and appearance, and to its accessibility. The fact that, for the vast majority of mainstream Christians, the altar table remains inaccessible to the whole assembly as a body is a clear indication of how far we have strayed from the foundational principles of our faith, and of how far we have yet to travel.

In most church buildings inherited from past generations, for the assembly to gather around the altar table, or even within sight of it, will require some degree of clearance to create sufficient space around it. The altar table needs space in which to stand and be seen and appreciated.

Alternatively, though less satisfactory, we can leave everything where it is and simply treat the abandoned east end as an 'architectural backdrop' to the liturgical space. If so, we must ensure that the flower guild are banished for ever from those regions, along with candlesticks and other paraphernalia which shout loud and clear that this old altar is not really dead, it's just resting. Such mothballing of east-end sanctuaries is, however, a recipe for trouble. It may seem an attractive compromise in the midst of a stormy parish meeting when the eggs are flying, but it will end in tears. A mothballed altar is nothing less than a cucumber field, and Moses could tell you all about those. Even 40 years on the children of Israel were still moaning and groaning about what they had left behind, most especially the cucumbers, and the nay-sayers of our own generation don't miss a beat in picking up the chorus.

The best position for the altar table is that which most honours its purpose and prominence in the space, and which most easily facilitates the gathering of the assembly around it to offer the eucharistic prayer.

In church buildings of the traditional nave and chancel formation, a frequent solution which may well accommodate these needs is to place the altar table in the midst of the chancel cleared of choir stalls and other furniture (although this will require the co-operation of the musicians who are frequently found to occupy this space; see section 8 below).

Much depends on the dimensions of this space, and what proportion of the assembly it is possible physically to gather round it at the same time. A lot will be determined by trial and error, seeing how things work and how they look once you have done them. For those who like things settled, neat and tidy, such experimentation is the equivalent of white-water rafting, but is probably unavoidable.

The altar table may well find a new home in the chancel, but not necessarily so. Even if the chancel is cleared of all rails and screens, the chancel steps remain, and although this may provide good visibility it also perpetuates bad theology. Altar steps have about them the smell of a hierarchical understanding of ministry which we are engaged in erasing in today's Church. I remember with some nostalgia the days of the High Mass, with priest, deacon and sub-deacon on different levels, each in his place and God in his heaven; but we are called now by the Spirit of God to sing a different song. Different ministries and vocations there will always be, and we rejoice in them, but they will be differentiated not by status but by service. The authority of those 'set over us in the Lord' is enhanced not diminished by a letting go of the trappings of power and privilege. The archbishop who sells his palace to live in a city rectory earns more Brownie points than he will ever know what to do with, and the pastor who leads from among his/her people is exalted not belittled in so doing.

If not in the chancel, therefore, the altar table must needs be placed on the floor of the house, on what Gordon Lathrop graphically describes as the 'liturgical pavement', the base level of the community's worshipping life. It is indeed a very noble aim to establish a single level throughout what might be called the 'arena' of liturgical action, that is, the central area on which will stand, in a variety of configurations, the font, the ambo and the altar table. This is the liturgical 'level playing field' where we can begin the training of the team in which we all have won a place by baptism.

This does not mean necessarily that the whole church building will be one level throughout, but the main liturgical axis will be level, with ancillary spaces (for example a platform to one side for the instrumentalists) grouped around the perimeter.

There is a wonderful dramatic effect to be gained here from reversing the traditional order – to come *down* into the centre of things instead of mounting up. In cases where a radical reorientation of the building is possible, the chancel is thereby converted into an entrance/gathering space, from which one steps down into the nave where the altar table is placed.

This experience echoes the Song of Mary, in the casting down and lifting up, and our Lord himself loved a good reversal of roles and expectations. Portsmouth Cathedral in England has created a remarkable liturgical space by this stratagem, and it is a delightful surprise to enter the doors of the cathedral onto a perimeter walkway around the central, almost square, nave which is at a lower level. There is something here that recalls the Pool of Siloam with its steps down to the healing waters.

In those situations where the final conclusion of the faith community is that it will

St Nicholas', Evanston, Illinois – view looking down from the former chancel

for ever remain impossible in this particular building to gather the assembly around the altar table, then two alternatives remain:

- To use the existing church building as one of two liturgical spaces for the Sunday Liturgy, the other space being located in a separate but adjacent space, for example the parish hall. In this way the assembly processes from one space where the ministry of the word takes place to the other space where the eucharistic prayer is offered and communion shared. Assuming that the assembly stands around the altar table (which is the whole purpose of the exercise) then no seating is required, except around the perimeter for the elderly or infirm, and so the latter space can be quite a bit smaller than the former. This kind of processional use of space is familiar to many parishes from the liturgies of Passion (Palm) Sunday.

- To retain the existing building as a liturgical space for weekday worship and for occasional offices such as weddings and funerals, while hiring an alternative space, for example a local school or community hall, for the Sunday Liturgy. This is the kind of strategic question that every parish should be addressing in terms not only of liturgy but of mission to the neighbourhood. The controversy that is likely to engulf such a proposal when first mooted can bring to life the education process by which a community of faith comes to terms with its real priorities. In this case, are we wedded to a particular space or to the sacred task of celebration and proclamation of good news?

Design

When the assembly arrives at the altar table, it has every right to expect that the table will fit the assembly, not the other way round. In Cranmer's liturgical renewal the altar table was turned through 90 degrees, end-on to the congregation in the nave, but that will most likely end up looking highly peculiar, and the chance should be taken to introduce an altar table that matches the theology of our own day instead of a bygone age. A rectangular table, which nearly all old altar tables are, is an unsatisfactory shape if we are trying to move on from the days when an altar had a front and back, a north and south, or a gospel and epistle end. By contrast, a square or round altar table declares by its shape and appearance a new deal.

> **See photograph in colour section: 'A table "where all God's people have equal access"'**

This altar table 'belongs' to no particular person or caste within the assembly, it belongs to all. This is a table where all God's people have equal access, at which 'all are welcome', to use the phrase from Marty Haugen's wonderful liturgical song.[1] The assembly of God's priestly community can approach the holy table because (at long last) it has come to realize its own holiness. For the assembly, like the children of Israel, 'beheld God, and they ate and drank' (Ex. 24.11). As Gordon Lathrop puts it, 'This is a meeting, an association, that is transformed in its mode and its content by being gathered into the very life of the triune God' (Lathrop, 1999, p. 39).

The altar table, like all liturgical furniture but especially so, should possess a 'sober splendor congruent with the assembly and its sacred purpose' (Kavanagh, 1990, p. 19).

If the altar is a worthy piece of liturgical furniture, let it be so. Allow it to stand up for itself, unadorned by frontals super or not-so-super.[2] Fear of upsetting the needle-workers of the parish is no justification for perpetuating ugliness and depriving the altar table of its rightful dignity and prominence. The altar table should not in fact be adorned by anything when not in use. No candlesticks, no cross, no flowers (!), no nothing. Despite the prevalence in English cathedrals of altar tables as long as a cricket pitch, the altar is not in fact a sideboard on which we display the family memorabilia, but a working table around which the assembly gathers. Not even the 'fair linen cloth' should stay on the altar table between services, but should instead be carried in procession at the offertory, a potent symbol of the 'laying of the table' by the community for its household meal.

7 Forming the assembly

All that being said about the centrality of the table in the liturgical life of the Christian tradition, Christians are called to be liturgically bifocal. Word and Sacrament are the twin pillars or poles that hold up our 'tent of meeting' with God, and ambo and altar are the two centres of our attention in the eucharistic action.

Both are 'tables' around which the assembly is invited to sit, at which we break open the words of Scripture and break the bread. As we unfold the Scriptures in our midst, the assembly devours and digests them, like the writer of Revelation who 'took the little scroll from the hand of the angel and ate it' (Rev. 10.10).

As the assembly reads, marks, learns and inwardly digests the Scriptures, it is formed and shaped by the Spirit of God. Jesus himself, not the written page, is the Word, and the Scriptures are a sacrament of this Word, by which we are fed and nurtured. As Bianchi reminds us, 'we find in both Biblical terminology and early Christian literature the idea of eating or "chewing" the Word, as a way of expressing the act of pondering the words of Scripture' (Bianchi, 2002, p. 19).

If we are to honour the Scriptures as the sacrament of Jesus the Word in the midst of the assembly, the greatest care needs to be given to the nature and design of the furniture on which the Scriptures are displayed, and from which they are read aloud, proclaimed and interpreted.

See photograph in colour section: 'An ambo "of prominence and simple dignity"'

To invest the reading and interpretation of the Scriptures with greater importance, a single piece of furniture, of prominence and simple dignity, and with adequate space around it, should be set up in the midst of the assembly as the place where the Scriptures are both proclaimed and interpreted.

The inherited pattern of both lectern and pulpit as dual foci of the reading and proclamation of the Scriptures is an unhelpful departure from primitive practice. One of them must be disposed of and the other pressed into service as an ambo, the word used in the early Church for the place of the reading of the word. Better still, a completely new piece of furniture could be installed that will do the job more appropriately.

The design of a new ambo provides all kinds of possibilities for recapturing earlier stages of our spiritual journey. One possibility is to create an ambo that will by its design (and perhaps by inscription also) recall us to the kind of reading desk (*bema*) that Jesus is described as using in the synagogues of Galilee. If so, we can construct an ambo with a very wide desk top to it (on which the scroll would have been unwound, but which for us can hold a multitude of books and papers for the various leaders of worship), and with a readers' bench, which comes in very handy when one has more than one reader, or an assistant to guide the readers who needs somewhere to perch.

The construction of a new ambo is thus an opportunity to strengthen our bonds with our neighbours of the Jewish tradition. At Philadelphia, our Jewish Adviser, Rabbi Ivan Caine, suggested the text from Psalm 16.8 ('I am ever aware of the presence of the Eternal One') which now adorns the front of our ambo, inscribed in Hebrew. He also found us an artist member of his synagogue to design the inscription, and was himself the first person to proclaim the Scriptures (from the Book of Daniel, read in Aramaic) from the new ambo at the rededication of our renovated cathedral.

If possible the ambo should be brought down into the midst of the people, at the west end facing east, where you would have found it in an early Christian basilica. This breaks once and for all with the 'performance model' of an east-end liturgical 'stage' from where the cast of the liturgical show addresses the audience.

8 Musical support

This section is headed 'musical support' rather than 'music', as we need to arrive at a place where those with musical gifts to share see their work as a liturgical ministry supporting and enriching the offering of the whole people of God. This may sound obvious enough, but the reverse situation all too often prevails in which the liturgy is seen merely as the setting for the musical jewels to be placed within it by 'the choir'. A five-minute setting of the Sanctus by Vittoria for example may be a delight as part of a concert, but in the liturgy it will in effect take an axe to the eucharistic prayer, destroying its essential unity.

The word 'choir' is here given inverted commas simply because its popular use is a misnomer that lies at the heart of the problem. There is only one choir in the assembly, and that is the assembly itself. What we have grown accustomed to calling the 'choir' is that section of the assembly which, in sharing its musical gifts, helps the whole assembly realize its potential to make music. Under the director of music, these singers and musicians give generously of time and talents to enrich the worship of the community of faith and to enable the whole assembly to find its voice.

The monastic tradition has for many centuries shown us the way: the whole monastic community of, say, a Benedictine abbey, forms the choir (and in medieval buildings 'choir' still refers to that part of the church or monastic building where the monks' stalls were placed). Within that choir formed of the whole monastic community, a small group of specially gifted singers will be on hand for 'special effects' when required, for example the singing of an intricate Gregorian alleluia, or a hymn sung in four parts. They will occupy their regular stalls along with everyone else, but may emerge to stand in the centre for a particular section where they need to be together. They face east because they are not 'performing' for a congregation but addressing God in praise. Having sung their 'party piece', members of the group return to their regular stalls and are once again lost in the crowd.

In this we see the pattern that should prevail in parishes. There is absolutely nothing in the role of singers and musicians described above that requires them to dress differently from the assembly, to sit in special seats, or to confine themselves to that part of a traditional church building (the chancel) where they have customarily been installed and from where, incidentally, they can be least clearly heard. The curious phenomenon of the robed choir is a romantic gothic fantasy dreamt up by the Victorians and now needs (at least as far as parish churches are concerned) to go the same way as the gas mantle, the hoop skirt and the pianola.

A parish dedicated to the renewal of the liturgy should address the music question as top priority. If confrontation is to be avoided, the leadership needs to spend time with those who have given loyal and devoted service in the robed choir, and

The singers emerge to exercise their ministry

preferably in a relaxed retreat setting rather than a hurried meeting after choir practice. Every effort should be made to get the musicians on board a comprehensive programme for renewal of worship, which will involve not just them but the whole assembly.

Musicians can play an extremely positive role in awakening the assembly to musical pastures new, and to a fresh understanding of how to share gifts and to minister to one another within the Body. 'Cantor, choir, and instrumentalists minister to and support Christians singing, serving the assembly before they serve their profession' (Kavanagh, 1990, p. 33).

Their enthusiastic support needs to be won, and their energies harnessed for the good of the communal life. Otherwise, it can take just a knot of disgruntled choir members, or a sulky organist determined to play every piece of new music at the wrong pace, for liturgical renewal to grind painfully to a halt. New music performed badly on the wrong instrument by a musical saboteur can be excruciating, but at worst this should mean only a slight delay in the introduction of new music, never its abandonment. Specialist singers may sing tunes, but in the community of faith they should never be allowed to call them.

A priority for parishes embracing liturgical renewal is that of an inclusive musical fare, in which we incorporate songs, hymns, chants, choruses and psalm refrains from a whole host of widely differing musical resources and from different periods in the development of sacred music. This is important not simply to provide much-needed variety, but also to ensure that in our liturgies there is something for everyone, thus avoiding the divisive polarization of separate services for separate age groups and interests. We may not like everything, but being required to learn something new each time we gather, or to sing the tunes we don't like as well as the ones we do, is no bad model for spiritual growth and development.

In the USA, to a greater extent than in the UK, Anglicans tend to clutch their copies of the official prayer book and hymnal (for Episcopalians, *The Hymnal 1982*) as a badge of pride by which they are defined. This has a stultifying effect on musical exploration in this particular corner of the Western Church, and is a reminder that once we issue to every member a hymn book of any kind we are providing a hostage to fortune.

The best hymnal in the world will always surprise someone by what it leaves out, and in any case tends to be out of date by the time it is printed. A far better solution is an order of service containing everything that members of the assembly will be required to say or sing together (though not the parts spoken individually), which frees up the whole thing wonderfully.

A further boon is for the assembly to be helped by its musicians to extend its repertoire of music that can be sung without books – chants from Taizé or Iona are good examples of this genre – which frees us up to sing more easily at those times when we need to be unencumbered with books (for example when we are on the move or standing around the altar table), or when we together need to respond spontaneously to something which moves or challenges us within the liturgy (for example when the communion takes longer than expected or when prayer and the laying-on of hands is requested for a sick member). In making music we need to develop the capacity to travel light.

For a pastor dedicated to liturgical renewal, the appointment of a music director is the most important appointment he/she will ever make. Appropriate liturgical music from a wide variety of sources is the sine qua non of liturgical renewal.[3]

Unfortunately the hiring of a new music director is a privilege bought with a price. The price is usually the trauma of firing the old one. Nothing in the training of a pastor has prepared him/her for this ordeal, and matters are made much worse if the outgoing director is, instead of an ogre (that kind usually shoot themselves in the foot sooner or later) the sweetest person you have ever met in your life. This scenario really does test the calibre of our long-term vision, but if we are serious about liturgy it has to be done. As in all matters pertaining to liturgical renewal, it needs to be undertaken not by a lone pastor set up by others for target practice, but by a small leadership team (including the pastor) committed to the vision and to the necessity of sometimes painful decisions along the way.

The question of appropriate leadership of the music department is of utmost importance therefore, not just in terms of musical fare, but in terms of the singers and musicians coming to know themselves to be a vital part of the assembly at worship, instead of an autonomous unit distinct from it. I am reminded of the change-ringers in the parish where I was trained, who summoned the town to worship with their peal of eight bells, but who then left for home as the liturgy began. They were attached to the church, but not of it. In the same way music departments can sometimes see themselves as separated out from the assembly, even over against it when the going really gets tough. Yes, they will of course always stay for the whole liturgy, but they can throughout inhabit a world of their own.

Small faith communities need not despair, and indeed can even lead the way in helping us all rethink our approach to liturgical music. Two things will be required of us, however: to let go of the safety net of an organist (however poor), and to expand our musical repertoire by exploring sources other than familiar hymns. Unaccompanied singing, after an initial training session or two from a good teacher, can be great fun and deeply satisfying, as the half-dozen or so present realize just what they are capable of. With selected hymns with easy harmonies, songs from contemporary composers and chants from places like Taizé or Iona, the musical fare can be rich and varied, and completely free of reliance on any one instrumentalist. It is a significant liberation from the constraints of the past.

Where singers and musicians are available, however, and where they are willing to think of themselves primarily as members of the assembly, with a ministry to bring to life the innate musicality of all its members, then a transformation takes place. There will be no need for painfully slow negotiations at interminable meetings to persuade them to relocate from the chancel; they will have already come to the leadership team to ask for a transfer from this place where their ministry is clearly ineffectual. Likewise there will be no need to get them out of fancy dress, or to dissuade them from pointless liturgical parades, because they will have already concluded that these things viewed in the cold light of morning are seen to be rather silly, diverting attention from the musicians' true and invaluable role.

Should one go in this direction, a word of caution is necessary. Having vacated the choir stalls, and with nature abhorring a vacuum, some bright spark may suggest placing the singers and musicians in a new configuration across the chancel behind the altar to 'make use of the space'. English cathedrals are very fond of doing this at their nave altars, thereby successfully scuppering any chance they ever had of imbuing the altar with solemn dignity or noble simplicity. The fantastic confections of curly- wurly joinery, devised to enthrone the choir in these locations in the manner to which they are accustomed, have actually been seen, otherwise they would not be believed. Visually speaking the presiding minister in such circumstances is simply lost to view, and can only be glimpsed now and again, 'not waving but drowning' in a sea of ruffs and red cassocks – the tail well and truly wagging the liturgical dog.

In more humble halls of worship the same applies. Even when singers and musicians have long since been liberated from their robes, the energy and activity of that section of the assembly disqualifies them from any position raised above and behind the focal point of the liturgical space. It's just too visually busy and intrusive. If the church building is reorientated, as has been done extremely successfully in countless church buildings on both sides of the Atlantic, then that's a different story. In that case the assembly will look inwards to the centre or in some other configuration, in which the chancel, formerly at the focal point, is now simply a raised platform to one side. In this case the chancel can indeed form a very useful raised platform for those providing musical accompaniment for the song of the liturgy.

9 Vesture

Determining the form of vesture appropriate for the occasion raises many theological issues which we should tease out before rushing to 'do what we have always done'. There may be some traditions to be rediscovered of greater authenticity than the habits of our own lifetime.

The alb is the basic liturgical garment of significance for the whole assembly. A recurrent theme of the Book of Revelation, or Apocalypse, is the white robe with which the blessed are vested ('they will walk with me, dressed in white, for they are worthy', Rev. 3.14) and as a result the white alb has been seen since earliest times as the robe of the baptized. Accordingly, there is much to be said for vesting the whole community in albs, or some other form of white garment more easily slipped on and off. The obvious disadvantage is the fate of the visitor who could easily feel excluded by such a custom, but it would be fun if a local congregation were to explore where this path might lead.

Attendance at worship at a Sikh gurdwara, for example, requires the removal of shoes and the donning of a headdress (if all else fails a handkerchief can be pressed into service), and this is accepted as normal, not exclusionary. Perhaps we have just become too squeamish and/or too casual in our desperate desire to eradicate from our worship any sign that this is a really special event for which we dress appropriately. This is not unrelated to low expectations in other areas of the Church's life, such as stewardship of our time, talents and treasure, and to a general shrinking from the notion that the baptized are enlisted men and women on active service.

An alb of suitable length and style

Normally, however, the alb will be worn only by those leading worship, but here it is a good thing to make as little distinction as possible between ordained and non-ordained leadership.

We need to be continually blurring the edges, in order to reassert at every turn the primacy of baptismal covenant, and in the process driving a further nail into the coffin of clericalism.

The wearing of an alb may sound straightforward, but the evidence of our eyes is that it remains beyond the capability of most leaders of worship. First, the alb is more often than not worn too *short*, revealing beneath a multitude of flapping flannels and unsuitable footwear ('too much visual', as Whoopi Goldberg would say). Second, the alb is too often held up with a cincture or girdle, which is both unnecessary and unsightly, giving the wearer a trussed-up appearance similar to a sack of potatoes.

Once upon a time, when the stole was worn by the presbyter crossed over the breast, a girdle was necessary to hold the stole in place. But no more; we can all be into free flow these days, and the effect is far more graceful.

The purpose of the alb is to distinguish one ministry or role from another within the assembly, not to announce the importance of the wearer. For this reason, a flowing alb, long enough just to touch the top of one's shoes, with full sleeves and a hood, is necessary to do the job. Yes, I know how much we loved those trips to the outfitters in Rome (I went myself), but those fancy albs with lace or patterned hems now need to be fed to the moths.

The stole is the symbol of authority and service of those called to the order of deacon or presbyter (and also of bishop, though they have various other goodies too). It is a universal custom that in the liturgy the ordained wear the stole in the manner appropriate to their order: across the shoulder for a deacon, round the neck for a presbyter. This custom should be challenged, however, if we mean business about recapturing the vision of the baptized community as a 'holy nation, a royal priesthood' as described in 1 Peter. This of course is not the same thing as the notion of the 'priesthood of all believers' dreamt up by the sixteenth-century Reformers in an understandable reaction against sacerdotal abuse going back many centuries.

The primitive vision is not of the Church as a gathering of individual priests (may the Lord preserve us!), but of a holy community which *when gathered as the community of faith to offer worship* exercises a shared priesthood, nay *becomes* a priest.

For centuries, clergy and laity have colluded in a deal to keep alive Levitical habits of priesthood because it is convenient for both camps: the clergy are kept in a job with a good pension, and the laity can offload all responsibilities to the priestly caste separated out from among them. It is high time we undid this cosy little deal.

One way of challenging this historic conspiracy in the liturgy is to take the highly significant step of reducing to one the number of stoles worn, no matter how many clergy are leading worship (this will be discussed in more detail in Part 3, section 5, 'The Liturgy of the Word').

In this way the stole becomes the stole of the assembly. It is worn by the presiding minister, as conductor of the orchestra, and then given in turn to any member of the assembly called forth to play a solo part in making the music of the liturgy. So then the reader, the deacon, the preacher, the intercessor, the cantor will each in turn come to the presiding minister to receive the stole before they play their part. In this way we make absolutely explicit the priestly nature and shared ministry of the *whole assembly*.

In so doing of course the presiding minister in no way loses authority, but in fact enhances it. For in the true spirit of the gospel, he/she relinquishes power in order to exercise it more nobly and humbly in a true act of *noblesse oblige*. To see the sharing

The preacher receiving the stole

of the stole as a belittling of leadership reveals a failure to understand the relationship between the priestly community and those within it called to preside over their assemblies in such a way that gifts and ministries are called forth and exercised to the full.

For the presiding minister the most usual outer vestment worn over the alb is the chasuble, the 'Sunday best' walking-out clothing of the well-to-do in the late Roman Empire (see Galley, 1989, p. 13). It has no sacramental significance in itself, and in recent years some have experimented with a variation of the Jewish ephod as an alternative. This latter garment resembles a sleeveless overcoat, open at the front, and for good measure can have tiny bells sewn to the hem, as with the ephod made for Aaron which was hemmed with 'pomegranates of blue and purple and scarlet stuff, around its skirts, with bells of gold between them' (Ex. 28.33). A further alternative is to dispense with the chasuble or ephod altogether, letting the stole stand alone as the symbol of presbyteral office.

It has to be said, however, that most presbyters would feel a little dismayed at any suggestion that the chasuble should be declared *infra dig.*, for not only is the use of the chasuble an early Christian tradition, albeit secular in origin, but moreover its restoration to use in England after the Reformation was an occasion for sorting the men from the boys. Those clergy of the English Church who first dared to wear these 'Popish rags' were sometimes thrown into canals by irate parishioners, or into prison by the state at the behest of vindictive Protestants. So the chasuble was hard won, and is not to be discarded lightly.

A very sensible distinction is to reserve the chasuble (or ephod) for Sundays and major festivals, using the stole alone over an alb on other days. When the chasuble is worn, it gives a sense of solemn dignity to the eucharistic offering entirely appropriate to Sunday or major Feasts. The chasuble cannot, however, be worn without a liturgical health warning.

The plain fact of the matter is that the chasuble should be entirely plain and unadorned. Far from reducing the chasuble's significance, this approach heightens, by dint of colour alone, the impact of the vestment as a major sign of the liturgical season or occasion. At the same time it diverts attention away from the presbyter, and his/her personalized vestment, to the presbyter's role and calling.

A chasuble 'plain and unadorned'

We face an uphill struggle here. Churches are bombarded weekly with catalogues of 'busy-bee' vestments, vestment-makers lie in wait at conferences and conventions, and in every congregation there are those who stand with needles poised to appliqué and embroider 'til the cows come home. All these people seem determined to seduce the Church with vestments, altar frontals, hangings and kneelers that will draw attention to themselves by their intricate designs and lavish use of colour and texture. They allow no peace for the soul and severely detract from the liturgy. They were the latest fashion in 1970 and should be consigned to the museum or to the dumpster, no matter who made them or how many members of the existing congregation clubbed together to buy them.

The chasuble should be very full, very large, plain and unadorned with orphrey or symbol. The art of the chasuble – and it requires considerable skill – lies in its cut, the choice of material and the choice of colour. If in doubt your local Cistercian monastery can usually be relied upon to give guidance or even produce them for you (for example, Spencer Abbey, Massachusetts, markets an excellent range of completely plain and classic chasubles).

This is no mere detail of fashion or style. The presider and his/her vestment have to come to terms. The time-honoured spiritual and liturgical rationale behind the use of the chasuble is that it helps to minimize the intrusion of the personality in the action of the Mass, allowing the office and function of the bishop or presbyter to speak louder than his/her person. The individual is 'buried' beneath the chasuble, that the assembly may rise from the dead. Many current trends in vestment-making depart from this ancient tradition, and end up enhancing, rather than down-playing, the cult of the personality.

10 Awakening the senses

a Touch

Enzo Bianchi says it well when he reminds us that the liturgy is

> an experience that involves all of the believer's senses. Those who participate *listen* to the word of God proclaimed, *see* icons, candles, and the faces of those around them, *taste* the eucharistic bread and wine, *smell* incense, and *touch* their neighbours as they exchange the sign of peace . . . the celebration of this mystery involves all of the senses, but requires that they be refined and transfigured so that we can perceive all of reality 'in Christ'. The senses are not eliminated, but ordered by faith, trained in prayer, grafted in Christ, and transfigured by the Holy Spirit. (Bianchi, 2002, pp. 9–10)

We have already spoken, in reference to musical support, of the vital ingredient of sound and song in our worship, and in reference to water, of the need to be tactile. To a large extent the appeal of the Liturgical Movement is to let go of our inhibitions – born either of the Enlightenment or of centuries of liturgical suppression – and to 'take hold' of the liturgy to make it our own. As David Philippart comments in his beautiful book *Saving Signs, Wondrous Words*, we need to recapture the power of human touch: 'In itself, human touch is very ambiguous. But by God's Spirit, human touch is redeemed. By the power of the Spirit, human touch is transformed and made a vehicle for the touch of God' (Philippart, 1996, p. 40).

b Sight

Unless we wish to strive to scale unnatural heights of cerebral purity and sensory renunciation, we shall take delight in visual beauty as a stimulus to our senses and emotions. We should not exclude worship from this universal experience of life.

Our worship spaces should be places of beauty in their form and in the simple elegance or noble simplicity of their layout. Within them should be found works of art which awaken our sense of delight and wonder in God, and in God's sharing of creativity with his creatures. They should be items which fulfil a variety of needs in our approach to God; sometimes drawing from us a response of prayerful devotion with their beauty, sometimes shaking us from our complacency with their intensity.

'Good images', writes Aidan Kavanagh, 'are meant to evoke the presence of mysteries the mind has glimpsed, to remind us of the ancestral heritage of worship, to tease us out of mere thought', in order that 'our memories mix with our longings and our joys to put us in touch with our deepest sense of home' (Kavanagh, 1990, pp. 20–1).

Previous generations, especially in the nineteenth century, tended to cover every surface and fill every niche with imagery of some kind, whether wall stencilling, stained glass or statuary. Layer upon layer of sugar icing was trowelled on the cake.

Today we are inclined to recapture the more primitive Christian approach of understatement, in which one or two exquisite pieces of art are given prominence in liturgical space by being set against a muted and uncluttered background.

No building I have seen has exhibited this process more dramatically than the 1960s' renovation by William Schickell of the Cistercian Abbey of Gethsemani in Kentucky, once the home of Thomas Merton. Here, a space of extremely busy high gothic detail crammed with images of every kind was transformed into a 'white box' in which the 'Christus' tapestry at the east end shines out in glorious power precisely because visually it stands alone.

Our visual aids to worship and spiritual formation – whether icon or statue or

Abbey of Gethsemani, Kentucky

textile hanging – should be given heightened significance by being few in number, and their introduction into the space should be a slow and cautious process. Countless are the contemporary light-filled worship spaces that have had their intrinsic architectural character subverted by the introduction of superfluous stained-glass windows by a well-meaning but misguided benefactor at a later stage. Countless are the spaces that are rendered visually neurotic and second rate by the insertion at every opportunity of homemade or catalogue art.

Let a large 'Go slow' sign be placed before any committee dealing with this subject, and let art be seasonal and temporary rather than a permanent fixture from which there is no turning back, and no escape.

Devotional art is particularly appropriate in spaces ancillary to the main worship space, set aside for devotional prayer or meditation. This may also be the same place where the Blessed Sacrament is reserved.

Here again, great care should be taken in choosing the item which will become the focus of prayer, and in avoiding unnecessary duplication of images. We should search and consult widely, seeking out artists (hopefully in our local community) with the proven skill to produce art that will feed the soul. All the main liturgical publishing houses will have resource books giving examples of fine work, and we need to circulate these publications to set our sights high.[4]

In such ancillary spaces, a facility for the lighting of candles should always be

Lighting a candle on the tree of life

provided. The simple act of lighting a candle, symbolizing the prayer which we offer and which continues after we have gone, is a custom which combines both visual and tactile awareness.

There are many ways of facilitating the lighting of candles, from a wrought-iron tray, or a container of sand, to a wrought-iron sphere, to a tree of life. In some cases, lights are mounted on small shelves integral to a wall. Whatever method is used, our worship spaces are enriched, and our habits of worship extended and deepened.

c Smell

As well as sight and sound and touch we need also to bring into play the sense of smell. 'Let my prayers come before you like incense, O God, and the lifting up of my hands like an evening sacrifice,' sang the psalmist (Ps. 141.2), and an enriched liturgy is one in which that image is made real before our eyes and under our noses.

The use of incense in worship is a custom of great antiquity which takes us back far beyond our own Christian history to the religions of the ancient world. Its adoption by the Christian Church was only gradual, but came by the tenth century to be synonymous with worship understood as sacrifice and with the mystery and total otherness of God. By involving the sense of smell in addition to sight and sound, the use of incense helps to make liturgy an all-round experience, involving all the senses. It is also simply beautiful. Incense is somehow deeply evocative of things beyond our understanding, as any New-Ager will tell you, and in our culture has long since passed out of the religious realm into everyday life.

Despite its impeccable biblical credentials (heaven is simply full of the stuff, as we know from Revelation 8.4, where we read that 'the smoke of the incense, with the prayers of the saints, rose before God from the hand of the angel'), incense is viewed with suspicion by those of a more Protestant persuasion, due probably to its visceral association with sacrifice and primitive religions for the great unwashed.

When I was first ordained, incense was considered *very* naughty in the Church of England, despite ingenious Scriptural interpretation by initiating clergy who pointed out a certain gift received by the Christ child from one of the Magi, and other hermeneutic tit-bits. The polarization around incense has largely passed, as it has around votive candles, mainly because as we have twittered on among ourselves about such details, the world has formed a queue in the local gift store to buy up every candle and incense stick it can lay hands on.

Incense should be part of our worship on Sundays and Holy Days, and we should quietly persevere in its use, no matter how many handkerchiefs are dramatically pressed into use as gas masks as the thurifer passes by. The pastor will find that the

*'Let my prayers come before you like incense
of God'*

sooner the better is the most useful rule of thumb where the introduction of incense
is concerned. On my first Sunday in an East Midlands parish, my announcement that
incense would be introduced the following Sunday was greeted with a loud shriek. Its
use there has continued now for 25 years.

New music resources greatly assist in the use of incense where no thurifer has
ventured before. For example, the exquisite setting of Psalm 138 by David Haas,
'The Fragrance of Christ' in *Gather Comprehensive* (GIA Publications Inc., 1998) is
enough to soften the hardest heart.

There are two significant differences in the liturgical use of incense today from the
days when it was a badge of a church 'party'.

First, it is handled in a far less fussy way than previously, mirroring the noble simplicity with which we aim to imbue the liturgy today. In the old days there was always
an (adult male) thurifer, usually in cassock and cotta, accompanied by a minuscule
boat-boy who carried the incense boat. The smaller the boat-boy the bigger the oohs
and aahs. There was much busyness, many genuflections, and a great deal of clank-
ing of chains. Today the pattern tends to be a single thurifer, most likely vested in alb,

involved in a minimal movement through the space, and using a simple open thurible, perhaps in pottery with a single chain.

Second, the revolution in thought about the nature of the assembly means that 'pecking order' in the use of incense has been radically reappraised. In the old days, incense was used primarily to cense 'things', most particularly the altar and that which was placed on it, as well as the Book of the Gospels in the ministry of the word. Today there is a shift in emphasis away from things to people. We have long known that the sacrament is holy, but can the community for which the sacrament is created and shared be any less holy?

Here is David Philippart again:

Always before the cross go the ephemeral curls of frankincense and myrrh, cedar and sage and pine. (They beckon us to follow.) The holy smoke carries our cries upward, raises up our praise, purifies the air of sin and sorrow. It dances delight-fully above our heads and waltzes into our nostrils, filling our lungs with thanks-giving. It puts petitions on our lips; we pray for the world like Christ. We rise like incense!' (Philippart, 1996, p. 68)

11 Lighting the space

As with the question of art, lighting the liturgical space demands the greatest care and attention (and as with art, this is discussed in more detail in *Re-Pitching the Tent*).

Lighting needs to be focused on the assembly and its needs and activities (not on the ceiling or rafters). It needs to be zoned, in order to break down the large space when only part of it is in use, giving an intimacy to the section where light is required. It needs to be focused on the main items of liturgical furniture and the assembly's action. It needs to respond to the different settings and moods required for different worship events, for example night prayer for 20 as opposed to eucharist for 200. It needs to consist of lots of little light fixtures rather than a few big ones. The light fittings should be set relatively low in the space, concentrating on a sense of intimacy and warmth rather than on uniform lux levels.

Finally, in the art of lighting liturgical space is likely to be the pastor or sensitive worship leader who will instruct the lighting engineer as to what is required, rather than the other way round. The worshipping community should therefore seek out spaces where lighting can be seen to be performing its liturgical task, and insist on more of the same. If in doubt, a lighting specialist who has worked in theatre is likely to be of more help than one who 'knows about churches'. Stand firm, brothers and sisters!

Notes

1 Marty Haugen, 'All are Welcome', *Gather Comprehensive* (GIA Publications, 1998), no. 753.
2 For Episcopalians at least, and no doubt for many other Anglicans, nothing subverts the sense of 'sober splendor' more effectively than that monstrous innovation known as the 'super frontal', the strip of cloth in the colour of the season stretched across the top 12 inches or so of the front of an altar otherwise laid bare.
3 American prayer books with the 1982 Hymnal bound in them should be burned – not because there isn't some good stuff lurking in the Hymnal but because the very notion that one hymn book could today contain all that an assembly will need is plainly ridiculous.
4 For example, Liturgical Press, Collegeville, Minnesota 56321; Liturgy Training publications, 1800 North Hermitage Avenue, Chicago, IL 60622, USA.

5 PREPARATION

1 Preparing the space

Before launching into the eucharistic action, the assembly needs to give painstaking attention to ensuring that everything is in place. This requires an amount of time that always exceeds all expectations, but without it the liturgy will be undermined by a sense of unpreparedness, with unscheduled dashes to the sacristy or the exchange of urgent messages at the Peace, and will lack that calm, sure and certain touch of a leadership team that knows where it's going and has everything it needs.

Preferably, as much as possible of such preparatory work should be done the night before, to avoid preparation against the clock, which makes no provision for the unforeseen hitch or hiccup. Certainly it is the task of a team rather than a lone presiding minister, and a willingness to roll up one's sleeves in the weekly chores of preparation should be the essential requirement for any aspiring worship leader.

The liturgy should be walked through by all those leading worship, checking on any special features of this particular event and the cues that will signal the involvement of each minister or the input of the musicians. Care should be taken to ensure that everything that is needed will be in the right place when the time comes, for example a fresh branch at the font for the sprinkling (showering the assembly with dried leaves can spoil the effect), or oil and purificator for anointing.

By the time the first worshippers are arriving, the ushers/welcomers should be at their posts, orders of service should be at the door, the readings should be ready on the ambo, and the Book of the Gospels on the altar table. The sacred elements of bread, wine and water should be placed on the credence table from where they will be taken to the altar table at the offertory. Everything that the presiding minister will need should be placed on a stool alongside the chair, together with orders of service on the seats of those assisting the presiding minister. Where a sound system is used, check batteries and microphones well before people start to arrive.

Candles should be lit about ten minutes before the liturgy begins, at both ambo and altar, and at other places as and when appropriate: for example the paschal candle in

Eastertide or when baptisms are to take place, the candles of the Advent wreath in that season, and candles associated with an image of a saint on the appropriate feast day. The manner in which the candles are lit can in itself contribute to the sense of calm preparedness. It should be done with a taper (never matches!) slowly and un-hurriedly.

Dashing about the liturgical space appearing distracted (or a little self-important) will get everything off to an atrocious start and infect the whole assembly with a lack of ease. If through unavoidable circumstances a minister should find him- or herself having to enter the space late on parade, nothing in the body language should give the game away. Continue to move slowly and purposefully, whatever the pressure, and everyone will come to believe things are hunky-dory, and relax.

2 Preparing the people

How do we begin to worship? We begin *before* the beginning. This is a process that involves the whole assembly, from top to bottom, end to end.

Worshippers behaving badly

We probably read a book sometime in the 1970s that told us God is everywhere, so now God is nowhere in particular. We have a lingering feeling that it is wrong to divorce 'sacred' and 'secular', so we are unsure quite what to do with 'sacred space' if we can still call it that, or with the silence that should precede worship. Add to that our natural congeniality when meeting with friends, and our patho-logical fear of silence, and hey presto we have a liturgical bear garden at the very moment we most need prayerful silence.

The 15 minutes or so before the beginning of the eucharist is in most Christian communities a squandered asset. It is simply thrown away. For most of us it is not even considered necessary to be present. Many delay arrival until the last minute. The vast majority of worshippers remain under the mistaken impression that if the principal act of worship is scheduled to begin at, say, 10 a.m., then that's the time when we show up, as 'nothing happens' before then. In fact, a great deal happens, if we let it.

The 'great deal' is the process by which the assembly is clothed with the sense of the presence of God. The 'conductor' of this electrical charge, the currency in which this exchange is transacted, is silence.

By silence we do not mean the personal silence of an individualistic or pietistic search for a spiritual experience independent of our fellow worshipper, but the silence which can fall upon the assembly when it waits upon God. The Acts of the Apostles says the Spirit of God 'fell upon all who heard the word' (Acts 10.44).

The experience of such silence is entirely corporate in nature, and it is the silence that can descend upon a liturgical assembly in our own generation, and allow room for us to hear God speaking to us in the present moment.

When people do arrive early for a few minutes of quiet reflection, they usually find themelves robbed of quiet by sacristans, servers or choir members fussing around the space to put in place what they failed to put in place in good time, loud hellos from the doorway, and the general hubbub of conversation between worshippers who should know better.

Among most Christians today there is an acute lack of awareness of the holy. God is treated rather like one of those poor piano players in a smart hotel lounge: we listen occasionally, but only when there's a lull in the conversation. This is a situation that requires a sea-change in our perception of what should happen when we enter liturgical space, and in our own habitual behaviour. The good news is that this is perfectly possible.

A word needs to be said at this point about the myth that time-keeping has an ethnic dimension. I was frequently told in my culturally diverse parish in northern England, and again in Philadelphia, that allowances must be made in the field of punctuality for people of different ethnic backgrounds. This is usually said by well-meaning liberals anxious to be sensitive to others, but I have always considered it patronizing to suggest that the genetic make-up of certain ethnic groups will prevent their being on time. It is in fact a subtle form of racial discrimination.

Once the assembly has the importance of its preparation and punctuality explained as an integral part of its offering of worship, there need be no further problem. Where habitual offenders remain, we can be sure that any sin-bin will not be populated by members of any one racial group alone.

Silence and children . . .

A further opt-out clause often cited, which poses a more difficult obstacle to silence generally, is the presence of children. This, however, is another false trail. Such an attitude supposes that children are incapable of awed silence, an asser-tion not borne out by anyone who has spent time with children who are moved by something which captivates them.

In this situation, the real problem is not usually the kids, but the parents who abdicate their responsibility to teach and nurture in their children a sense of the holy. In a culture of video games and instant gratification, a taste of silence is an essential ingredient in the nurturing of a whole and well-rounded person. The ability to maintain silence is a social skill which should be intentionally encouraged in the young, if we ever want to take them to the ballet or the theatre, let alone to the church's assembly.

In this, parents will need a great deal of help from pastors who give a strong lead, backed up with some solid teaching and practical tips, and faith communities with the love and patience to concentrate on the eventual goal rather than the immediate setback. Of course there will be disasters along the way, for children, as well as being teachers themselves of the ways of God (according to our Lord), can also develop a knowledge of how best to embarrass their parents with a well-timed stage whisper. These are but growing pains, however, and given a shared sense of purpose in this matter an all-age appreciation of a few moments of stillness is not beyond any faith community.

Even with periods of silence built into worship, the overwhelming experience of liturgy remains that of word, song and movement, so quiet listening is still the vitamin in short supply in our diet. In any case, don't Quakers have kids?

Presiding minister

Proper preparation begins at the top, and the presiding minister and other leaders of worship need to be beyond reproach in the matter of establishing a sense of reverence and anticipation within the worship space. They should never appear rushed or unprepared, and must ensure that they arrive in the building with more than enough time to carry out the tasks of preparation for which they are responsible.

Proper preparation for the presiding minister therefore begins with the purchase of an alarm clock that never fails, and that is set for a good 30 minutes earlier than is considered 'reasonable'. This allows for the unforeseen circumstance – the leak, the heating system failure, disarray from the previous evening – that lies in wait to rob us of time and of composure. The worship leader should in his/her person embody the spirit of centredness in God to which he/she calls the whole community.

Greeting people at the door before worship is a task to be delegated to others.

Before the liturgy, the presiding minister should be vested in alb (but not other vestments), and maintain a quiet presence in the worship space, engaged in spiritual reading or praying. He/she should not be in the sacristy frantically trying to catch up on undone tasks, or holding court to people with messages and reminders. The presiding minister needs to embody economy of movement, and by his/her body language give expression to a deep inner stillness.

Worship support team

Following the presider's lead, all those with ministries that make worship happen – sacristy team, servers, musicians – should have finished their preparatory tasks by a prearranged time, for example 30 minutes before the eucharistic liturgy is scheduled to begin.

The assembly

If the example is clearly set, the message filters down through the whole assembly. Once prayerful preparation is what people expect to find on entering the worship space, a new norm is established.

Those who hail fellow-worshippers across the room should be responded to silently, with a smile, and approached to be told in a whisper that prayer is in progress. Those who carry on conversation must be asked, gently but firmly, to respect the prayer time of others, or to talk in the narthex. This requires a certain toughness (as it's often the most disarming senior member who is the offender) but there is no avoiding a few awkward moments if we are to effect a culture change.

Where seating is reduced to a level appropriate to the size of the assembly (rather than set at a level to accommodate numbers at a Midnight Mass or a celebrity wedding) it becomes difficult if not impossible to avoid one another. In these circumstances, going our own sweet way – talking when everyone else is silent, for example – becomes that much more unlikely, if not unthinkable.

Preparation ahead of time will include prayer in the home, either individually or as a household, and reflection on the Scriptures set for us by the Church for the coming Sunday. To encourage such preparation, it is a helpful practice to distribute *on the previous Sunday* the printed leaflets which set out the readings for the next Sunday. In this way the community can keep the readings before them throughout the week, even researching them a little if they so wish, and so arrive at the eucharist grounded in the Scriptures they will hear proclaimed.

In this way the reading of the Scriptures becomes a kind of corporate liturgical Bible study, rather than the recitation of sacred words to a bemused flock. In addition, as we shall see later, having the readings circulated the week before makes for an alert and informed assembly, in liturgical dialogue with the reader, instead of one with noses buried in books and bulletins.

Preparation on the day itself will be primarily a corporate affair, the sacred business of the assembly to pull itself together and dust itself down before it addresses God.

To do this we need to create a climate of prayerful preparation and anticipation long before the eucharistic liturgy actually begins. There are many aspects to this.

Posture

The posture appropriate to the assembly in the time of preparing for worship is that of centred or meditative prayer – sitting erect, relaxed yet alert, with hands resting on one's lap, with palms open and upturned in a gesture of acceptance.

The great disadvantage of retaining pews is that the posture of prayer they facilitate is (in theory) kneeling or (in practice) the 'shampoo position', leaning forward in one's seat, brow clutched in one hand, in a posture suggestive both of suicidal tendencies and a dismissive attitude to things spiritual. This is no posture for the sons and daughters of God.

Music

Carefully chosen recorded music, provided the sound system is adequate, is an effective means of stimulating a prayerful atmosphere, and reduces the embarrassment level of those not used to silence.

In many ways, recorded music is to be preferred above live music at this point, as it completely removes the performance element, which may be intrusive at this God-centred moment. The singers and musicians will have their turn later.

The Divine Office

Another way of building up an atmosphere of God-centred prayer before the eucharistic liturgy is to sing the Divine Office in a meditative manner. The monastic model of using the office of Lauds as a preparation for the eucharist, with a short gap in between, can be translated into a parish setting by using a simplified version of Morning Prayer in the same way.

Lauds (Morning Prayer) at Philadelphia Cathedral

This is not a moment for a choir to sing Stanford in F, or to hog the psalms with Anglican chant. Rather, it is a time for the assembly to learn how to sing the psalter together, with accessible chants or responsorial psalms. Although a cantor or two will be advantageous, the psalms should be sung in a manner which downplays the role of individual soloists in order to enhance the corporate musical expression of the whole community. The assembly becomes the choir. No one singer or musician should interject his/her personality into a prayerful conversation between the assembly and its God.

The Office of Lauds or Morning Prayer should be tailored to end around seven or eight minutes before the beginning of the eucharist. This makes a clean break between the two, enabling people to enter quietly for the eucharist, but not providing enough time for worship leaders to start doing jobs. Instead they remain in the liturgical space, sitting quietly waiting for the eucharist to begin, and leading by example in helping the assembly to maintain prayerful silence.

Having prepared ourselves as an assembly as best we may, how do we begin the eucharistic liturgy?

PART 3   THE EUCHARIST IN SLOW MOTION: THE MEETING

Set out here is a suggested ceremonial for the eucharist of the Sunday assembly, following the ordo of the Western Church while drawing upon the resources of Anglican, Lutheran and Roman traditions. The ceremonial is accompanied by a commentary which discusses alternatives available at each stage of the eucharistic action and sets forth a preferred set of options, with explanatory notes touching upon historical, liturgical and theological aspects of the rite.

   The criteria for this preferred path through the liturgical minefield are:

1 the common experience of the Western Church – Anglican, Lutheran, Roman;
2 the assembly as the primary minister of God's transforming grace in the eucharist;
3 the need for beauty, simplicity, dignity and grace in our worship;
4 the Sunday assembly as good news for the world, not just as reassurance for itself.

1 The entrance

Ceremonial

The presiding minister and other ministers vest in albs and occupy their seats in the assembly, for a period of quiet preparation.

When the Liturgy is about to begin, the presiding minister goes to the presider's chair, accompanied by the other ministers, and puts on the chasuble and stole which have previously been placed over the chair.

On special occasions, and always when the bishop is presiding, a solemn entrance procession from the main doors to the bishop's or presiding minister's chair will be appropriate.

Chasuble laid ready on presiding minister's chair

Commentary

Customarily, the Liturgy begins with an entrance procession accompanied by a suitably rousing hymn. We do well to pause and examine what message is given when the 'altar party' processes in this way. Although a familiar and enjoyable custom (it's one of the 'highs' of the week for many clergy – the nearest we get to a triumphal entrance into the stadium), it should be used only on high days and holidays. In the cold light of day it is seen to perpetuate a perception of the ordained as the people who 'do' worship for the benefit of the 'audience' gathered before them. Once caught in this role-play, no matter how much 'audience participation' we include, the audience remains an audience.

Performing prelates

Thomas Day has an amusing account of the dangers of what he calls the 'rapport Mass' beloved of populist clergy, a cautionary tale for bishops tempted to forget who they are and what they are doing, and for all presiding ministers to heed:

> The rapport Mass is no aberration among the lower clergy. It starts at the top.
>
> Let us go to a famous cathedral and watch the way one particular prelate shows the priests of his diocese how rapport will allow them to 'steal the show'.
>
> At Midnight Mass the prelate charges into the great church; he shakes hands on his way up the aisle. The chorus, organ, timpani and congregation are supposed to be jubilantly gathering the faithful in song or announcing the theme of the Mass, but a stronger impression is that they are proclaiming the arrival of the star performer, the prelate. (Day, 1998, p. 136)

As a corrective to such triumphalism, the sight of the presiding minister and assistants, vested in albs, seated as members of the assembly in a time of quiet preparation works wonders for the recapture of the vision of the baptismal community offering eucharist together. It is also extremely effective in stilling the storm of mindless chatter that usually assails our ears as we enter a place of worship.

Except for high days and holidays, when an entrance procession rightly signifies the importance of the occasion, the vestments to be worn by the presiding minister over the alb should be placed on the presider's chair and donned just before the eucharist is about to begin. In this way the vestments will be seen less as symbols of authority and more as 'overalls' for the task in hand, a task designated to the presiding minister by the whole assembly.

On occasions when the bishop is present, and on other special festivals, an entrance procession sets apart the eucharist as being of particular significance, and heightens the sense of anticipation. When a procession takes place, every effort should be made (no matter what the weather is doing, nor how tortuous the route via the boiler room) to ensure that the procession begins at the main entrance doors with some éclat. Any hope of dramatic effect is lost if the first sight the assembly has of the procession is that of the worship leaders slinking down the side aisle, trying to make themselves invisible.

Great self-discipline is required of those leading worship if a procession is to work effectively as a solemn occasion. All those taking part need to keep their eyes on the ball, which usually means straight ahead. The presiding minister needs to remember that he/she is not canvassing votes or kissing babies at this point. He/she has no need to make eye contact with anyone, let alone wave or grasp hands.

Nor is there need for those forming the procession to carry hymn books to wave around in a burst of energetic hymn singing. Those forming the entrance procession need to impress no one, except in their concentration on what the assembly needs them to do – to model God-centredness at the beginning of worship to lift the whole assembly to a new plane and a new level of spiritual consciousness.

Incense should lead the procession, followed by the cross, which should be carried into the midst of the assembly to be 'planted' in a position central to the action, probably near the altar table. The cross should then remain there throughout the eucharist, and should not be taken on any walk-about, for example at the gospel or offertory. It should go without saying that there should only ever be one cross visible at any one time, either in the procession or in the liturgical space. The needless duplication of symbols is a primary cause of their having been devalued.

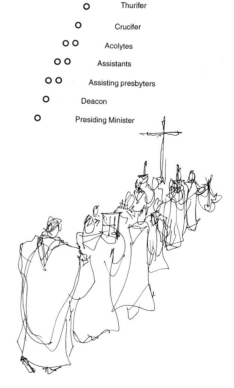

Thurifer

Crucifer

Acolytes

Assistants

Assisting presbyters

Deacon

Presiding Minister

Order for processions

The procession will not necessarily be very long. Lights may accompany the cross, and then follow the vested ministers of the liturgy, the presiding minister bringing up the rear. As discussed in Chapter 4 (section 8), there is no need for the singers to vest or to process, as their voices will be heard more effectively from elsewhere. It may, however, be appropriate for musicians (for example percussionists) to join the procession to add a bit of oomph.

2 The greeting

Ceremonial

The presiding minister bows to the assembly, and greets the community with the opening acclamation followed by words of welcome and an introduction to the theme of the day.

Commentary

The first word from the presiding minister's lips should be a liturgical greeting, not his or her words, but the words of the liturgy, reminding the assembly from the first moment that they are here engaged on special business far removed from the regular and the mundane.

Too much good cheer

A cheery 'good morning' is not the way. If the very first words the assembly hears are those ad-libbed by the presiding minister, attention is automatically drawn to him- or herself instead of to the liturgy the assembly is about to offer.

The first moment of Triumphalism, the first grabbing of attention, comes with the 'Good morning' (i.e. 'Welcome to my presentation') and the little rapport speech at the beginning of the liturgy . . .
  A university chaplain I knew had the simplest trick of all for making sure that everyone remembered he had top billing: he would begin Mass just with one little word: 'Hi!' Now how does a congregation proceed to the confession of its sins after an opening line like that? (Day, 1998, p. 140)

Because actions speak louder than words, it is a highly significant gesture for the presiding minister, before he/she says anything, to bow deeply to the assembly, once to each side of the seating area. This simple act by the presider of honouring the fellow members of the baptized community, the fellow ministers of the liturgical action that is now beginning, speaks volumes of the inherent holiness of the assembly and of the presiding minister's role within it as convenor and conductor of the orchestra.

In this simple act of courtesy, it is proclaimed loud and clear that all members of the assembly are *co-celebrants* of the liturgy.

Opening acclamation

The opening acclamation should be pronounced slowly and deliberately and with an air of expectation, as if the glory of God is at any moment about to break through. As these words are spoken, the presiding minister should make the sign of the cross upon him- or herself, unhurriedly and deliberately, and with 'large letters', renouncing for ever the 'quick scratch' that passes for the sign of the cross with so many of those who lead worship.

Introduction

Once the assembly has been greeted liturgically, it is time for a slightly more informal opening announcement. In a greeting that might begin 'my dear friends', or 'my dear brothers and sisters' (am I alone in thinking that the unvarying use of 'my sisters and brothers' ends up sounding just a little coy?), the presiding minister reminds the assembly what Sunday or other day it is in the liturgical calendar, draws out something of the theme of the readings, and inserts a key phrase from the Scriptures that is to be used in the homily. The presiding minister may also at this point welcome visitors or special guests. This is a brief introduction – just three or four sentences – and concludes by drawing the assembly into the next component of the liturgical action.

This little introduction to the liturgy of the day is in fact quite a crucial test of the presiding minister's abilities. First of all, although the presiding minister will need to assemble his/her thoughts beforehand to avoid getting into a theological sentence from which there is no exit, the introduction needs to be given ad lib and in an informal and easy manner.

At the same time, the presiding minister is the bearer of the assembly's sacred and solemn task in the eucharistic liturgy, the embodiment of its corporate persona and action, and the community has a right to expect him/her to maintain a certain distance. The presiding minister who is at all other times the life and soul of the party needs, on donning those vestments, to learn what is appropriate behaviour for the task in hand. When we begin the liturgy we are ready to be taken out of ourselves into the realm of God. We want a good driver who knows where he/she is going, rather than one who can crack jokes. At the same time, the good presiding minister is one whose natural personality and sense of humour is always about to break out: it's lurking there, *just* under the surface.

3 The penitential rite

Ceremonial

The presiding minister leads the assembly, assisted by deacon or cantor, in a rite of penance.

The penitential rite is led either from the chair or at the font. When the font is used, the assembly processes to the font and gathers round it, and is sprinkled by the presiding minister with water from the font.

Commentary

From the opening introduction the eucharistic action can go in one of several directions, depending on the liturgical season or occasion.

Throughout the Western Church the most common starting point is the penitential rite. It has taken a little time for Anglicans to fall back into line here, although it is now clearly the preferred option in the contemporary rite contained in *Common Worship* (2000).

Now or later

American Anglicans clearly had the best of intentions in the *Book of Common Prayer* (1979) when it provided a separate 'Penitential Order' (p. 351) placed immediately before the order for the eucharist 'for use at the beginning of the Liturgy, or as a separate service'.

As is often the way, however, options have to be spelt out with great clarity or else they are not followed. The vast majority of Episcopal parishes persist in placing the penitential rite in the alternative position between the prayers of the people and the Peace. Perhaps this is because this remains the only place where the penitential rite is specifically mentioned within the eucharistic rite itself, despite the clear attempt to provide an alternative at the beginning.

The rubric at the later place states that ' a Confession of Sin is said here if it has not been said earlier'. Without wishing to add yet another conspiracy theory to the already sizeable American stockpile, the wording of the rubrics of the eucharist seems to have ensured that the later (very intrusive) position is invariably adopted. Perhaps no one has ever found page 351?

There is within us all a natural tendency to want to 'get the apology over with' before we can enjoy an easy and relaxed conversation. This goes as much for our conversation with God in liturgy as it does with a friend after a misunderstanding. Therefore the earlier position is usually to be preferred. However, every effort should be made to avoid it becoming a mere perfunctory preface to the liturgy proper.

It is at this point that the issue of journey in liturgy becomes unavoidable. As we discussed in Chapter 2, journey is an essential component of our worship of God in the Judaeo-Christian tradition, and until recently it has been either excluded from our rites altogether or ritualized in such a way that it lost all meaning.

A liturgy that contains a journey for the whole assembly – even if just a forced march from ambo to altar table – does a great service to the people of God by reminding us of who we are and where we came from. It sets our folk memory going, and gets us off our spiritual backsides. We are woken up to discover who we are.

Gathering at the font

The first journey of the assembly should be the journey to the river, to the waters of the well without which no settlement on planet earth is possible. The water in our well, the baptismal font, has waters welling up to eternal life, and so is more precious even than the town water supply.

For the assembly to gather at the font is a powerful image of its remembering that we are called by a faithful generous God who 'turned the hard rock into a pool of water, and flint-stone into a flowing spring' (Ps. 114.8). Here also we recall our beginning as a follower of Jesus the Christ, for most of us at a time when we were totally unaware of God's grace, and we thank God for the baptism into which we have only slowly grown. It is a good place to make peace with God before we continue our journey.

The assembly gathered at the font

Fighting your way to the font

In many church buildings, to gather round the existing font is almost a practical impossibility, but do it nevertheless. Do it when only a few can get within touching distance, do it with people standing on pews or sitting on window sills. Do it until the cry goes up, 'How long, O Lord, how long . . . before we can build a proper font?'

Resist the idea of a movable font. That just demeans the sacrament of baptism and puts off the evil day of ever doing anything about putting things right.

Even the meanest, silliest, little bird bath, or the ugliest brute of a monster, can be given a (temporary) reprieve if you take off (and lose) its lid, and fill it with water until it overflows.

So then, once we have manhandled the stone font from the transept into the entrance, and removed a few pews in the near vicinity to allow for at least a vestigial crowd to gather at the well, we can begin.

The essential thing is for the people of God to have to *move*, and for the people of God to get *wet*. These two shocking notions, enough to cause any self-respecting congregation to chase its pastor out of town, are sufficient to set in motion a wholesome renewal of our liturgy. Over the last fifty years or so, the three mainstream liturgical traditions of the Western Church have had a shared experience of the rediscovery of the baptismal covenant as the primary defining characteristic of the holy community of faith. This is something that must be made explicit and celebrated in our rites.

Confession and absolution

Our prayer books give us many excellent orders of confession, but the limitation with all of them is that they do not bear repeating week in, week out. They will be effective the first time we use them, because we are moved by the words on first hearing, but they rapidly decline in effectiveness with each repetition. Once we know them off by heart we are practically done for.

Instead, those penitential rites that allow flexibility for the leader to stir our imaginations and to prick our consciences, space in which we can quietly reflect, and a well-known response which we can say or sing, are more likely to achieve the purpose of this part of our liturgy. By such means we are likely to become more realistic about ourselves and more certain of our need for God's mercy.

Examples of these alternative penitential rites can be found in Appendix B.

Sprinkling

In the old days, the asperges were thought of as mysterious and very 'High Church' ceremonies engaged in before the beginning of Mass. We now have an opportunity of reviving this ancient custom but within the eucharist proper and as part of the penitential rite. It's time for us all to get wet.

The rite of sprinkling is a superb example of a component of the liturgy in which actions speak louder than words. What we actually say is less important than what we do. This is not the time to get over-anxious about correct texts or procedures.

> **See photograph in colour section: 'Sprinkling the assembly from the waters of the font'**

The basic elements of the penitential rite are the expression of our longing for God in our need, the calling on God's mercy, the reaffirmation of God's forgiveness to the penitent, and the rejoicing of God's people in the knowledge of God's unconditional love.

Singing our thirstiness

Some of the most beautiful liturgical songs of recent years have been written to enhance the Sunday assembly's gathering at the font, the 'village well' of the community of faith, and music should play a big role in this part of our Sunday ritual. We can sing as we process together to the font, as we offer a responsorial litany of penitence, and as we rejoice in the gift of water, this basic element of life that speaks so powerfully of both death and birth in the life of the Spirit. Particularly fine examples are: 'Springs of Water' by Marty Haugen in *Gather Comprehensive* (GIA Publications Inc., 1998), 'O Blessed Spring' by Susan Palo Cherwein in *Wonder, Love and Praise* (Church Publishing, 1997) and *With One Voice* (Augsburg Fortress Press, 1995).

The ritual actions of this 'gathering at the well' are of immense significance, and there are many options.

The presiding minister might fill a suitable container of water from the font, from which the people are sprinkled, using a small branch. The container, like everything else in liturgy, should be chosen with care. A ceramic pot of simple dignity is preferable, either small enough to be carried in one hand by the presiding minister, or large enough to be carried by a liturgical assistant as the presiding minister proceeds through the assembly.

Alternatively, the people might come to the font one by one, to dip their finger in the water and make the sign of the cross on themselves, or better still, make the sign on each other, as an interactive symbol of God's choosing and God's forgiveness.

Ringing the changes

The penitential rite with sprinkling is most common and most effective at the beginning of the eucharistic rite, but it is good to ring the changes, and gather at the font *after* rather than before the ministry of the Word, on the grounds that only after having heard Scriptures read and expounded are we awakened to penitence and renewal. This is a change we may wish to use to heighten awareness of the changing seasons of the Church's Year.

That being so, the logical place for this to occur is therefore after the homily, when the assembly can process to the font for the affirmation of faith and the renewal of the baptismal covenant. Here the emphasis will focus on the re-affirmation of faith and commitment, with water used as a sign of the renewal of baptismal vows. In this case, some form of question-and-answer credal formula can be effective, such as that found in the renewal of the baptismal covenant in the Easter Vigil of the *Book of Common Prayer* (1979) (see Appendix E).

Where the gathering at the font takes place at this point, the prayers of the people can follow, still around the font, and (in the Anglican and Lutheran traditions) the rite then culminates, most fittingly, in the sharing of the Peace.

One position for the Penitential Rite that remains puzzling is that included in both American and English prayer books, that is, between the prayers of the people and the Peace. This seems most intrusive in the flow of the liturgical action, but stems I suppose from a laudable desire for reconciliation before approaching the altar, in the spirit of Matthew 5.24. This, however, appears too close to a 'doubling up' of rituals, the Peace itself being a means of reconciliation, and to smack just a little of a Calvinistic creep to the altar.

4 The opening prayer

Ceremonial

The presiding minister, from the presider's chair, sings or says the prayer of the day.

Commentary

This opening prayer has a couple of names, both deriving from a Latin origin. Anglicans are still accustomed to the term 'collect' (L. *collecta*), with the sense that this prayer 'collects together' the thread of the liturgy of the day. Both the *Book of Common Prayer* (1979) and *Common Worship* (2000) retain this heading. Rome, however, has modernized, using quite simply 'prayer' (L. *oratio*), and in the *Lutheran Book of Worship* the Lutherans have followed suit. On the grounds of 'if in doubt be contemporary', the less obscure word is used here. Although explaining 'collect' can be fun in a study group, there is no sense in retaining an obscure word when a simple one will do.

Different traditions, and different periods within the same tradition, approach the prayer of the day in different ways. All three liturgical traditions of the Western Church have tended to provide Sunday collects of general application to the season, but with no direct reference to the readings appointed for the day. In this, the *Roman Sunday Missal*, the *Lutheran Book of Worship*, and both the *Book of Common Prayer* (1979) and *Common Worship* (2000), are as one.

On the other hand, the prayers of the day compiled by the International Commission on English Texts take a different approach, and are related to the themes of the three-year lectionary, with phrases from the readings woven seamlessly into the text of the prayer. These are an incredibly rich resource, composed with grace and a masterly use of language.

Although sadly the Roman Communion has not yet adopted them officially, they are now published in the UK under the title *Opening Prayers* (Canterbury Press, 2001). Examples of collects from this source, set alongside those for the same Sunday from our official rites, can be found in Appendix C.

In many cases the Sunday collects provided in the official rites of all three traditions are sometimes sadly lacking, and may strike us as perversely dull and unworthy of the occasion. This is especially so where the collect is a redrafting of an ancient prayer bearing no relation to the readings (from a newer lectionary) with which it is now unhappily yoked.

For this reason we should here become unashamed magpies or jackdaws, picking up gems wherever we find them. The beauty of an opening prayer or collect is that it is relatively short, and with a bit of luck is over before the liturgical thought police can get it on tape and clap us into irons.

The prayer for the day may seem a simple thing, but it has a significance out of all proportion to its length in setting the tone of the whole eucharistic liturgy. It collects our thoughts and lays out the theme. Having made our peace with God and rejoiced in God's mercy, we are ready to begin the serious business of the liturgy.

Two questions

First, should the prayer of the day be said or sung? On Sundays and Holy Days it should always be sung as a sign of the solemn dignity of the day, and as a link with the early formative centuries of the Church's liturgical life. Where the presider claims to be musically challenged (my musician friends tell me there is no such thing as 'tone deaf') he/she should be confined to barracks with a patient but firm music teacher until they emerge as the little songbirds they really are.

There is much to be said for the view that if a person cannot sing, they cannot preside at the assembly of the faithful. The Ethiopian Church would say the same goes for liturgical dance, but we may get to that later.

Second, how are the words of the prayer of the day to be presented to the presiding minister? Although the assembly has no need to see the words (but only to *hear* them beautifully and clearly intoned), the presiding minister needs to have them placed before him/her in a convenient manner.

The presiding minister should always avoid holding the book, as this precludes the appropriate gestures of invitation and of prayer, as well as looking slap-dash and casual. The book must therefore be held for the presiding minister by an assistant, who should stand directly in front of the presiding minister with the book held at a suitable angle and height. This is preferable to the assistant standing alongside the presiding minister in a kind of 'leaning over' posture with the book, which looks awkward.

The book itself is of course of prime significance, and liturgical resources are now published in so many different shapes and sizes that it is extremely unlikely, except in the most prescriptive of communions, that a single imposing cere-monial book will contain all that an assembly needs. It will therefore probably be advisable to purchase a ring binder in the liturgical colour of the season in which the various elements of the Mass required by the presider (possibly from a number of different sources) can all be contained. Such binders can cover a multi-tude of canonical sins.

The presider first greets the people, with hands extended by singing (or saying) 'The Lord be with you', not in a perfunctory manner or timidly, but boldly, with a sense of excitement and awe at what is to follow. *Enriching our Worship*, a supplement to the *Book of Common Prayer* (1979) concerned particularly with inclusive language, substitutes 'God be with you' for the greeting, but as yet stands alone in this.

The presider invites the assembly to prayer with the words 'Let us pray', and we pause from the frantic activity of daily life to ponder the mystery of God and God's call to us.

There then follows a period of SILENCE with hands brought back together. This period of silence is perhaps one of the most telling indicators of whether a presider is praying or parading his/her way through the liturgy. If the presider is nervous of silence, has no sense of 'waiting upon God' but is intent only on 'pressing ahead' in case anyone might otherwise feel uncomfortable, then all is lost. Let the silence descend mightily upon the assembly, like the soothing oil that 'ran down from Aaron's beard to the skirt of his clothing'.

Extending hands once again, the presider intones the prayer of the day, slowly, majestically and drawing out the significance of the key phrases which will shape the thinking of the community that day. The greatest care should be taken over this. Never mind practising the sermon out loud (God forbid!); practise the singing of the collect, with the parish musician standing at the other end of the space. Let it be glorious.

The hands are brought together again for the doxology.

Intoning the prayer of the day

5 The Liturgy of the Word

a The readings

Ceremonial

The assembly listens attentively to the Scriptures of the day.

Each reader approaches the presiding minister's chair, and the presiding minister and reader bow to one another.

The presiding minister places over the reader's neck the stole, symbol of the presbyter's authority to lead the assembly.

The cantor for the psalm does likewise.

The deacon, or other minister appointed to proclaim the Gospel, does likewise.

Commentary

The assembly now begins the solemn process of being formed and quickened and shaped by the words of the sacred Scriptures of both the Hebrew and Christian traditions, in which God down the ages has made himself known. For the Christian community, Jesus alone is the Word of God, but through the Scriptures, despite their flawed passages when the messengers got in the way of the message, the words of God can still be heard through those who have set down a record of their encounter with the God who remains forever beyond words.

The assembly listens to the Scriptures with rapt attention, not because they are a set of inerrant and unassailable definitions of truth with but a single meaning (what an astonishing notion!), but because they are a series of stories with many meanings, inexhaustible in their richness and application.

The telling of the story in this rite is never intended to take out all the poetry, to say 'it means just this, or just that.' We stick with the Scriptures, and not books of theology or lives of the saints, precisely because they open up, rather than limit or define. They are not historical data, or someone else's piety. They are free to be about me, about anyone, about us. They can be my story, our story, when as the church we hear and reflect.' (Huck, 1998, p. 77)

The heading for this section of the eucharist in both the *Roman Missal* and *Common Worship* (2000) is 'Liturgy of the Word', whereas the *Book of Common Prayer* (1979) rather clumsily uses 'Word of God' to cover the whole synaxis, with no sub-heading provided for the section following the prayer of the day.

It is important that the assembly 'sits up straight', ears pinned back, undistracted by books and bits of paper, to engage the reader in a dialogue of giving and receiving, and to listen with great attentiveness.

After centuries of passive captivity, the members of the assembly are now rediscovering their true role as celebrants of the liturgy, and at the end of the collect we come to a fork in the path. Here is a pregnant moment when we decide which way to turn.

One way forward is for everyone to sit down and wait for the reader to go to the ambo and begin the first reading. An alternative way forward is for everyone to remain standing while the reader comes into the centre of the space, and approaches the presiding minister. Presiding minister and reader bow deeply to one another, and the presiding minister vests the reader in the presiding minister's stole. This is a forceful sign of the empowerment of the baptized to lead worship in the context of the New Testament understanding of priesthood residing in the whole community of faith. For the presiding minister it is a powerful reminder that authority, like love, is enhanced by sharing, diminished by keeping to oneself.

> **See photograph in colour section: 'The reader is vested with the stole'**

For many, on both sides of the encounter, this is a scary moment, when the theological chips are down. Do we really believe the New Testament, or will our innate clericalism win the day? Dare we let go what subsequent centuries of Christian practice have preserved? Will the whole house of cards come tumbling down? Only you can tell.

Readings and readers

There is a multitude of reasons why the Church is full of bad readers. Pastoral concern for those who have always read, political issues about those whom we wish to honour by asking them to read, and above all, a general feeling that the reading of the Scriptures is merely something to be got through as well as we can.

In fact the reading of the Scriptures is a solemn act of proclamation of life-giving words, and is of equal, if not greater, significance in the liturgy than, say, leading the intercessions (which is usually considered a more difficult and exalted task) or administering communion (for which a special licence is required). Ensuring that the Scriptures are heard and understood by the assembly is a ministry of life-changing importance, a task of highest honour, and is too sacred a task to be left to any hapless volunteer.

Both pastoral and political considerations can be effectively resolved by the simple expedient of enhancing the role of the reader in the life of the parish by making mandatory for all readers a short and simple training course. This may consist of one annual session, offered on perhaps a weekday evening and a Saturday morning, at which help is given in the art of reading, covering posture, voice projection, pace and emphasis, and in which the ministry of the reader is given a sound spiritual foundation. Such a course serves both to raise standards and to thin out the ranks, as those who resent or resist training will probably not show up and exclude themselves from further participation in this ministry. But the course has to be mandatory to be effective, and the pastor needs to make clear to the whole community that no show equals no read.

The Sunday readings leaflet having been handed out the previous week (and emailed for good measure), the assembly is ready to listen with at least some idea of what is to come, but with a sense of anticipation at what both readers and homilist will draw out of the texts set before the Church.

It is important that we should not be too snooty about scriptural texts. What matters is that the people of God are gripped by the power of the Scriptures, and begin to see them as applicable to their own lives and situations. Paul VI quoted Augustine of Hippo in declaring that 'It is better that we should be blamed by literary critics than that we should not be understood by the people' (Hebblethwaite, 1993, p. 309).

Translations such as Eugene Peterson's *The Message* may not win friends in academic circles, but there is at least one Philadelphia parish where they leave the assembly spellbound.[1]

The first reading

The reader, commissioned for this ministry by the presiding minister in the name of the whole assembly, and wearing the stole of the assembly's shared priesthood, now approaches the ambo. The reader approaches the ambo therefore like a national president approaching a podium to announce a significant policy decision. It is a tense and exciting moment, and the text to be read needs to be announced with a sense of élan. This is big news.

The reader, wearing the stole as a sign of the authority vested by the assembly, reads from the ambo

The reading itself needs to be dramatic, but not over-dramatic, slow and purposeful without being sleep-inducing. The reader needs to capture and keep the attention of the assembly, and to show evident delight in savouring, chewing on, these holy words. A good reader will make us want to rush home to read the passage again, and to understand it perhaps for the first time.

At the end of the reading, silence is once again a vital component. Far too often it sounds as if the parting words of Jeremiah or Paul were 'the word of the Lord'. The reader is in such a hurry to get the thing over and done with that he/she runs the reading into the liturgical concluding announcement. The train crashes into the buffers and the sense spills out.

At the end of the reading itself, a lengthy pause is essential. Only then may the reader meaningfully proclaim, and with a proper sense of wonder, 'The Word of the Lord', 'Hear what the Spirit is saying to the churches' or 'Holy Wisdom, Holy Word.'

Readers can also add much to the character of the liturgy by the way they approach the ambo, and by their posture. Movement should be unhurried and purposeful, with a sense that nothing is going to impede them in this task. At the ambo, the reader will take time to settle before launching into the reading, taking a brief look around the assembly to establish contact with those for whom the Scriptures are to be proclaimed. The reader will take hold of the ambo rather than the book. The lectionary, or Bible, or liturgical binder needs to lie flat on the ambo as a liturgical object of significance, not held up in one hand like a paperback. Readers who come to the ambo clutching a Sunday readings leaflet need to have them snatched away by an eagle-eyed and merciless liturgical assistant.

Where sufficient levels of trust and expertise have been attained, it can be very effective for the reader to give a *brief* introduction to the reading. Not a mini-sermon, or a testimony, but perhaps a word on the context of the passage, historically or theologically. This can of course be a perilous venture, requiring a fairly tight leash, but is worth the risk if the assembly is really to become a community of mutual ministry and listening. It is the pastor's role to deal with abuses of such opportunities, but that's why he/she is paid the big bucks and gets to wear the fancy outfits.

After the reader has returned to his/her place in the assembly, having been divested of the stole by the presiding minister, a short period of silence is observed. This signals the assembly's acknowledgement that when the Scriptures are broken open, something significant happens which demands silence, silence in which the community of faith reflects on what it has heard, in the pattern of Mary who 'treasured all these words and pondered them in her heart' (Luke 2.19).

The psalm

Between first and second readings the Church has traditionally sung a portion of the Hebrew psalter. The 'Psalms of David' are not only an incredibly rich source of liturgical material covering every mood of humankind's stormy relationship with God, but they are also, it should be remembered, the prayers that our Lord himself used. This tradition takes us back to the roots of our faith, to the time when the Hebrew psalter was the bread and butter of Christian worship, having been appropriated by the Church and given an unequivocal christological meaning. The monastic tradition then caught the ball and ran with it, using the psalms to provide the Christian tradition with the romantic but potent notion of the continual song of praise of God's people.

The psalm should be seen not as an optional extra, but as 'an integral part of the Liturgy of the Word' that 'holds great liturgical and pastoral importance, because it fosters meditation on the word of God' (*General Instruction of the Roman Missal* II.61).

To achieve this meditative setting, the assembly remains seated, in a posture of quiet recollection. It is essential that the liturgy does not rush headlong from reading into psalm, but pauses to allow the assembly to settle and centre itself:

> The responsorial psalm grows out of the silence. It does not come as a sharp break. It is not a time to have a book in hand. The psalm simply flows from the silence, without announcement or disturbance. It continues the reflection. (Huck, 1998, p. 78)

Singing the Lord's song

'As the deacon's book is the four gospels, as the lector's book is the lectionary, so the choir's and cantor's book is the psalter' (Kavanagh, 1990, p. 33), but although the Roman Communion has remained steadily faithful to the liturgical use of the psalter, Anglicans have sadly wavered. *Common Worship* (2000) makes a stab at it and looks promising: 'the psalm or canticle follows the first reading', but then falls at a later fence '. . . other hymns and songs may be used between the readings'. The *Book of Common Prayer* (1979) is even more supine: 'a psalm, hymn or anthem may follow each reading'.

There is a simple explanation for this. In the Anglican tradition, a particular snare and delusion lies in wait at this point, ready to derail the liturgical action – the method of singing the psalms known as Anglican chant.

Anglican chant for Choral Evensong in an English cathedral can be a magical experience, but it is wholly inappropriate for the local church at its Sunday Liturgy, chiefly because it is difficult to do well, and excludes rather than involves the assembly. Directors of music are usually keen on the idea because it gives the choir one of its few moments of significance in what is otherwise a 'people's Mass'. But that is no justification for a 'party piece' at this juncture in the liturgy, and directors of music who suggest such a thing need to be reminded that in the Sunday Liturgy the whole assembly is the choir.

Another anomaly is the *saying* of the psalm even when there is a goodly number of people present. Although this is usually appropriate on a weekday celebration of the eucharist, when numbers are small, the Sunday Liturgy demands a little more effort on our part, even (dare we say?) the learning of something entirely new. A psalm is a song, and a song needs to be sung. There is surely nothing in the world quite as trite and deadly as a song read out loud as a piece of prose. Let's get our act together here!

We should therefore seize the opportunity to renew the singing of the psalter. There is now a myriad of different ways in which the psalter may be sung today, ways which are as accessible as they are tuneful and delightful. The biggest breakthrough came with the responsorial psalm, in which the assembly can pick up the refrain immediately, even without prior practice.

It is important to persevere with different ways of singing the psalms because this is our moment in the eucharist when we are plugged in to this rich Judaeo-Christian tradition, and it should be relished. The psalm can be sung in a number of ways.

It can be sung by a cantor(s) from the ambo and, if so, the cantor should come to the presider to be vested in the stole as a sign of the importance of this ministry. The most effective psalm is responsorial, in which the assembly responds with an easily learnt refrain, and the cantor will also act as conductor, bringing in the assembly at the appropriate moments. The response should be learned if possible by ear, releasing the assembly to look up to the cantor rather than down to its order of service.

The cantor, wearing the stole as a sign of the authority vested by the assembly, leads the singing of the psalm

Alternatively, the psalm might take the form of a liturgical song based on the text of a particular psalm, and again these are often written in responsorial form.

The second reading

The second reading follows the psalm, and all that was said above regarding the first reading applies here also. A second person should always be used for the second reading. Even if the assembly should have within its membership an actor from the Royal Shakespeare Company, this would be no excuse for hogging the ambo. Shared ministry, rather than perfect elocution, is the name of the game.

The Alleluia

After the second reading, it is time to prepare for the reading of the Gospel, and here the liturgical tempo gets geared up a few notches. The assembly stands, quite properly so, for it is at this point that symbolically the Lord enters the room in the form of the words of his Gospel, and the assembly rises, eager to greet him as he comes to stand among us.

In Lent, when the Alleluia is omitted, the Gospel is greeted instead by an alternative gospel acclamation, which may be a portion of a psalm, a sentence of Scripture or a specially composed refrain. A good example of the latter is 'Praise to you, O Christ, our Saviour' by Bernadette Farrell in *Gather Comprehensive* (GIA Publications, 1994). Other examples are listed in Appendix D.

The singing of the Alleluia repeated around a verse of the gradual psalm or some other psalm appropriate to the season or the theme of the day goes back to the third century or even earlier. It was perhaps heady stuff for the dour Reformers, and so for most Anglicans it has been fully restored to use only in recent decades. That is the reason why the deplorable custom of wedging in hymns before

The percussionists give some 'oomph' to the Alleluia

and/or after the Gospel still persists in some dark corners of our communion, and among Lutherans too. A hymn is no substitute for our ecstatic greeting of the words of Jesus by singing this ancient Hebrew word of praise to God.

There are today countless contemporary as well as traditional versions of the Alleluia, and we are spoiled for choice. This is a good opportunity to change tempo with some march or dance rhythms, accompanied by drums distributed through the assembly. With the blessing of incense and the procession through the space, as the assembly rises to its feet, the alleluia can be made quite something. By song, posture, movement and smell, the assembly is told in no uncertain fashion that something important is about to happen.

The deacon, or other minister, now comes forward to the presiding minister to be blessed before going to the altar to take hold of the Book of the Gospels. He/She then proceeds to the altar table, where the Book of the Gospels is displayed, and turning to face the people carries it, solemnly and lifted high, through the midst of the assembly.

Of deacons and gospels

Traditionally, it is the deacon whose ministry it is to proclaim the Gospel, but if a deacon is not present, what do we do? Different traditions have different answers to this question.

Rome is adamant that, in the absence of a deacon the priest himself proclaims the Gospel, indeed all the readings if no lector is present (*General Instruction of the Roman Missal* IV.135). For English Anglicans *Common Worship* (2000), while reiterating the tradition of the deacon's role, seems to leave the door ajar, allowing that the presiding minister may 'delegate the leadership of all or parts of the Gathering and the Liturgy of the Word to a deacon, Reader or other authorized lay person' (p. 159).

For American Anglicans, clericalism is taking a little longer to die, and the *Book of Common Prayer* (1979) stipulates that 'the Deacon or a Priest' reads the Gospel. However, the Additional Directives concerning situations where communion is omitted, allow that, in the absence of a priest, the eucharistic rite up to and including the prayers of the people 'may be said by a deacon, or, if there is no deacon, by a lay reader' (p. 407).

In the Lutheran tradition, in the absence of an order of deacons, while there is no restriction as to the reading of the Gospel, in practice it is usually the preacher who reads it, which nine times out of ten means that it remains in the safe clerical hands of the pastor as presiding minister.

At the risk of being thrown into jail, we need to ask whether such a restrictive covenant is any longer sustainable in view of the supposed theological primacy of baptism, and begin plotting a quiet but effective liturgical *coup d'état*.

One way forward is to train and commission a limited number of 'liturgical assistants' who will undertake a number of specialized liturgical tasks including the reading of the Gospel. The liturgical assistant will be vested in alb, and receive the stole for those parts of the eucharist when he/she leads the assembly. It is always best if this ministry can be tied to an already recognized role in the parish – for example warden or other form of lay officer, or seminarian – which then removes from the equation any subjective selection on the part of the pastor.

Such a team of liturgical assistants remains highly desirable even when a deacon is regularly available. For a deacon's role is not to reserve unto him- or herself honorific roles, but to *enable* liturgical participation. The deacon's role in the life of a parish would therefore be greatly enhanced if the deacon were to train and co-ordinate the team of liturgical assistants, taking his/her turn at reading the Gospel with the rest of them.

Where there is a deacon available on the parish team, he/she will obviously take a turn with the liturgical assistants in reading the Gospel, and this raises a practical question concerning the stole. Deacons traditionally wear the stole across the left shoulder, but for the presider to attempt to place the stole on the deacon in this way may be awkward or time-consuming, and in any case, in the scenario outlined above, lay people have just been wearing the stole over the neck, so why not the deacon? This is a case of course where local custom will in the end prevail, but one outcome may be that we lose sight, except at ordinations, of the historic but quaint distinction between presbyter and deacon in this regard.

The Gospel

The reading of a passage from one of the four canonical Gospels now follows, a reading accorded highest honour by coming last, and by the acclamations addressed to Christ which precede and follow it. Furthermore, the assembly always stands to hear the Gospel, a custom which survived from early Christian practice even when other postures had become customary for other parts of the service. Although the first two English Prayer Books made no mention of posture to hear the Gospel, the 1662 Book, through the godly influence of Bishop Cosin, includes the rubric 'the people all standing up'. In addition, it is customary for the people to turn and face the Book of the

Gospels as it is carried through the assembly and then proclaimed, and it is a dead give-away of a liturgically illiterate congregation when the crowd, apparently either dazed or determined, looks anywhere *but* at the Gospel.

The Book of the Gospels needs to be as gorgeous as possible, and where funds don't run to engraved metal covers, this is a good moment to make the needleworkers of the parish feel wanted, having cruelly deprived them of kneeler and frontal production.

Before the beginning of the liturgy, the Book of the Gospels should be placed on a suitable table in the midst of the assembly, and stood on its end, to be clearly visible to all. Customarily the 'suitable table' would be the altar table itself, but in a processional or stational liturgy, the assembly has not reached the altar table at this stage; the altar table remains just over the liturgical horizon.[2] So the Book of the Gospels needs to be placed in the midst of the assembly seated for the ministry of the word around the ambo. Care needs to be taken as to how we place the book, as it is difficult for a small table not to end up looking like a secondary altar table. Perhaps a solid cube, perhaps a stand of some kind, will be the answer. Once again, the local community of faith can have fun coming up with its own solution to this little problem.

The Book of the Gospels is then taken by the deacon or liturgical assistant, after the blessing by the presiding minister, for the solemn procession to the ambo. Although we are all now accustomed to the procession of the Gospel Book to the middle of the space, to a station in the middle of nowhere requiring an assistant to hold the book, it should now be possible to process instead to the ambo, provided this is now in its proper place in the midst of the people towards the west end.

The presiding minister blesses incense, and the thurifer leads the deacon to the ambo. In carrying the Book of the Gospels the deacon or liturgical assistant holds it in front of him/her as high as possible, signifying the treasure which is carried among the people. Because lights are already in place at the ambo, it should no longer be necessary for lights to accompany the Book of the Gospels in procession.

At the ambo, the deacon or liturgical assistant places the Book of the Gospels on the desk, opens it and announces the Gospel. There are a number of variations on how exactly this is done, but by far the most effective I have ever heard is 'Hear the Good News of our Lord Jesus Christ according to . . .'.[3] This has a nice dramatic ring to it, and gets us off to a good start. The reader makes the sign of the cross, using his/her thumb, on the Book of the Gospels and then on his/her forehead, lips and breast. Members of the assembly should be encouraged to sign themselves in the same way, with this ancient gesture powerfully indicative of our prayer that the words of Christ take hold of our minds, mouths and hearts. The deacon or liturgical assistant then takes the thurible from the thurifer, censes the Book of the Gospels and hands back the thurible.

Although the singing of the Gospel may be thought to render its meaning less accessible, to hear the Gospel sung majestically and yet effortlessly is a memorable experience, and it is a worthy aim for every assembly to hear it sung at least on special occasions. If a high standard remains elusive, however, it is better to read it exceptionally well than to sing it moderately well. At the end of the day, communicating the good news is what counts.

At the end of the Gospel, a moment of silence is again observed before the closing acclamation. As the words are spoken, 'The Gospel of the Lord', the deacon or liturgical assistant kisses the page he/she has just read, and holds high the Book of the Gospels, turning to show it to the whole assembly.

At the end of the Gospel, the Alleluia is repeated as a song of thanksgiving, and we come to another fork in the path. Either the Book of the Gospels is at this point left on the ambo for the homilist, if so required, or it is carried through the assembly by the deacon or liturgical assistant, to be touched (or even kissed!) by the faithful. This is a good place for us to lighten up liturgically.

The reader holds high the Book of the Gospels

Kissing the Book of the Gospels

Those of us of Anglo-Saxon stock may find it hard to be demonstrative in our spiritual life, but my own education in this regard was given a push forward when serving in a parish in Stevenage, one of England's 'new towns' – perceived as rather soulless places created out of nothing amid what was yesterday a green-field site. In the basement of our modern parish church was a screen dividing off a small chapel, on which were painted some mediocre depictions of the Holy Family. We never gave them second glance.

One day I found this elderly woman in black, complete with black headscarf, slowly edging along the wall, arms uplifted, kissing with utmost devotion and gentleness the faces of the figures depicted. I have never forgotten it. She was a Greek Orthodox from Cyprus, visiting her son who kept the local fish and chip shop. Amid the mundane, the humdrum and the second-rate, she had created her own little window into heaven.

So to kiss the Book of the Gospels as it passes by may be a leap for us, and should not be attempted without adequate explanation and encouragement, but is worth a try nevertheless. Even if only half successful, it can serve to release within us that natural sense of tactile devotion in which the Eastern Church has long put us to shame.

See photograph in colour section: 'The reader takes the Book of the Gospels to the assembly'

b The homily

Ceremonial

A homily, based primarily on the Gospel of the day, is given by the presiding minister, or other minister. In the latter case, the preacher comes to the presiding minister to receive the stole.

Commentary

The word homily rather than sermon is used here deliberately in the hope of recalling all those who interpret the Scriptures for us, that they are called here to comment liturgically and theologically on the import of what has been read and what the assembly is about in its offering of the Liturgy.

The homily is an essential part of the liturgy, even when only 'two or three are gathered together' but especially at the Sunday Liturgy, 'for it is necessary for the nurturing of the Christian Life' (*General Instruction of the Roman Missal* II.65).

Kavanagh reminds us that the homily is 'inherent to the rhythmic ritual of the liturgy' (Kavanagh, 1990, p. 27). It is not an educational treatise inserted into the liturgy, but is itself part of the flow of the liturgical action. The homily needs no invocation or prayer at the beginning (Galley, 1989, p. 90), for it is set within a whole liturgy of prayer.

The preacher can simply invite the assembly to be seated to listen to the homily. Likewise no concluding invocation is required, other than perhaps a 'Thanks be to God' or brief doxology, which Galley reminds us was the custom of many of the Church fathers. If the homily is any good at all, it should evoke a nice loud 'Amen!' on the part of the assembly, and all the homilist should need to do is provide a clear cue that the homily is over.

On preaching

There is a most unfortunate tendency, especially evident in the United States, for the preacher to feel obliged to offer a doctoral thesis instead of a fairly brief word of commentary and application to daily life. Many hours are spent by clergy (or so they would have us believe) locked away in studies amid commentaries and reference books, hunting down arcane definitions and meanings and clever quotations, all apparently to no effect. All too often, neither is the liturgy enhanced nor the Scriptures opened up to us by such *magna opera*, and the faithful are sent away with mere scraps of food as their rations for the week, with which they are supposed to work out how the gospel makes a difference to daily life.

A good homily should help us 'chew over' the Scriptures, taking a phrase or incident which is savoured, delighted in and applied to real life. Moreover, the Scriptures broken open for us in the homily are the liturgical Scriptures, those the Church gives us for the eucharist on that day or for that occasion. The liturgical homilist never cheats by selecting passages that suit his/her purpose. The (literally) fatal consequences of such selectivity can be seen all too clearly in the preaching of right-wing fundamentalists who restrict themselves time after time to the Johannine canon and the Letter to the Romans. You can cook up quite a nasty little religion that way, and identify quite a few infidels for extermination, but it won't be the good news of Jesus of Nazareth. 'The homily therefore', says

Kavanagh (1990, p. 27), 'must be soaked with the gospel in its liturgical context.' The homilist will take what is given and enjoy the challenge of wrestling a piquant message from the unlikeliest of texts.

The homily should make us hungry for more; not more of the preacher, but more of the Scriptures, of the spiritual life, of further horizons on our journey. Like John the Baptist, the preacher should be self-effacing, restraining any tendency to be too clever or humorous, that he/she may decrease so that the Christ in the midst of the assembly may increase. Ten minutes is usually more than enough; a good preacher knows that the toughest sermon to prepare is the shortest.

On weekdays, with smaller numbers in a more intimate setting, it is good practice for the homilist (usually the presiding minister) to prepare nothing until the moment the Gospel is read, and then speak by the Spirit of God on a phrase or incident that has 'sprung from the page'. Occasionally at the Sunday Liturgy, too, the preacher should, after prayerful preparation, do likewise. Garrison Keillor's delightful story about pastor Inqvist of Lake Wobegone is instructive. After carefully preparing his sermon, the good pastor arrived in the pulpit to find to his horror that he had with him only a card marked 'conclusion'. He extemporized bravely on, and afterwards received more remarks of appreciation than ever before in his ministry. After all, any person ordained after years of professional training ought to be able, at a moment's notice, to respond to the exhortation to 'make a defence to anyone who calls you to account for the hope that is in you' (1 Pet. 3.15). If not, he or she is in the wrong job.

In addition to addressing the content of the homily, we need also to examine the alternative postures for delivering the homily, which, depending on the occasion, may include the preacher on the move, and the preacher seated. Although it may be necessary at the Sunday Liturgy, on grounds of visibility, for the homilist to stand at the ambo to preach, that can sometimes smack too much of the public lecture, and it is good to ring the changes.

Posture

Some preachers are adept at the wandering homily, out there among the crowd, with the help of a radio mike (or that fancy French name they use in the States). Although highly effective on an occasional basis as a wake-up call, if overdone it can bring out the showman in the preacher to an unhealthy degree, and we need to guard against the homilist as comic entertainer/conjuror.

Another effective way of breaking the mould, and with primitive Christian practice behind it, is for the homilist to remain seated. 'In the early church,' Galley reminds us, 'following Jewish custom, the preacher usually sat in a chair to preach' (Galley, 1989, p. 91), and he recalls us to the scene in Luke 4.20–21 where Jesus, having returned to his home town of Nazareth, and in the synagogue on the sabbath, 'stood up to read' from the prophet Isaiah. What comes as a surprise when we come to examine the text, is to find that, having stood to read, Jesus 'sat down' to deliver his homily bringing to life the words he had just read, a piece of preaching so effective that he was driven out of town.

> **See photograph in colour section: 'The Bishop of Pennsylvania preaching from his *cathedra*'**

The seated posture for preaching is particularly appropriate for a bishop addressing his/her diocese from the *cathedra* of the diocesan cathedral. This requires, however, a bishop's chair placed in the eastern presidential position, in accordance with primitive custom, not stuck in a corner. At Philadelphia we have been fortunate in being able to build a new stone *cathedra* for the Bishop of Pennsylvania that is like something straight out of a fifth-century basilica in Asia Minor. This helps us set our common life in a proper historical context, and it is a fine sight to see our bishop address his diocese from his *cathedra*, flanked on the *presbyterium* by his presbyters and deacons, living out the teaching office of the episcopate.

St Gregory's, San Francisco

The seated posture is not, however, restricted to bishops. Certainly it is true that, for me, the preaching that 35 years on sticks in my mind from seminary days is not the pulpit sermons at the eucharist, but the addresses given, always seated, after the Office of Night Prayer (Compline) in the chapel at Cuddesdon. In some strange but telling way the preacher was, in this posture, able to *engage* the listener, as a friend alongside rather than a lecturer over and above. The pace also becomes slower and more measured, the message more intimate and direct, and the whole experience more potent and memorable.

In adventurous parishes like St Gregory of Nyssa, San Francisco, the preacher not only sits, but following an introductory homily invites members of the assembly to enter into dialogue with their own insights into the Scriptures of the day. This requires in an assembly a high degree of cohesion, of mutual trust and discipline, but is worth the risk now and again when circumstances suggest it. This is not for the faint-hearted, but perhaps the good people of St Gregory's would help with a workshop or two on 'taming the parish bore' and other such techniques.

The homilist has therefore several options when it comes to posture. Perhaps the best thing is for the preacher to keep us guessing, sometimes standing at a raised ambo to proclaim the prophetic word, sometimes moving among the assembly as God's fool to awaken us to a keener sense of our calling, and sometimes sitting in the midst of the assembly as a trusted teacher and friend to gently unfold the Scriptures to us. Different occasions will call for different approaches, but however we do it, let the Scriptures be broken open at every eucharist, as the bread is broken at the table.

A further question is, 'Who should give the homily?' How does the role of the homilist relate to that of the presiding minister?

The homilist

The St Gregory's model assumes that it is the presiding minister doing the preaching, as the chair used by the homilist is not any old chair, but the presiding minister's chair, and it would not be seemly for presiding minister and preacher to fight for it, as if they were a couple of medieval archbishops.[4]

We need to ask, however, is it appropriate that the presiding minister should always be the homilist? The Roman Communion assumes that 'the homily should ordinarily be given by the priest celebrant himself' (*General Instruction of the Roman Missal* II.66), although he may on occasion 'entrust it' to a fellow concelebrating priest, or to a deacon, though 'never to a lay person'. Anglican rites make no such restriction, and indeed *Common Worship* (2000) throws the doors wide open: 'The sermon shall be preached by a duly authorized minister, deaconess, Reader or lay worker or, at the invitation of the minister having the cure of souls and with the permission of the bishop, another person' (p. 159).

For Anglicans, therefore, the notion that it should ordinarily be the presiding minister who delivers the homily may seem a little odd if we are in a parish with a clergy team where the liturgical tasks are shared at the principal eucharist.

Kavanagh is undoubtedly right, however, in asserting that we need the presiding minister to preach if we are to attain that 'seamless robe' of liturgical continuity: 'The homily follows directly on the gospel of the day because the former is simply the continuance of the latter by the assembly's president amid his peers in faith. He preaches because he presides in the assembly' (Kavanagh, 1990, p. 26). Although there will be times when this rule is set aside – for a deacon or a visiting preacher, for example – it is a practice that ensures cohesion of the liturgy. Where there is more than one presbyter resident on the parish staff, it is preferable to encourage this comprehensive approach to presidency rather than the notion that all clergy need to justify their existence by being 'dressed up and up front' at every eucharist.

If we ask, 'What is a presbyter to do who is neither presiding or preaching?' the answer is most certainly not to dress him/her up as some form of pseudo-deacon, to administer communion or lead the prayers of the people or some other task hijacked from other (lay) members of the assembly to whom they rightly belong. Neither should he/she 'concelebrate' unless invited by the bishop on some grand occasion in, say, the cathedral. Concelebration was an inspired brainwave of the Roman Communion to release their ordained priests from the treadmill of the daily Mass which they were obliged to offer, even if only one other person was available to 'hear Mass' for them. This travesty of all that the eucharist was meant to be was ended (for all but the stubborn of heart) by the introduction of concelebration as the norm for priests in community.

This appealed also to many Anglicans because it somehow served to elevate liturgically the distinct ministry of the presbyterate, and of course because we rather like dressing up and processing in and out of grand spaces. Theologically, however, concelebration is bad news, because it sets apart the presbyters as a priestly caste rather than setting apart the presiding minister as orchestrator of the liturgical action of the whole assembly. It undermines the theological truth that *all* members of the assembly are celebrants alongside the presiding minister. Kavanagh says of concelebration: 'its theory is flawed, its form verbally obsessive, its practice clericalizing' (1990, p. 61).

What, therefore, should a second presbyter do? He/She should sit with the rest of the assembly, dressed like a regular human being, and take part alongside everyone else in the assembly's offering. Apart from being sound ecclesiological theology, it provides brilliant feedback for staff meeting!

c The silence

Ceremonial

A significant period of silence is announced by the sounding of a gong or bell or other instrument.

Commentary

The periods of silence observed after each of the previous readings are but trailers for the main feature that now follows. At the conclusion of the whole section of the liturgy in which the Scriptures are proclaimed and interpreted, an awed and reflective silence falls upon the assembly, the 'thunderous quiet' of people 'communicating that which escapes being put into words' (Kavanagh, 1990, p. 51). Silence at this point is not an optional extra, but an integral part of the liturgical rite.

The charka is sounded to announce the period of silence

The fact that the mainstream liturgical churches have customarily charged headlong through the eucharist without pausing for breath is the main reason we meet so many people who say that they have left to become Quakers. They felt they needed to get away from the noise. They would rather abandon entirely their liturgical birthright than see it mangled any further. In this frantic world, in which we are subjected to audio violence at every turn, we must have silence, and in the eucharist silence needs to be deeply embedded.

Actively quiet, purposely still

In the liturgy, we are silent, silent *together*. This is not an individual silence, even though each of us – as best as each of us is able – is quiet. This is not a passive silence, even though we try to be as still as we can be. We are silent together, actively quiet, purposely still.' (Philippart, 1996, p. 21)

This is more difficult than it sounds. Until the practice of silence is taught and made part of our lives, it is highly probable that, should a period of silence be introduced, a server or church warden will come forward to check that the presider is not feeling unwell, or at least offer to find his/her place in the book.

Everyone feels a little awkward around liturgical silence (as we do around empty space in liturgical places). We like everything to be filled, labelled and accounted for. Silence therefore needs to be *announced*, for liturgical silence is not just a gap in the proceedings but a silence 'purposeful, pregnant and controlled' (Kavanagh, 1990, p. 51).

Such announcement should not be by the spoken word, which somehow defeats the object, but by a prearranged signal. Here we can have fun hunting down on the web a Buddhist gong, or in the flea market some suitable urn or vessel to make a melodious sound. The traditional sanctuary bell is not a good idea, since it has programmed us since medieval times to a different posture and purpose.

While the ringing of the gong to announce the silence is a liturgical ministry usually fought over by the younger members of the assembly, the ending of the silence is a different matter. It has taken me four years, and many silences that end as soon as they have begun, to learn that to ensure a period of silence of appropriate length, the presiding minister alone needs to gauge the length of the silence. The end of the silence can be marked by the sounding of the gong (at a given signal from the presiding minister), or simply by the presiding minister standing up in order to move on to the next stage of the liturgy.

When we try this for the first time we feel an incredible pressure to bring immediately to an end this weird and wonderful experiment. Every second feels like a minute, but that is merely our unfamiliarity with what should be second nature to us, and the presiding minister must appear totally unmoved and unruffled. A period of at least two full minutes, hopefully three, is needed if the silence is to do its work. It must not be a momentary interruption, but a component of liturgy to be savoured and enjoyed. After the assembly has been at it for a while, we shall feel cheated, rather than relieved, when the silence ends.

The keeping of an appropriate period of silence is a test for the presiding minister as much as for the assembly. The sensitivity required to keep the silence just right – neither hurried nor tedious – is the hallmark of a good presiding minister. The gauging of the length of the silence cannot be pre-timed. It is a response to a number of factors, requiring experience, sensitivity and a strong nerve. It's a gift, but one that can be developed.

d Affirmation of faith

Ceremonial

The presiding minister leads the assembly in an affirmation of faith.

Commentary

After the period of silence, the presiding minister stands to signal a move into the next part of the liturgy. If the assembly did not gather round the font for the penitential rite, now is the time to go walkabout. At this stage in the liturgy, however, the gathering at the font will have a different emphasis.

As well as causing us to reflect on our weakness and our need for God's mercy, the reading and unfolding of the Scriptures will also move us to rededication in the collective remembering of our baptismal calling.

The *General Instruction of the Roman Missal* states:

The purpose of the Profession of Faith . . . is that the whole gathered people may respond to the word of God proclaimed in the readings taken from Sacred Scripture and explained in the homily and that they may also call to mind and confess the great mysteries of the faith . . . before these mysteries are celebrated in the Eucharist. (II.67)

For this reason the creed has customarily followed at this point on Sundays and major festivals (but *not* on any other occasion, a basic liturgical rule ignored by those who trot out the creed at every opportunity, like a ham-fisted gardener over-watering plants that are trying to breathe).

Roman and Anglican traditions maintain this requirement in their new liturgies, but the *Lutheran Book of Worship* states, 'a Creed may be said'. Its rubric continues, however, with precise instructions as to which creed is appropriate in which season, so it is probably true to say that there is an expectation of a creed here, if not an absolute requirement.

If at this stage of the liturgy we gather at the font, we are given a glorious opportunity to relive the Renewal of Baptismal Vows in the Great Vigil of Easter. In the American *Book of Common Prayer* (1979) the presiding minister enters into a dialogue with the assembly, using the Apostles' Creed in question-and-answer form, together with other supplementary questions concerning the assembly's commitment to be good news in Jesus the Christ by the power of the Spirit of God. If not sprinkled already, the assembly may be sprinkled at this point, brought into direct contact with the waters welling up to eternal life.

The renewal of our baptismal covenant makes particularly good sense at the font, especially in view of the fact that most creeds began life as baptismal formulae (see below). If, however, we have already processed to the font for the penitential rite, then the presiding minister will lead the profession of faith from the chair.

'Profession of faith' is the contemporary, and more appropriate, name given to the corporate recitation of a statement of faith we formerly called the 'creed' (from the Latin *credo*, 'I believe'). This was an awfully individualistic way to regard Christian belief, and the new translations of the Nicene Creed in all three liturgical traditions all begin with the words 'We believe'. This does justice to the corporate nature of belief, and to our need for one another in wrestling with the mysteries of the faith. The exhortation of Paul that we should 'bear one another's burdens' (Gal. 6.2) can apply very well to those sticky bits of the creed, where we may feel we need all the help we can get.

Seeing is believing

The widely felt need for the believer to confess with the whole community that which unites them before God has its roots in the synagogue tradition of reciting the Jewish confession of faith known as the *shema*, from the first word of the first passage of Scripture (Deut. 6.4) from which it is taken: 'Hear, O Israel: The Lord is our God, the Lord alone. You shall love the Lord your God with all your heart, and with all your soul, and with all your might.'

In the *shema*, the believer confessed with all Israel that Yahweh is One, on which basis Israel distinguished itself unequivocally from the surrounding tribes and nations.

As a result it was natural for the early Christian communities to require candidates for baptism to profess their belief in Jesus in the presence of the assembly, though in very simple form, proclaiming, for example, 'Jesus is Lord!' (1 Cor. 12.3). 'The need to confess one's faith according to a fixed text', wrote Oscar Cullmann, 'manifested itself in every gathering of the community.'

These short and sweet baptismal creeds developed into a confession we now know as the 'Apostles' Creed', and were later supplemented by conciliar creeds in which councils of bishops (or at least those with the emperor's ear) attempted to define the true faith as opposed to the teaching of heretics. We may have been taught that such creeds are inviolate and unerring, but we should remember that they represent what was then the latest round in an ongoing theological dispute, and bear both the strengths and weaknesses of a document forged in the heat of battle.

The Nicene Creed, whatever the precise arguments as to which text and when and by whom, remains the contentious product of the almighty row that engulfed the fourth-century Christian world as to who Jesus called the Christ really was. It was an age of fierce and often violent controversy with the full range of dirty tricks, including imperial interference, the exiling of perverse bishops, the inflaming of mobs and the commissioning of theological thugs who would beat error out of you if you couldn't do it for yourself.

There is no need for us to approach the Nicene Creed with bated breath. It was not handed down to us from God on tablets of stone, and its use in the liturgy was a gradual and piecemeal development spread over a long period between the fifth and eleventh centuries. As Galley reminds us (1989, p. 91), the more primitive Christian tradition 'regarded the eucharistic prayer as the church's profession of faith'.

The Lutherans have a point in taking a step back from the mandatory creed. To recite parrot-fashion the Nicene Creed is no way, however, for grown-ups to reaffirm their faith. We can do much more with this important aspect of the liturgy.

Those Christian traditions which today insist on the Nicene Creed as the only permissible credal formula exhibit a mind-blowing insensitivity to how far humankind has since travelled, as well as a marked lack of creativity. Since that period the greatest Christian minds have for sixteen centuries looped the loop and turned somersault in an unceasing attempt to make sense of fourth-century thought forms and issues which no longer have much meaning for us. There is now a growing number of people in our Sunday assemblies who will simply mouth certain parts of the Nicene Creed, or remain silent altogether. Others outside the Church will cite the requirement to say the creed as an indication of the perverseness of the Church in obscuring Jesus behind a smokescreen of fourth-century philosophical jargon.

If the Christian assembly is to be a community of authenticity and honesty, what is to be done? The assembly is not an aggregate of individuals, but a community of faith. It needs to hold fast to its historical origins and treasure the unity that comes from a common understanding of the wonder of God at work in the person of Jesus the Christ. An oft-recited credal formula that we solemnly repeat when we assemble on the Lord's Day is an essential ingredient to our common life. But it has to be something we are proud to say, not an embarrassment.

One way forward is for the Church to provide alternative affirmations of faith, such as those found in the Church of England's *Common Worship* (2000). Here are a rich variety of alternatives, some crafted from baptismal promises, some from historical documents, and some (the most successful) directly from the Scriptures. If we seek trustworthy historical documents, then the Scriptures will serve us better than the official statements of fourth-century bishops' meetings. Philippians 2.6–11 (an early credal hymn), 1 Corinthians 15.3–7 and Ephesians 3 form the basis of three excellent ways to affirm our faith in God and in the risen Lord Christ without having to cross our fingers behind our backs. Although alternatives of this kind cause us to depart from Cullmann's 'fixed text' (see above), if Scriptural they can be said to unite us in the single text of the canon of Scripture.

Alternatively, the community of faith might take on the project of writing its own creed, giving unique expression to the life and power of God in its midst. Using both the Scriptures and other historical texts to help them, the community will thus fashion from its own experience images and language that do justice to the revelation of God in our own generation. Such a 'creed' may never emerge beyond the parish boundaries or beyond a limited period in its communal life, but the community that wrestles with these issues will necessarily be a community of vitality that knows itself to be on a journey.

For examples of alternative affirmations of faith, see Appendix E.

e The prayers of the people

Ceremonial

A member of the assembly leads the assembly in the prayers of the people, first coming to the presiding minister to receive the stole.

Commentary

These prayers are named differently in the three liturgical traditions. The *Roman Missal* refers to them as 'The Prayer of the Faithful', while *Common Worship* (2000) names them 'Prayers of Intercession', a far too narrow definition for the nature of the beast. The *Book of Common Prayer* (1979) is the most satisfactory with 'The Prayers of the People', chiefly because it emphasizes the grass-roots nature of these prayers: the prayers of the whole assembly.

Every effort should be made to develop the skills within the assembly necessary to enable set forms of prayer to be laid aside in preference for prayers composed by the leader for the particular Sunday in question.

The member of the assembly leading the prayers of the people will do so from the ambo, with the presiding minister remaining at the chair.

Alternatively, if the assembly has gathered around the font for the affirmation of faith, it should remain there for the prayers of the people, the member of the assembly leading the prayers remaining in his/her place in the circle around the font, assisted with a portable microphone if necessary.

Praying by the people for the people

As with the creed, so with the prayers of the people: elements of the rite once contained within the eucharistic prayer were extracted from the second part of the liturgy, that is, the offering (Gk *anaphora*) at the altar, and given their own distinctive section in the ministry of the word (Gk *synaxis*).

Being raised on the English *Book of Common Prayer* (1662), I grew up with a rite in which the 'Prayer for the Church' came *after* the offertory, as the first part of the *anaphora*. Strange though this now seems to us, the 1662 rite was merely perpetuating the pre-Reformation order.

Before the Church rediscovered, thanks to the Liturgical Movement, the liturgy as the work of the people of God, the 'Prayers for the Church' were a solo performance by that jack-of-all-trades, the priest celebrant. They were said by the priest for the people, and were tucked safely away in the canon of the Mass, on the assumption that the laity could not pray for themselves, and needed, like good children, to be seen and not heard.

In the post-Vatican II era, new prayer books have given the prayers back to the people and have often provided several alternative forms. The American *Book of Common Prayer* (1979), for example, supplies six forms of the prayers of the people, and *Common Worship* (2000) five. As things have turned out, this is a pity.

In both cases the resources start out well, content in the eucharistic rite itself merely to provide a heading 'The Prayers of the People' (USA) or the more constrictive 'Prayers of Intercession' (UK), with beneath it a list of suggested ingredients. This should be more than sufficient for a mature community of faith, yet in both cases the compilers cannot resist providing in appendices a selection of pre-cooked dishes for this little feast. As a result it is often difficult to persuade those leading the community in prayer to let go of these props. After a time, these fixed texts, no matter how often we ring the changes, become stale and hackneyed.

By contrast, the community that encourages the ministers of this part of the liturgy to do their own thing, and to bring into play their imagination and creativity, finds itself blessed with prayers that can captivate the assembly instead of sending it to sleep. Of course, guidelines are necessary to provide a useful framework with a few ground rules, and those who attempt to smuggle in a sermon or a soapbox have to be given one last chance and one only. Nevertheless, the occasional disaster or embarrassment is well worth the liberation experienced by any community of faith with the courage to undergo in this regard an appendectomy of its prayer books.

Suggested guidelines for writing good prayers are contained in Appendix F.

f The Peace

Ceremonial

The presiding minister, or deacon if one is present, recalls the assembly to its vocation to be a community of peace and reconciliation.

Extending his/her hands, the presiding minister invokes the peace of God upon the assembly.

The deacon, or other assistant minister, invites the members of the assembly to share with one another a sign of God's peace.

Commentary

The Peace is the ritual enactment of New Testament exhortation to 'Greet one another with a holy kiss' (Rom. 16.16), an appeal linked directly to peace in 1 Peter 5.14 where we read, 'Greet one another with a kiss of love. Peace to all of you who are in Christ.' The Peace is no mere gesture, however, for it embodies that reconcili-

The assembly shares the Peace

ation one with another that Jesus taught was a prerequisite of our eligibility to offer worship. The command is about as explicit a liturgical rubric as you can get:

'So when you are offering your gift at the altar, if you remember that your brother or sister has something against you, leave your gift there before the altar and go; first be reconciled to your brother or sister, and then come and offer your gift.' (Matt. 5.23–24)

Anglican and Lutheran traditions share the Peace before going to the altar, Romans at the altar, immediately before Communion. Anglicans like to believe that in this they enjoy the original position, sustained not only by the Matthean text but also by the early tradition of the Church. In the second century Justin Martyr in his *Apology*, describing for others what Christians do in their worship, tells us that 'at the conclusion of the prayers we greet one another with a kiss. Then bread and a chalice containing wine mixed with water are presented to the one presiding over the brethren.' Likewise the third-century *Apostolic Tradition* of Hippolytus, a document highly influential in the renewal of liturgy following Vatican II, places the Peace at the conclusion of the initiation rite. In all Eastern Orthodox rites the kiss remains in this position.

The gesture considered appropriate for exchanging this greeting will vary from culture to culture. Although today (some decades after the restoration of the Peace to the people) we are accustomed to tailoring this exchange to the norms of our culture, Paul Bradshaw reminds us that for Christians in the early centuries the Peace was an expression of the deeply held conviction that relationships within the Church super-seded those with natural family members who were not believers. He quotes Justin Martyr as describing the kiss of peace as no mere formality, but 'the exchange of a kiss on the lips – an unusually intimate action for those unrelated to one another' (Bradshaw, 1996, p. 43). In other words, whether in the second century or in the wake of Vatican II, the kiss of peace can take us to the liturgical cutting edge, and to the nub of the issue of our identity as a community modelling the Kingdom of God.

The kiss of peace should not therefore be a greeting kept behind a religious glass case, with ritualized gestures used in no other walk of life, but the kind of warm greet-ing customary on a social occasion in other circumstances. It should be natural and sincere: better not share the Peace than share it and not mean it. My all-time favourite is the version preferred by the cheerful little Italian woman in black – the sacristan I think – at the daily Mass in a church down a Rome side street. At the Peace, she simply paused at the sacristy door and blew kisses to us all.

When we offer each other a sign of *Christ's* peace, we are saying with our bodies that we hold dear the One who is our peace. We are believing with our bodies that the barriers between us have been broken down, the divisions undone, the ruptures repaired. We are pledging with our action that we will leave this place and spread the peace of Christ to the sidewalks and the supermarket aisles, to the dance club and the hospital ward. (Philippart, 1996, p. 49)

The breakout of peace

The restoration of the Peace among all Western liturgical traditions is the single most dramatic difference between eucharistic rites 'before and after' Vatican II. Thomas Day, as we might expect, has another liturgical legend of our times which deserves to be quoted in full:

> In the early 1970s a friend of mine attended Mass in one of Philadelphia's grand old parishes, an immense pile of stone built to last for eternity. In the same pew, right next to him, was an elderly lady who energetically fingered her rosary beads all during Mass . . . The time came for the Handshake of Peace, one of those 'new things' which made everyone feel a bit silly. My friend turned to the elderly lady at this point and, holding out his hand in friendship, said, 'May the peace of the Lord be always with you.' The old lady scowled. She looked at the proffered hand as if it were diseased. 'I don't believe in that shit,' she replied. (Day, 1998, p. 6)

Yes, the Pax lurked in the Roman rite, after the canon, but was a desiccated husk of a gesture confined to the sanctuary, while Anglicans had given up on it altogether in 1552. The Peace was also the most controversial innovation, and when I arrived in my West Yorkshire parish in 1987 a notice in the sacristy still read, 'The Peace is not shared in this church.' For some people it was a case of just too much humanity.

On my first Sunday in that parish, it was a lonely walk that the presiding minister took down the central aisle, looking hopefully for anyone who would look him in the eye, or perhaps even give a half-smile. Occasionally an individual, in response to the proffered 'Peace be with you', would reply 'No thank you' – a response not known to the Liturgical Commission. It should be noted that in this regard pews are an excellent defence against the Peace, and all kinds of half-hearted and unsuccessful attempts to move out and around can for some people put off the evil day of encountering fellow Christians for months or years. Insistence and persistence soon prevail, however, and in West Yorkshire the pews were not long for this world.

A more prevalent problem today lies at the opposite end of the spectrum, when the Peace is too enthusiastic for its own good, thereby obscuring its purpose. The Peace is in the final analysis a *gesture* of love and reconciliation, not an exhaustive workshop on the subject.

Each stage of this restoration process has therefore provided pitfalls where the Peace is concerned. At first the reluctant assembly had to be persuaded and cajoled; now the over-enthusiastic assembly has to be restrained.

In congregations of reasonable size this significant liturgical moment can be undermined by the ridiculous notion that every individual must share the Peace with *every* other person present. Failure to do so will indicate exclusion or a falling out of friends. It is thereby reduced to an anxiety-filled time of seeking out and double-checking that all bases are covered.

The Peace can also degenerate into a time of self-indulgent chatter when we catch up on the news with our buddies, an activity which should be confined to the (equally essential) coffee hour. The Peace can also be a time for some very selective hugging and kissing, and we would do well to remember dear old St Francis and his leper. There can be no hint of discrimination in sharing the Peace: how we share it with those we especially like is how we should share it with everyone.

The Peace should be relaxed and disciplined, and as with the observance of the silence, it is the presiding minister's task to be sensitive enough to determine its appropriate length. Priority should be given to greeting those immediately around us, those we haven't seen for some time, or those with whom there has been an awkwardness of some sort. At particularly emotional times, for example following a bereavement, queues forming to greet an individual should be avoided at all costs. There will be plenty of time at the coffee hour to catch the people we cannot greet at the Peace. The whole thing should last no more than two or three minutes; anything much longer than that and we will have hijacked the liturgy for our social calendar.

The Peace is not a time for the presiding minister to relax; in fact it calls for the utmost vigilance, especially in the Anglican and Lutheran position, to ensure that at this point the whole liturgical action does not become unravelled, like a woolly sweater caught on a rusty nail.

As with the gauging of the periods of silence, so with the Peace; the presiding minister needs to develop an acute sensitivity to the needs of the assembly as a whole, a second sense about pace and rhythm. The presiding minister needs to give special attention to the introduction to the Peace, the manner in which it is handed on through the assembly, and its conclusion.

Introducing the Peace

The presiding minister has a particular contribution in alerting the assembly to the true purpose of the Peace by the manner in which the Peace is introduced. This is extremely important if we are to avoid the mistake of the American *Book of Common Prayer* (1979). Evidently the compilers of this rite were practical jokers who liked to creep up on us quietly and suddenly shout out to make us jump out of our liturgical skins. After the prayers of the people, out of the blue, with no introduction or preparation or setting in context, the command is given, 'Let us confess our sins against God and our neighbor.' It has all the subtlety of a box around the ears. Likewise after the confession and absolution there comes another sudden salvo out of nowhere, 'The peace of the Lord be always with you.'

English priests on parish exchanges in the USA are greeted by adoring and grateful crowds after the liturgy simply because they will have introduced the Peace (and the confession earlier on) with suitable words culled from the Scriptures to give the assembly half an idea of what we are engaged in. This is sensational news for the Americans but old hat for the English, where the renewed rites have always set the action in a Scriptural context. In Rite 2 of the *Alternative Service Book 1980*, for example, the presiding minister first sets the scene with these words: 'We are the Body of Christ. In the one spirit we were all baptised into one body. Let us therefore pursue all that makes for peace, and builds up the body of Christ.' *Common Worship* (2000) goes further, with seven alternatives quarried from appropriate passages in the New Testament. This after all is the tradition of Cranmer's prayer books, in which offertory and confession were clearly set in a scriptural context.

Perhaps the compilers of the American book took the view that the presiding minister would add his/her own words, but sadly that just doesn't happen. We appear riveted to the words on the page, and those words only, like rabbits transfixed by the headlights of a car bearing down relentlessly upon them.

A suitable scriptural framework to the Peace can appropriately be given by the deacon or other assistant, with the presiding minister announcing the Peace itself, after which the deacon invites the assembly's participation. In this way, the dialogue between presiding minister and deacon is itself a precursor of the exchange that is to follow between members of the assembly.

Some appropriate texts are included in Appendix G.

Sharing the Peace

The responsibility of the presiding minister is to oversee the sharing of the Peace in an appropriate manner. Care must be taken to let the Peace flow naturally in a way that disabuses anyone of the clerical notion that the Peace must originate with the presiding minister alone, with waves of embraces spreading out from the chair in some kind of 'apostolic succession' of blessing and reconciliation. Of course the Peace begins with the greeting and invitation of the presiding minister, but after that it is a free-for-all; we can exchange the Peace with anyone who comes our way.

Concluding the Peace

It is frequently the case that the presiding minister will have the greatest difficulty in bringing the Peace to an end, to reclaim the liturgy for the good of the assembly. Quite literally, the liturgy may have got out of control, and it takes a determined presiding minister, with perhaps a little help from friends in the music department, to bring things back together so that the liturgical action may resume.

   The Peace is not for the sole benefit of the gregarious among us, who may show no sign of tiring, but for the whole body. The presiding minister's task is to remember those introverts who are praying for release, not just those extroverts who could go on for hours, and to recall the assembly to its sacred purpose, as it moves forward to its next task in the wondrous offering of the liturgy.

Notes

1 Gloria Dei, Philadelphia, under the leadership of David Rivers.
2 We at Philadelphia Cathedral are grateful to Professor Paul Bradshaw for graciously pointing out this anomaly after his participation in our Sunday Liturgy in January 2004. In such ways are liturgies continually honed and improved.
3 First encountered at the Benedictine Community of the Priory of Our Lady, Burford, England.
4 For 300 years the Archbishops of Canterbury and York, Primates of England, fought, on one occasion quite literally, for possession of Augustine's chair and the primacy that went with it. The matter was eventually settled by Innocent V who in 1360 decided in favour of Canterbury, who henceforth was titled 'Primate of *All* England'.

PART 4 THE EUCHARIST IN SLOW MOTION: THE MEAL

The Liturgy of the Sacrament

1 The offertory

Ceremonial

The assembly processes towards the altar table, and (a) gathers at a suitable location en route, at some distance from the altar table, where a small credence table has been set up and on which offerings of money are placed in a large basket.

When the offerings have been made, the whole assembly, standing near the credence table, faces towards the altar table. Appointed members of the assembly hold up the gifts of bread and wine and money, and the whole assembly raises hands in a gesture of offering. The presiding minister says the offertory prayers and the assembly sings a suitable refrain, chant or chorus.

Or (b) the gifts are offered at the altar table, at which point the presiding minister says the offertory prayers and the assembly sings or says its response, or (c) the gifts are offered at the altar table in silence.

The assembly offers its gifts to God

Commentary

'Then I will go to the altar of God, to God my exceeding joy' (Ps. 43.4). This sounds a very simple thing to do, a very joyous thing to do, and in planning the liturgy we should move heaven and earth to make it so.

Once again, David Philippart puts it simply and beautifully:

> I give you a gift because I have come to know that you are a gift, a gift to the world; that no one ever or anywhere else is you, that none give me what you give me, means to me what you mean to me.
>
> And so it is in the assembly of the church. And so it is when we – as individuals yes, and more so, as a people – give our gifts to God. But what do you give to a god? What do you give to the Living God who made everything and has everything and needs nothing?
>
> We offer the simple things of bread and wine, 'which earth has given and human hands have made'. (Philippart, 1996, p. 28)

Nothing is quite that simple, however, and the offering of our gifts brings us to a defining moment, a fork in the road. The academics will tell us that the eucharistic prayer includes the offering, and that no further 'offertory prayers' are necessary, the gifts being placed on the altar in silence. This is undoubtedly true, and yet as we have seen, what we now call the 'creed' and the 'prayers of the people' were both original-ly lodged in the eucharistic prayer before being given a home of their own. Furthermore, while it might be a useful corrective for the Roman Communion to go softly on to offertory prayers at this moment, it might be just as useful a corrective for Anglicans to do the opposite. After a 500-year period of hang-ups about unworthi-ness, never being allowed to bring anything to the party, perhaps it is about time we showed up with a smile on our faces, with a bouquet of flowers in one hand and a bottle of wine in the other.

Unfortunately, we have several things stacked against us at this point in the eucharistic action, and it will be necessary to make a couple of short digressions to address the issues that lurk in the liturgical bushes, waiting to jump out on us.

Offering: the theory

Although this moment is popularly called the 'offertory', the very suggestion that the assembly might be offering something at the altar (well, maybe money, but certainly not bread and wine) sets the alarm bells ringing, especially if we are at the Evangelical end of the Anglican spectrum. Tainted as our tradition is by the great Calvinist error of the 'utter depravity of man', an infection which someone at Geneva must have picked up on a package holiday to North Africa ('In the footsteps of St Augustine'), we can still get all jittery at the thought of a mere human being bringing anything worthwhile to God's table. God's grace is all-sufficient, to such an extent that we are smothered by it, deprived of any instinct or contribution of value in this travesty of the doctrine of creation. No wonder that Anglicans are often suspected of being covert semi-Pelagians. Thank God we are.

This is not the place to unpack all the baggage of the sixteenth century, but we give a nod to those controversies as we try to piece together an appropriate response to God's invitation to feast at his table. For Anglicans and Lutherans, arriving at a theological fault line at this juncture, it is revealing to see what words we use to describe this action. The *Book of Common Prayer* (1979) dodges the issue by calling the whole second part of the eucharist 'The Holy Communion', with no heading to cover the presentation of the gifts. *Common Worship* (2000) speaks of the 'Preparation of the Table' which nicely diverts attention away from what we are putting on the table. Interestingly, the American Church, springing from the loins of the Scottish Church, is perfectly happy to speak in its eucharistic prayers of 'offering' bread and wine, while the English Church is not, still hung up on this semantic detail 500 years on from when it was a hot-button issue. It is about time we moved on.

Whatever is decreed by the keepers of the dogma, it is clear to most people participating in the eucharistic action that in some way which we can only dimly discern, we are taking part in the offering of a spiritual sacrifice of some sort. Obviously we are not killing animals, and neither are we indulging in some medieval extravagance of dragging Christ down from the cross to be sacrificed all over again. We are simply returning home to God, bringing to the family table what we have earned and made, what is precious to us and what we are rather proud of, and giving it back to God with hearts brimming with joy and thankfulness.

Having been trained in a parish of the Catholic tradition in the late 1960s, I never presided at the eucharist without inviting the assembly, having placed the gifts of bread and wine on the altar, to pray with me 'that my sacrifice and yours be acceptable to God the Almighty Father'. These words will not be found in the *Book of Common Prayer* (1662), but in the *English Missal*, an Anglo-Catholic text of the 1930s, not authorized by the Church of England (which in those days was precisely the point) and still in print.

In those days it was fun to be a little naughty, and sometimes liturgical customs were retained not just for their theological content but also to annoy those who understood the Anglican heritage differently. Nevertheless there was a sense, however dimly understood or inadequately conveyed, that in the eucharist we stood in awe at the gate of heaven to do something more than 'fiddle about with vinegar bottles' (as one churchwarden in rural Northamptonshire was heard to describe the holy mysteries).

We talked then, in introducing the eucharistic rite, of 'offering the holy sacrifice of the Mass', but we were probably a little hazy about what we meant. I guess we were hovering around the idea that in the Mass the one perfect sacrifice of Christ was recalled, through which we 'pleaded' (another favourite High-Church word) for ourselves and for the world. Above all, we didn't want to be mistaken for Protestants, and the use of such extreme sacrificial language seemed a good way of ensuring that.

Yet why is sacrificial language regarded with such suspicion and hostility among the Churches of the Reformation, and among many Anglicans? Rowan Williams describes the Church as 'a sacrificial reality' (see Stevenson, 1996, p. 16), and we know from our own experience that any love worth winning, any thing worth having, any cause worth embracing, will entail sacrifice, and sacrifice joyfully given.

Kenneth Stevenson, in his masterly treatment of this subject, *Eucharist and Offering*, affirms the basic sacrificial nature of the New Covenant of Christ as laid out in the New Testament. Adapting the Jewish (and originally pagan) concept of offering, the early Christians saw Christ as the sacrifice, 'and in response to his death the Christian is either a living sacrifice (Rom. 12.1) or offers "spiritual sacrifices" (1 Pet. 2.5)' (Stevenson, 1986, p. 17). Stevenson goes on to warn against the 'spiritualisation' of sacrifice by which, in many Christian traditions, it is robbed of its meaning, 'internalised to the point of being little more than psychological' (p. 17). Such spiritualization 'could not be further from the intentions of New Testament writers, particularly the author of the letter to the Hebrews', and furthermore, adds Stevenson, 'the sacrifices required of the Christian are more real than those performed under the Law' (p. 17).

Stevenson defines sacrifice as 'the destruction or surrender of something valued or desired for the sake of something having a higher or more pressing claim' (p. 4). That sounds very like a stewardship appeal, and it is no bad description of the eucharist either, as we place more than we can afford in the offertory basket and our freshly baked loaf into the presiding minister's hands. If such a definition is denied us because 'sacrifice' is a trigger word letting loose all kinds of pre-Reformation abuses and superstitions, then we need to re-examine our liturgical priorities.

Philadelphia Cathedral: liturgical configuration

'Sufficiently prominent... sufficiently large'

The assembly on the move

Sprinkling the assembly from the waters of the font

A table 'where all God's people have equal access'

An ambo 'of prominence and simple dignity'

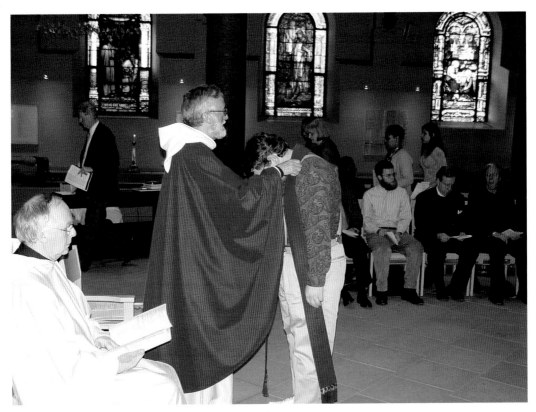

The reader is invested with the stole

The reader takes the Book of the Gospels to the assembly

The Bishop of Pennsylvania preaching from his cathedra

The assembly encircles the altar table

Censing the gifts

The assembly offers the eucharistic prayer

The communion

Communion: administered and taken

Offering: the texts

Not that our prayer books help us. Both the *Book of Common Prayer* (1979) and *Common Worship* (2000) reduce us to stunned silence at this point, instructing that we place on the altar table various objects. It is instructive to note that (surprise, surprise) the English cannot bring themselves to name the bread and wine as gifts or offerings, but in *Common Worship* (2000) distinguish carefully between the 'gifts of the people' (presumably money) that are to be 'gathered and presented', and 'bread and wine' which just mysteriously appear to be 'placed upon it'. Thankfully the *Book of Common Prayer* (1979) is bold by comparison, its Scottish heritage shining through nicely, as it speaks of 'the people's offerings of bread and wine, and money or other gifts' to be brought forward to be 'presented and placed on the Altar'.

Many Anglican presiding ministers, having got rather fed up with this mealy-mouthed approach, can be found using the Roman offertory prayers of the *Missa Normativa*. These two prayers are reminiscent of the *berakah*, the characteristic Jewish prayer of blessing or thanksgiving over food. The *berakah* was so familiar to the early (predominantly Jewish) Christian communities that their custom of giving thanks (making eucharist) over bread and wine quite naturally became their defining central ritual.

These prayers are meaningful and popular, especially in the intimate setting of a weekday eucharist. Stevenson (1986, p. 203) draws attention to the earlier 1965 version, in the first flush of Vatican II, when the offertory was made even simpler, the priest reciting quietly over the bread and wine two poetic formulae with a congregational response. The first is from the *Didache* (9.4), the second from Proverbs (9.1–2):

> As this bread was scattered and then gathered and made one,
> so may your Church be gathered into your kingdom.
> **Glory to you, O God, for ever.**

> Wisdom has built a house for herself,
> she has mixed her wine,
> she has set her table.
> **Glory to you, O God, for ever.**

Now to say some such thing as we bring gifts to God's table seems to my simple mind like a very nice thing to do. It's good manners, after all, as we know from when we attend a party at someone's house. No matter how many times the host may say, 'just bring yourself', we take a small gift. At this point the question as to whether we are 'worthy' to offer this gift does not arise. We are glad to be going, and the gift is a small token of our delight. Such gifts, big or small, appropriate or missing the mark, are appreciated because they arise from a desire to give pleasure, and they somehow strengthen the bonds between us.

Likewise the 'little presents' we bring to God's table have no connection to our worthiness or otherwise. They are inadequate and in some ways pathetic. And yet they are our heartfelt gestures of love, and we do the best we can, knowing that in this simple act we have stumbled on the heart of worship:

> What can I give him, poor as I am?
> If I were a shepherd, I would give a lamb
> If I were a wise man, I would do my part
> But what I have I give Him; give my heart.
> (Christina Rossetti)

It would appear that in resisting this instinctive response, the academic liturgists of the Reformed Churches have led us down a blind alley, and in the process have made our eucharistic liturgies the poorer. To eliminate from the eucharist such a natural human instinct seems perverse.

Here is an opportunity for each of us in our own small corner to do something to correct the imbalance. We can 'say nowt' (as they would put it in Yorkshire), or we say our liturgical 'please' and 'thank you'. It's good manners, after all.

Some arrangement by which the assembly, as it moves forward, gathers at a 'station' in the centre of the axial space, where it collects and offers, may be an appropriate response to the puzzle. At this point the whole assembly, including the presiding minister, pauses in the journey, faces liturgical east – towards the altar table – as the offerings of money, bread and wine are raised up. The presiding minister says the offering prayers cited above, in response to which a suitable chorus of thanksgiving or praise (something known by heart) is sung. In this scenario, the offering prayers are said not at the altar but on our way to it, and once we arrive there 'the gifts are placed on the altar in silence, as a functional act with symbolic overtones' (Stevenson, 1986, p. 226). In such an arrangement perhaps everyone has something, and the academics are appeased. But perhaps that's asking a lot.

Collecting the subscriptions

The first aspect of offertory, and the word's usual connotation in popular parlance among Anglicans at least, is the gathering and presentation of gifts of money. Kavanagh considers that in Western society today 'cash offering probably is more vigorously symbolic of a modern assembly's gift of itself than even the eucharistic gifts of bread and wine' (Kavanagh, 1990, p. 65). As a result, the inclusion of money along with bread and wine should be standard procedure.

This simple acknowledgement of how life is and what makes us tick is, however, a concept which meets with determined resistance when we do liturgy. In the cathedral at Philadelphia we place the money offering on the altar table every Sunday, and almost every Sunday a well-meaning server will attempt to take it off before the eucharistic prayer begins. This appears second nature to us because we somehow imagine that money is 'dirty' and should not taint the 'holy' gifts alongside it. It is a strange thing, but we need to do our best to overcome it. Money that represents the toil and endeavour of God's holy people is, in this offering, made holy too. For better or for worse we need lots of this dubious commodity if we are to sustain our communal life and transform the world.

Exactly *how* we gather the money raises an interesting question too. The *Book of Common Prayer* (1979) certainly assumes that a collection will be taken at this point, and provides a selection of 'offertory sentences' to get the ball rolling (after which a hymn or anthem takes over to cover any unseemly noise arising from this questionable ritual). This provision of words to encourage the faithful to dig into their pockets is familiar from the earlier English prayer books, but in *Common Worship* (2000) has been dropped.

The facts-and-figures people will affirm that taking a plate or basket around the assembly will obtain the maximum yield, and they are quite right. However, is the taking of a collection the right and proper thing to do in the assembly?

If we think of ourselves as the household of faith, then we shall have already made provision in our budgeting for the work of the Church. Indeed, if we have done so by using some form of direct debit then we shall bring nothing with us to the assembly. That is how a household works; we don't pass the hat at Sunday dinner at home. Therefore this is a point in the liturgy which tests the practical application of our theology. Do we mean what we say, or are we simply after maximum return? I have always found the collection, when visiting other church communities, a form of harassment that I have not enjoyed. It is extremely inhospitable. Guests shouldn't be asked to contribute, and the home team should have it all taken care of.

Any alternative – for example a collection basket in a central position in which the assembly places its gifts on the way to the altar – will of course lose us some income, as some people inevitably slip through the net. The collection plate, extended menacingly under our chins, will, however, lose us more: our good name for unconditional hospitality and theological authenticity.

2 The approach to the altar table

Ceremonial

The assembly, led by the presiding minister, processes to the altar table.

Members of the assembly carry in procession a clean white cloth, the bread, wine and water, the basket of money, and a thurible.

Commentary

Whatever we say or do not say at the offering of the gifts and the preparing of the table, the assembly, in company with the psalmist, approaches the altar of God with joy. Two questions immediately arise: can we actually *get* to the altar? And if so, how should we go?

First, we need to *approach* the altar table, and here of course we mean an approach by the whole assembly, not just a highly selective sample. Furthermore, we need to be able, not merely to glimpse, but to *stand around* it, for 'this consecrated table, this altar stands here, Christ in our midst, the center of our life, our life lived for the sake of the world' (Philippart, 1996, p. 6). I was tempted there to add 'if at all possible' but refrained. By hook or by crook we have to make it possible. How we might do so has already been addressed in Part 2.

Second, how should we travel as the people of God? One reason why the assembly needs plenty of *space* is that it gives us room to manoeuvre; it allows the assembly the freedom to express itself in its own authentic way as it proceeds joyfully on its liturgical journey.

At this point some parishes will opt to sing, beat drums, even dance, as they travel. St Gregory of Nyssa has made the dance to the altar its trademark, and sadly few parishes have followed. St Gregory's dance is in fact very restrained – two steps forward, one back, with hand on the shoulder of the person in front, all to a simple drum beat – and we should work harder at devising our own parish traditions in this field, even if only on special occasions.

Everyone dances

In my West Yorkshire parish we were blessed one year by having as leader of our annual parish retreat a member of the Iona Community, that wonderful force for renewal in the British Isles and source of the haunting worship songs produced by Wild Goose Publications. The Iona line on liturgical dance is that it is a dance for the *whole assembly*.

'Everyone dances, or no one dances' was the message scrawled on a dance hall reduced to a shell by revolutionaries somewhere in South America, and they were onto something. Kavanagh calls the liturgy itself 'a complex and solemn form of communal dance'.

That being the case, 'liturgical dance' as we have come to know it – a dance performed by a few for the whole – is taking us down the same false trail as the robed choir. We should all be in this together, and we need dancers to help us dance, as we need singers to help us sing, not do the dancing or singing for us.

I don't believe I am totally alone in this world in finding liturgical dance by the few a strangely disconcerting experience, and sometimes unintentionally comical. For a start off, where is one supposed to *look*? Will we have to report to a sexual awareness class if we gaze too intently at the gyrating human form? Or should we gaze into heaven? Or close our eyes and look pious but unheeding of all the hours of practice? It is a minefield best avoided, says Kavanagh, for it is 'liturgically superficial' and has the effect of 'reinforcing the assembly's passivity' (Kavanagh, 1990, p. 33).

3 Preparation of the table

Ceremonial

The assembly, at the invitation of the presiding minister, moves forward to form a circle around the altar table. The presiding minister takes up a position at the head of the table (usually on the liturgical east side).

The deacon (or other liturgical assistant) oversees the spreading of a clean white cloth on the altar table. A corporal is then spread, on which are placed the bread and wine, with the basket of money placed elsewhere on the altar table.

The presiding minister censes the gifts on the altar table, and then the whole assembly.

When the censing is completed, the deacon or other assistant comes forward with a bowl and pitcher to enable the presiding minister and other ministers to wash their hands.

Commentary

It is at this point that our renewed theology of the priestly community needs to take root, and to be expressed in the manner in which the assembly takes up its position as a community of co-celebrants encircling the altar table.

> See photograph in colour section: 'The assembly encircles the altar table'

On special occasions when very large numbers are present, and it is physically impossible to gather the assembly around the altar table, the presiding minister should do everything possible to encourage the people, even if standing in their places at some distance, to make the prayer their own. The whole assembly should be asked to face the altar table, with hands lifted in prayer, and to enter into the liturgical action no less than if they were alongside the altar.

The procession of gifts to be placed on the altar is led by the thurifer, followed by the person carrying the 'clean white cloth' specified by the *Book of Common Prayer* (1979). This cloth covers the whole altar table, and should reach to the floor (but just short of it) on either side. It is placed on the altar table by the deacon, or if there is no deacon, by a liturgical assistant. If the altar table can be kept entirely bare up to this point, its clothing with the white cloth is all the more dramatic and meaningful.

At the centre of the altar table on the side at which the presiding minister will stand, the corporal is spread. The corporal is a white linen cloth about 20 inches square, and its name comes from the Latin *corpus* (body), for on it the sacramental Body of Christ will be laid. The corporal should be of finest linen, simple and without adornment, least of all edged with lace.

The paten and chalice (or other vessel) containing the bread and wine are then placed upon the corporal, together with a purificator (a small linen towel or napkin) laid alongside the corporal. The basket containing the monetary gifts is also placed on the altar table, though not of course on the corporal.

The presiding minister takes no part in the table-laying, standing back to allow the deacon or other nominated assistant to supervise this task. This is because it is helpful to signal at this point that presidency does not mean doing everything personally, but ensuring that everything gets done. Furthermore, the laying of the table puts the deacon (or those serving as quasi-deacons) in touch with the New Testament roots of the diaconate, which had its genesis in the early Church's need to feed its community physically as well as spiritually, dual demands which were beginning to swamp its leadership:

The deacon fills the chalice

And the twelve called together the whole community of the disciples and said, 'It is not right that we should neglect the word of God in order to wait at tables. Therefore, friends, select from among yourselves seven men of good standing, full of the Spirit and of wisdom, whom we may appoint to this task.' (Acts 6.2–3)

Even though visibility is not a primary concern when the assembly encircles the altar table, it is good practice to place the paten and chalice side by side, rather than one in front of the other. This accords with ancient practice of the Eastern Church and with the modern Roman rite.

The chalice and paten placed side by side on the corporal

Censing

When everything is ready on the altar table, the presiding minister receives the thurible, brought in procession at the offertory, from a member of the assembly (this need not necessarily be a robed assistant), and, bowing before the altar table, censes the gifts. This needs to be done very slowly, simply and with dignity, in whatever pattern comes naturally and fits the occasion. Fortunately there is now no need for the convoluted patterns laid down in the old missals, clockwise and anti-clockwise, which now seem more Masonic than Christian. The censing could consist of the presider describing a circle with the thurifer three times around the gifts, and then encircling the altar table once, with a minimum of fussy motion, yet with simple dignity.

See photograph in colour section: 'Censing the gifts'

The presiding minister then bows to the assembly and censes the holy people who are offering the holy gifts. If this point about the assembly's intrinsic holiness is to be brought home, it requires more than a nod in their direction. The presiding minister should proceed slowly around the complete circle of co-celebrants, censing throughout, and, returning to the centre, should bow to them before handing back the thurible.

Needless to say, there is no way that the presiding minister should ever delegate this privilege of so honouring his/her co-celebrants. To do so downgrades the assembly and takes us back to the bad old days when the priest-celebrant, having been censed himself in great style, would then hand over to lower orders (perhaps a deacon, or failing that an MC or thurifer) to finish off with a nod (that is, a much briefer censing than accorded the gifts or the ordained priest) the common herd, the liturgical hoi polloi.

All this was of course sacerdotal elitism, and a strong corrective is needed to redress the balance. This can be achieved if the presiding minister, having completed the censing of the assembly, should then hand the thurible to the thurifer or other assistant to be the last person censed, in token of the presiding minister's servanthood of the assembly.

Washing of hands

The ceremonial washing of hands is traditionally called the lavabo, the first word of the Latin version of the scriptural text recited at this point by the priest: 'I will wash my hands in innocence, O Lord, that I may go in procession round your altar.' Originating no doubt in the Jewish rites of washing before meals, the adaptation of

Censing the assembly

this practice to Christian use dates from the patristic period of the Church, and was concerned basically with ritual purity rather than hygiene.

In the fourth-century *Apostolic Constitutions* the washing of hands comes before the offertory, not after it, signifying that only the pure can approach the altar of God. (This practice survives today in the Ethiopic rite, in which interestingly the priest does not dry his hands, but shakes out the remaining drops in the direction of the people, just in case no one got the message.)

This remained the practice until the Middle Ages when the Roman Church changed the emphasis to the cleansing of hands after the reception of the gifts, and moved the lavabo to its present position. Today, therefore, the lavabo has a more utilitarian purpose in the cleansing of hands after the censing and before the handling of the gifts in the eucharistic prayer.

Against this rich background, the washing of hands deserves a more prominent place, correcting the tendency for the washing of hands to be carried out somewhat furtively. Often this ritual goes unnoticed, the presiding minister perhaps muttering the traditional words of Psalm 26 while the assembly is busy singing. Furthermore, the ceremony is often carried out using vessels inadequate to the task – a tiny container of water and finger bowl.

This washing of hands should be done with purpose and with style, and as ever with simple dignity. A large pottery bowl and pitcher should be used, with water flowing generously, not trickling meanly. When all is ready, let silence be kept while the deacon (or some other appropriate person) and assistant come forward carrying a pottery pitcher of water, large bowl and towel. Let water be poured in generous proportions over the presiding minister's hands while he/she says aloud, and with meaning, the words of Psalm 26:

> I will wash my hands in innocence, O Lord;
> that I may go in procession round your altar.
> Singing aloud a song of thanksgiving;
> And recounting all your wonderful deeds.

After the presiding minister has dried his/her hands, those who will also be handling the bread of the sacrament come forward to have their hands washed too.

We should not lose sight, however, of the possibility of reverting to the more ancient custom of washing hands *before* the assembly approaches the altar, in the spirit of Psalm 26. If we explore this option, the whole assembly should take part, not just the presiding minister and assistants. In this scenario, a large bowl with towels alongside would be placed on a small table, in the place where the assembly gathers before approaching the altar table. This is an excellent example of where it is necessary to play with the possibilities of a ritual act before it can be brought to life in the context of a real and actual community at worship. But in the exploring and the experimenting lies the fun of making the liturgy the work of the people of God.

Vessels

There is a renewed emphasis today on the use of symbols which explain, rather than obscure, what we are trying to do. For this reason the *Book of Common Prayer* (1979) takes the trouble to specify that 'there be only one chalice on the Altar' and, by inference, only one loaf. A flagon is also permitted when numbers demand it from which other chalices may be filled later.

Silverware is the most common material for the sacred vessels of the eucharist, but in today's emphasis on simple dignity the patens and chalices from previous generations can appear fussy and over-ornate. Simple potteryware can give the desired effect of the new aesthetic, but needs to be chosen carefully to achieve a simple but noble appearance and, in the case of the chalice, to avoid a thick rim which makes drinking from it more difficult.

There is also a school of thought which says that in this 'transparent' liturgical age, the vessels should be of glass, so that everything may be seen clearly by the assembly. There is power to that argument, but it is not as easy to find glass vessels of simple dignity as it is pottery ones. So some form of trade-off may be necessary here.

Elements

Great care should be taken with the choice of the elements of bread and wine to ensure a cohesion of what we talk about in the eucharist and what we see and handle. The use of bread made from wheat flour and wine made from grapes is essential to the understanding of the eucharist in all mainstream liturgical traditions. The substitution of non-alcoholic grape juice has long been the custom in many Protestant traditions, but has now reared its head in a few corners of the Anglican and Lutheran traditions, though as an alternative not a substitute, out of deference for those with problems of alcohol abuse.

This concession to the few should be resisted for the good of the whole. Our entering into the mystery of these elements as sacraments not only of the Body and Blood of Christ but also of God's good and powerful and fruitful creation should not be sacrificed or diminished for the sake of a tiny minority. As we shall see when we come to communion, we also need to teach more effectively the simple truth that the fullness of Christ's sacramental presence is given in two kinds and is imparted fully in either.

Bread can be leavened or unleavened, but leavened is far preferable. It gives a sense of everyday reality and 'ordinariness' to the substance to be transformed by God in the eucharist into something extraordinary. A single loaf helps bring alive for us those stirring words of Paul to the Church in Corinth: 'Because there is one bread, we who are many are one body, for we all partake of the one bread' (1 Cor. 10. 17). The one loaf also makes more sense of the fraction, when the single loaf is broken to become food for the many.

Unleavened bread (usually in the form of wafers) is less satisfactory symbolically, both in terms of not being 'one bread' except at very small gatherings, and because it is at base a religious, rather than a natural, commodity. It has very little that is 'ordinary' about it in the daily lives of most Christians. The essence of the sacramental life is the transformation of the ordinary, and unleavened bread is one step from the ordinary, a step too far.

Unleavened bread is nevertheless very convenient for exceptionally large assemblies, or for a small weekday eucharist when even a soft bread roll might be too large. If it is felt that, on such special occasions, unleavened bread is the most practical solution, every attempt should be made to obtain unleavened bread in an appropriate form. Unleavened bread should be totally plain, and fairly thick and biscuit-like. Wafers which are covered in little crosses or patterns, or which are so thin and insubstantial that they melt instantly on the tongue, should be avoided at all costs. (In the United States, plain thick wafers are (like tasty Cheddar cheeses) almost impossible to find, but in England I remember that the Carmelite sisters at Wetherby always got it just right.)

At the end of the day, only the best will do, and David Philippart reminds us powerfully and poetically why we need the taste in our mouths of real leavened bread, and full-bodied wine, if we are to enter fully into the mystery and into the living-out of Christ broken for us, within us:

> We become Christ's body, bread broken for a world that is obese with a materialism and still dying of malnutrition. We become a leaven in the world's bread, an agent of change that helps the reign of God to rise, fragrantly, like a loaf browning in the oven. We become Christ's blood, wine poured out in sacrifice and celebration, poured out for the sake of a world drowning in division and still dying of thirst, a thirst for union and *communion*. We become the brewer's yeast, the zest that unlocks the extraordinary in the ordinary, the tingle that makes sober people giddy with joy, the sweet smell and taste of the vintage. (Philippart, 1996, p. 20)

4 The Great Thanksgiving

The preliminary prayer

Ceremonial

The presiding minister leads the assembly in a preliminary prayer.

Commentary

The table is laid, the gifts prepared, the people censed, and hands washed. Now the presiding minister pulls together the various and multi-coloured threads of the assembly's worship so far, to weave them together into a tapestry of the eucharistic offering.

Whereas at this transitional point the Roman and Lutheran rites provide a prayer – the prayer over the gifts – to tidy things up before moving on, Anglican rites do not, and thereby leave a slightly awkward transition. It always seems hurried to launch directly into the *sursum corda* ('Lift up your hearts') without some form of prayer or passage of Scripture which describes what we are about to do together, and just how wonderful it is.

Preliminary prayer

One example of a such a transition piece is the beautiful passage from the apocrypha rediscovered by St Gregory of Nyssa parish, San Francisco. This can be transposed from where they use it (after communion) to this point where (dare I say?) it is even more effective. The passage is from the Book of Baruch:

Arise, O Jerusalem, stand on high and look toward the east,
and see your children gathered from west and east,
at the word of the Holy One,
rejoicing that God has remembered them.
For they went out from you on foot,
led away by enemies,

but God will bring them back to you, riding high in honour,
as children of the kingdom.   (Baruch 5.5–6)

Spoken at the conclusion of the preparation of the table, as the assembly gathers around to take its part, the passage serves as a proclamation of the glorious inheritance of the children of God. The emphasis on liberation and triumph of God's chosen, 'who come back to you riding high in honour', sharpens our awareness of the sacred act in which we are about to take part, and increases the electricity in the air. These words also act as an antidote to the five hundred years of unworthy grovelling we have been told is our lot, charging the assembly with a sense of irrepressible joyful hope and expectation.

For examples of alternative preliminary prayers, see Appendix H.

The eucharistic prayer

Ceremonial

The presiding minister takes his/her place in the circle of the assembly, standing back from the altar, in a position behind it equivalent to the place at the head of the table, remaining there throughout the eucharistic prayer. The presiding minister recalls the assembly to its vocation to exercise a priestly ministry.

Raising his/her hands to the orans *position, the presiding minister invites the whole assembly to do likewise, a posture maintained by the assembly throughout the eucharistic prayer.*

The presiding minister begins the eucharistic prayer with the dialogue of the sursum corda.

Commentary

Here we come to the heart of the eucharistic action. Although hopefully we have by now banished all notions of 'magic moments', aware that the whole eucharist is the act of consecration just as the whole assembly is the agent of consecration, nevertheless there is a natural sense of progression to this stage of the liturgy, for which we have been prepared and formed in the the ministry of the word (or *synaxis*).

While *Common Worship* (2000) adopts, along with the Roman Rite, the term 'Eucharistic Prayer' to describe this section of the eucharist, the *Book of Common*

Prayer (1979) in addition inserts above the eucharistic prayers the heading 'The Great Thanksgiving'. This has a noble ring to it (as does its description of the Easter Vigil as 'The Great Vigil of Easter') and has the advantage of emphasizing the predominant note of thanksgiving which, after all, the eucharist should be about.

It is essential that the assembly, not just in thought but in deed, should claim all that follows as its own, instead of continuing to see the eucharistic prayer as a strictly clerical preserve around which 'no admittance' is writ large.

All eucharistic prayers begin with the ancient dialogue between presiding minister and assembly known as the *sursum corda* ('Lift up your hearts'), in which the whole assembly enlists in the eucharistic action. This dialogue can be effective either said or sung, but either way it needs to be done boldly and with a sense of anticipation by the musicians.

The assembly stands in a circle around the altar, without crowding it, but at a distance of at least ten feet if space permits. There may not be space to allow the assembly to form a single circle, so that in places the encircling assembly may be two or three deep.

Forming a circle

At every stage the overriding liturgical principle is to use every means at our disposal, in gesture, posture and voice, to make an unequivocal statement that the eucharistic prayer is offered by the whole people of God. The assembly's forming of a circle around the altar table is a prime example of this principle.

The encircling is made solemn and reverent and impressive, not because of the neatness of the circle, but because of the revelation of God's presence made real to those standing in this dynamic encirclement. The circle can be ragged, kids may choose to sit on the floor, a chair may be brought forward for anyone who needs one.

It will be a circle of all shapes and sizes, ages and colours, a rag-tag-and-bobtail collection of humanity, as untidy as you like. Nevertheless it will be simply wondrous in that it is a circle intent upon the liturgical action into which they are called. It is a circle of celebrants:

> This the Lord's doing;
> it is marvellous in our eyes. (Psalm 118.23)

The presiding minister at this point needs to say a brief word, especially for the benefit of newcomers, setting the assembly's role in the eucharistic prayer in the context of the 'royal priesthood' of 1 Peter 2.9. A lecture is not necessary, neither is any reference to which prayer is being used. A couple of sentences will suffice, but in these few words the presiding minister can 'light the blue touch paper' of the priestly calling of the holy community of the people of God.

A typical introduction might be as follows:

We invite you now to place your orders of service on the floor, and to raise your hands in the posture of prayer and thanksgiving adopted by the first Christians. In so doing we make the Great Thanksgiving the prayer of the holy community of God's priestly people: no longer my prayer, but *our* prayer.

It is helpful if the presiding minister's word of invitation and explanation is given before the dialogue of the *sursum corda*, otherwise the flow of the eucharistic prayer will be disrupted. There can then be a nice co-ordination of 'Lift up your hearts' with the lifting up of the hands of the people.

The presiding minister should raise his/her hands in such a way that the whole assembly is moved to raise hands too, in a bold 'gathering-up' motion indicative of the presiding minister's true role as the conductor of the orchestra. This can usually be achieved by the presiding minister raising his/her hands slowly and deliberately, making eye contact with those in the circle, then pausing (if necessary) to allow everyone in the circle time to follow suit. There are always likely to be a few who prefer not to adopt this posture, but as long as the majority do so, the effect is a powerful sign of the mobilization of the whole assembly.

As always, actions speak louder than words, and the presiding minister needs to announce this introduction and invitation *from within the circle*. By standing back from the table throughout the eucharistic prayer, alongside his/her co-celebrants who together form the assembly, the presiding minister will make a dramatic statement, more eloquent and telling than a lecture. Here is a mystery not wrought by human hands, but by God working through the holy priestly community of faith.

The presiding minister remains in his/her place in the circle of celebrants for the entire eucharistic prayer, not going forward to touch the elements on the altar table at any point. Whenever the text of the eucharistic prayer makes it appropriate, the presiding minister reaches forth his/her hand(s) to indicate the elements or the assembly.

We can get very blasé about what we do together on a Sunday morning, forgetful of the privilege. The presiding minister's words and tone should excite us once again about the mystery into which we are called. This should be a wondrous moment at every Sunday Liturgy.

In offering together the eucharistic prayer, posture is of supreme importance in achieving a quiet revolution. The invitation given by the presiding minister to the assembly to adopt a posture that will enhance their sense of being part of the offering of the eucharistic prayer is a *kairos* moment of liturgical formation.

> See photograph in colour section: 'The assembly offers the eucharistic prayer'

Posture

For many centuries the community of faith has been accustomed to observing the eucharistic prayer from afar, kneeling in the pews of their liturgical compound. Sometimes, peeping between fingers arched in prayer, they have stolen a look at the priestly caste doing its thing in the holy of holies; at other times they have simply wondered what was for lunch.

Today, members of the assembly are invited to encircle the altar table at which the presiding minister stands alongside them. They are to stand instead of kneel; and by their body language to engage in the prayer as if it were the prayer of the whole assembly rather than that of a single designated person.

In their slim but seminal book, *The Postures of the Assembly during the Eucharistic Prayer* (1994), John Leonard and Nathan Mitchell do the Church inestimable service by recalling us to what John Baldovin in his introduction calls 'the communal choreography of liturgy' (p. 3). They point out that 'in every instance of human eating and drinking . . . differences in roles are recognized by differences in posture'. They remind us of the biblical tradition that it was always considered fitting to stand in any encounter with the presence of God, and that standing erect with hands raised in the *orans* position was for many centuries the universal practice of the Christian assembly when praising God in prayer.

It comes therefore as something of a surprise to discover that it is in fact kneeling, not standing, that is the more recent posture for the community at prayer. As the eucharist slowly evolved from an act of joyful praise and remembrance by the whole assembly into a dramatic re-enactment of the Last Supper by a principal player taking the role of Jesus, posture changed dramatically. The community withdrew from the action, reduced to the role of passive spectators, and kneeling took over from standing as the posture considered appropriate to the assembly. The *orans* posture of prayer, once considered the norm for all, became the sole prerogative of the presiding minister.

It is not an exaggeration to say that until the assembly can be drawn into the offering of the eucharistic prayer 'body and soul', the renewal of the liturgy will not take root in our lives. It is not enough for our minds to be educated and enlivened by new texts of depth and beauty; our bodies need to be caught up in the process too. As Leonard and Mitchell show us, there needs to be a direct connection between our theological understanding of who we are and the bodily posture we adopt to give these thoughts physical expression. A disconnection will eventually lead to frustration and dissatisfaction, as the liturgy is seen to be reduced to a cerebral exercise, not an experience that involves body, mind and heart.

> Standing this way, lifting up our hands, we stand like Christ . . . so let us all stand this way when the great eucharistic prayer is prayed. Thus we are ready to serve God at this table and in the world. Thus we are willing to offer up our very bodies along with our bread and wine, and in turn, receive from God the body and blood. And let us stand this way when we pray the words that Christ taught us. Let us stand as Christ. (Philippart, 1996, p. 42)

Eucharistic prayers

All the mainstream liturgical churches now provide a number of forms of the eucharistic prayer or *anaphora* ('offering') as it is known to the scholars. Each of these arises from a different historical or liturgical tradition, or bearing a different emphasis. This helps make the Church more sensitive to different kinds of occasion at which the eucharist is celebrated, and enables a higher degree of appropriateness in terms of liturgical language. Sadly, human nature being what it is, most presiders get stuck in the groove of a particular favourite that gets played too often at the expense of the others.

At the risk of sounding ungrateful for the dramatic improvement in the Church's increasing our ration of authorized eucharistic prayers from one to six, it also seems a great pity that each mainstream tradition (officially at least) gets so snooty about borrowing from another. I well remember how effective it was in a new church plant situation on a housing estate in England to use, for those who had probably never been to a eucharist before in their lives, the matchless and beautifully simple Roman eucharistic prayers for use with children. These proved tailor-made for the eucharist as a formation experience for those who had grown up in a post-Christian culture. In the Anglican Communion we have from across the world many rich resources to enjoy in the field of eucharistic prayers. It would seem common sense that we should swap eucharistic prayers as we would swap good stories if they help bring alive the Christian way. Every sacristy should contain a ring binder containing eucharistic prayers from different traditions and cultures, from which the presiding minister can select a prayer appropriate for the occasion. Bishops should relax about this one: it's not worth the fight.

As with the creed, so with the eucharistic prayer: it should not be considered beyond the pale that in certain circumstances, for example when the community is spending time away on retreat, the assembly might try its hand at composition. Not that we don't already have a splendid selection of eucharistic prayers at our disposal, of course, but they have one thing in common. Being compiled by learned scholars commissioned by a particular tradition, they must by definition give expression to that church's tradition and stance on a number of theological issues. They must hold the theological line, and the language and imagery used must be familiar and acceptable to the majority of that tradition's members. In the face of an across-the-board diminishing membership of liturgical mainstream churches in the Western world, and in the face of the rapid growth of an alternative culture of what might be called mechanical-biblical Christianity in which liturgy plays little or no part, 'holding the line' is not where we should be at.

Instead we need adventurous communities of faith willing to push out the liturgical boat a little and new ways of giving thanks to God over bread and wine in the assembly. The language and thought forms developed will need to be not only fresh and dynamic but also sufficiently rich to sustain us in faith and deepen our spiritual formation. Above all the challenge is to create eucharistic prayers that are full of meaning but free of jargon.

It would be a creative and formative exercise for any community of faith to tackle on a day away from the parish the task of formulating a new eucharistic prayer which *for that particular community* met the criteria outlined above. Is it possible to speak, for example, of the experience of being rescued and liberated in Christ without mentioning the atonement, or of the experience of God's overwhelming and all-pervading love for us without mentioning the Holy Trinity? We should have a go, even if we fail, for out there are people hungry for spirituality while feeling discouraged by the Church's insistence on limiting the description of the truths of God to certain classic expressions now etched in stone. They are waiting for us to make the attempt.

For many of us, the rites of the Church were sacred unalterable texts handed down from on high, where the eucharistic prayer was a text in which every word counted, fine tuned to the infinite degree in long sessions of a national committee at which there was blood on the carpet. Clergy spent a lot of time pondering which historic rites were 'sound' and carefully assessing new rites according to certain criteria pronounced by the liturgical guru of the day. At all costs Catholic order must be maintained, and this could only be ensured by the right words in the correct sequence.

In this context, to conceive of a local faith community creating its own eucharistic prayer may seem a shocking thing, but we need to rediscover our own tradition. Byron Stuhlman recalls us to the 'early tradition of freedom in the formulation of prayers for the eucharist', and points out that although 'the compiler of the *Didache* presents a set of prayers', he also advises that 'in the case of prophets, however, you should let them give thanks in their own way' (Stuhlman, 2000, p. 7).

Creative writing class

When a faith community has reached the point of wanting to have a go at creative liturgical writing to produce a eucharistic prayer appropriate to its own situation while honouring the Church's tradition from the first centuries of the Common Era, how does it begin?

The community should start by examining the basic themes common to the majority of eucharistic prayers produced by the many different churches and traditions within the Christian fold over the last two thousand years.

This may seem a tall order for an average local church, but the untidiness of the early Church's eucharistic prayers should give us heart: we are not alone. Bradshaw reminds us that there is nothing neat and tidy about the arrangements of these rites, and indeed there is wide variation in the components and primary emphases of the *anaphoras* of the early rites (Bradshaw, 1992, pp. 159–60).

So, with the guidance of a pastor open to the possibilities, there are plentiful resources to help us, especially liturgical dictionaries and other reference books of a liturgical nature (see, for example, Bradshaw, 2002).

Within these basic themes specific components can be identified, together with the order in which traditionally they are placed. We shall need to re-examine in the light of current experience, often reinforcing their significance, but occasionally re-arranging them, or even jettisoning one or two altogether.

Even a cursory glance down the centuries will reveal a basic pattern of ingredients which we need to assemble and stir well into the liturgical casserole.

a Engagement. At the outset of the eucharistic prayer, the presiding minister, as conductor of the orchestra, needs to ensure that all the players are alert and ready to begin making music. The presiding minister must receive the assembly's authority to do what needs to be done by one individual in the name of all.

This engagement of the assembly in the common purpose of God's people to make thanksgiving takes the form of what is known as the dialogue or *sursum corda* ('Lift up your hearts'). The dialogue derives from the Jewish forms of thanksgiving, and is common to all eucharistic prayers from every corner of the Christian liturgical map. At first sight the dialogue may appear to be a mere preamble to the eucharistic prayer itself, but it is in fact integral to it.

In the dialogue, the presiding minister first checks with the crew that everyone is on board and ready to roll. It's equivalent to the message alerting all passengers that 'doors are closing' before the subway train can move.

b *Thanksgiving*. The whole eucharistic prayer is of course a prayer of thanksgiving (the 'Great Thanksgiving' as the *Book of Common Prayer* (1979) calls it), and the theology of the eucharist in the *Didache* is one of God's superabundant blessing, in the context of which 'the bread and wine are consecrated for their sacramental purpose by giving of thanks over them' (Stuhlman, 2000, p. 13). Nevertheless a portion of the whole is given over to this theme with particular emphasis. This has two aspects to it.

First, the presiding minister recites the story of the saving acts of God in what is known as the preface. Once again, 'preface' sounds to our ears like a preamble, but the original Latin word *praefatio* for this first part of the eucharistic prayer means proclamation. The preface is a proclamation of thanksgiving to God, and is the foundation of all that follows in the rest of the *anaphora*, or eucharistic prayer.

Historically the Eastern and Western traditions of the Church developed different emphases in the matter of the preface. The Eastern rites provide a comprehensive thanksgiving for the whole action of God in creating and rescuing humankind, while the West prefers a more thematic approach, tying the proclamation of thanks to a particular feast or season of the Church's year. Both traditions have much to teach us: the East is more balanced, the West more brief and focused.

Second, the assembly joins its voice in assent in the *Sanctus*. This ancient anthem, 'Holy, holy, holy', is probably derived from certain Jewish thanksgiving prayers and echoes passages in both Hebrew and Christian Scriptures (Isa. 6.3 and Rev. 4.8). No one is quite sure when this anthem (together with the *Benedictus*, 'Blessed is the one who comes in the name of the Lord', with which it has traditionally been coupled) made its way into the Christian eucharistic rites. Although the oldest surviving texts omit these anthems, they have for the most part held sway ever since.

The *Sanctus* and *Benedictus* are at the same time both good and bad news. They give the assembly a voice in the eucharistic prayer, enabling it to let rip with a little communal thanksgiving to complement that of the presiding minister. They also interrupt the flow, however, and give credence to the old superstitions about 'magic moments' and special sections of the eucharistic prayer. For evidence of this one needs look no further than those antiquated liturgies (even those which use contemporary language) where the assembly, at the completion of the *Sanctus*, drops to its knees for the 'really holy' bits.

Some eucharistic prayers, most notably Eucharistic Prayer I of the Roman rite, and Eucharistic Prayer G in *Common Worship* (2000), place the *Sanctus* at the conclusion of the whole eucharistic prayer, as a coda sung by the whole assembly. There is much to be said for this practice.

When the *Sanctus* remains in its most familiar position in the middle of the eucharistic prayer, it will be necessary to round off the thanksgiving section with a link passage (known as the post-*sanctus*), to make a smooth transition from the verbal thanksgiving to the ritual thanksgiving over bread and cup which follows.

c Recollection and making present. This is a clumsy title, but with good reason. The scholars call this section the anamnesis, but they are unanimous in telling us that this Greek word for a Jewish concept is almost untranslatable into English. Basically it appears to mean an objective act by which we recall the past but at the same time make the past present. This confusion of past, present and future is very much part of the mystery of the eucharist, so we have to grapple with it, doing our best to keep all the balls in the air.

The two essential elements in this act of recalling and making present the life and self-offering of Jesus the Christ are remembering and offering. We remember all that Jesus, God's Anointed, has done for us and for humankind, and we explicitly state (as best as our historical hang-ups allow us) that by offering this bread and cup, we are intent upon making real for us here and now the timeless sacrifice of Christ. Past, present and future (in the hope of the heavenly banquet) become one.

Traditionally, an essential component of this recalling and making present is the recitation of the institution narrative, the words of Jesus at the Last Supper described first by Paul (1 Cor. 11.23–26) and later in the Synoptic Gospels. Although often listed as a separate component, it seems logically to form part of the anamnesis, lying at the heart of the recalling and the making present.

For the vast majority of Christians, the omission of the institution narrative would be unthinkable, but there are good reasons why we should pause for a moment at this point. First, New Testament scholarship is less certain that the words of institution can be traced back to Jesus himself, and in fact only Luke's account of the Last Supper contains the command to 'do this in remembrance of me'. It is likely that these words have a liturgical rather than historical origin. Second, the earliest eucharistic rite available to us, the *Didache*, dating from the first century, omits the institution narrative. Third, the institution narrative, as we shall see later, has been so abused by generations of Christians looking for a 'magic moment', that it was elevated to a position of importance that threatened the cohesion and unity of the whole eucharistic prayer. To omit the narrative altogether, at least occasionally, might be a shock to the system, but it would be a healthy corrective that might stir our thinking and praying.

d Transformation. For the faithful Christian, the crux of the whole business of the eucharist is the belief that, in some mysterious way that cannot be fully explained, the gifts on the altar table are invested in the eucharistic action with a reality that goes beyond their external appearance: bread and wine become, sacramentally at least, body and blood. To effect this transformation, the Spirit of God is invoked by the presiding minister on behalf of the whole assembly, an action known as the *epiclesis* ('invocation').

Although many Reformation liturgies (including the English *Book of Common Prayer* (1662)) were weak, or even silent, on the action of the Holy Spirit in the eucharistic transformation, the *epiclesis* is integral to the contemporary rites of all the main liturgical traditions. In times gone by, there was much liturgical snobbery about the 'proper' place for the *epiclesis*, and today we seem to hedge our bets. Of the eight eucharistic prayers in *Common Worship* (2000), for example, five have the *epiclesis* before the institution narrative, and three after it.

This renewed emphasis on the action of the Holy Spirit is another nail in the coffin of the institution narrative as *the* defining moment.

e Prayer and praise. Eucharistic prayers through the ages have usually included some element of intercessory prayer, and culminated in a doxology as a concluding hymn of praise.

The intercessions were traditionally called the diptychs, from the hinged board found in the earliest Christian church buildings, on which were written the names of those, living and departed, for whom the assembly wished to pray. Board or no board, it is an excellent corrective to pietistic self-indulgence, on the part of individual or community, for the whole assembly's thanksgiving for Christ's self-offering to flow out in loving concern for the world. Such prayers are an immediate first fruit of our communion with God in Christ, and help ground us in the reality of existence in this created order where we 'groan inwardly as we wait for adoption' (Rom. 8.23).

The eucharistic prayer customarily ends, where it began, with the accent on praise, here in the form of a solemn trinitarian doxology, to which the assembly's 'Amen' is as essential an assent as the response to the opening dialogue. When the *Sanctus* concludes the whole eucharistic prayer, the trinitarian doxology may be replaced by it, or amended to flow into it.

In attempting to construct its own eucharistic prayer, an assembly will need to weave together the elements outlined above, while never losing sight of the cohesion of the prayer seen as a *single united whole*. No one element should predominate over or intrude upon the others. It is the whole action, by the whole assembly, that effects this work of God.

One example of such an attempt, crafted at our cathedral and inspired by Arthur Peacocke's *Paths from Science towards God*, is included in Appendix I. Peacocke speaks powerfully of our need to repackage the Christian message in words and thoughts that stand a chance of being understood by the people. This instinct is one of which Cranmer would have approved entirely, and our Philadelphia efforts might prompt others to do much better.

Unlike Cranmer's time, the vast majority of our fellow citizens inhabit a world of residual Christianity, seeing in organized religion but a faint echo of a bygone Christian era. Our task is therefore the more urgent, and arguing over the 'soundness' of a eucharistic prayer, or whether it has the *epiclesis* in the right place, makes the Church in this cultural setting look plainly ridiculous. Our overriding need is to articulate this wondrous and timeless message in language and forms that will take hold of people's imaginations today.

Praying the eucharistic prayer

Attention can be given as to the manner in which the eucharistic prayer is offered. Singing or saying the eucharistic prayer are not the only options. A very effective way of involving the whole community, and which can be beautiful if done well, is for the assembly to sustain notes sung or hummed in a chord, beneath the words of the prayer. This works equally well with the prayer said or sung, but requires determination to keep going when all around you lose their nerve. Alternatively, the words of the eucharistic prayer can be accompanied instrumentally, which makes for a nice change, but is not so participatory for the assembly.

On a quiet weekday with a regular group of worshippers who know each other well, it is not unknown (tell it not in Gath!) for the eucharistic prayer to be shared by the celebrants, that is, by the members of the assembly. To keep the bishop's hair on, the presiding minister takes care to begin and to conclude the eucharistic prayer, and to be responsible for the words of institution (if these form part of the prayer, as they usually do). Before the eucharist begins, however, numbered cards are distributed among the group, on each of which is printed the words of just one of the paragraphs of the eucharistic prayer to be used, together with the last line of the person who will go before, to cue them in. As a way of sharing the eucharistic prayer among a group of friends who meet regularly for the eucharist, this method can be moving and formative. If used with discretion, it need not ruffle too many liturgical feathers during this period of gradual liberation, as we wait 'with eager longing for the revealing of the children of God' (Rom. 8.19).

Magic moments

In situations where different members of the assembly share the leading of the eucharistic prayer, the retention of the words of institution to the presiding minister is an understandable custom, given how far we have come in so short a time, but it is essentially a concession to tender souls which is out of tune with everything else that is going on in that setting.

As we have seen, the institution narrative, which we are accustomed to regard as the heart of the eucharistic prayer, did not form part of the earliest known forms of the Christian eucharist. The earliest known text of the eucharist is found in the *Didache* (probably first century), and clearly shows how the eucharist began life as a thanksgiving over bread and wine in the Jewish model. Jesus, described simply as 'Servant', is central to the prayer, but there is no connection made to the Last Supper. This came later with the separating out of the infant Church from the Jewish culture, and with it an assertion that this meal was no mere Jewish *seder* (Passover meal) adapted to Christian use, but a new beginning commissioned by Jesus himself. The authority for this came from Paul's second letter to the Church in Corinth where he describes what he 'received from the Lord' and also 'handed on to you'. In so doing he provides the earliest known account of what was said and done in the upper room at the last meal Jesus took with his closest followers. These are the words which we call the 'institution narrative' and which form part of every subsequent eucharistic rite available to us.

With the coming of the Middle Ages, the institution narrative became *the* consecration, instead of part of the whole eucharistic action by which consecration is effected. Hence the missals still going the rounds when I was ordained had the words of institution written in capitals, to indicate clearly that *this* was the 'magic moment' in which bread and wine were transformed at the hands of the priest, and he alone, into the Body and Blood of Christ. The Mass practically came to a standstill as we elevated and genuflected with much heaving and groaning, and with many a dramatic pause and ringing of bells. (Modernist though I am, how I love to read accounts of the medieval congregations who would shout out at the elevation of the Host, 'Heave it higher, sir priest!'). All this to declare that '*this* was *it*'.

Holding the Host in both hands between the first fingers and thumbs, he pronounces the words of consecration secretly, distinctly and attentively over the Host, and likewise over all of them if a number are to be consecrated.

| HOC EST ENIM CORPUS MEUM. | THIS IS MY BODY WHICH IS GIVEN FOR YOU. Do this in remembrance of me. |

Having uttered these words, he straightway genuflects and adores the consecrated Host: he rises, shows it to the people, replaces it on the Corporal, and again genuflects and adores: he does not henceforth disjoin his thumbs and first fingers, unless he has to handle the Host, until the ablution of the fingers. Then, having uncovered the Chalice, he says:

| SIMILI modo postquam cenátum est, (Ambabus manibus accipit Calicem) accípiens et hunc præclárum Cálicem in sanctas ac věnerábiles manus suas: item | LIKEWISE after supper, (*He takes the Chalice in both hands*) he took the Cup, (*He bows his head, and then holding the Chalice in his left hand, he signs over it with* |

A section of the 1662 eucharistic prayer as laid out in the English Missal

Hopefully we have moved on a long way from that stage in our evolution towards a more holistic understanding of the eucharist, seeing the *whole* eucharist, not just two sentences, as the means by which transformation is effected, and the *whole* assembly, not just the priest, as the agent of transformation. We are also objects of transformation, for in the eucharist it is not just bread and wine that are transformed, but the people of God.

For these reasons the institution narrative adopts a lower profile in contemporary liturgies attempting to recapture the cohesion of the pre-medieval period. The narrative is not printed in capital letters, neither is there a slowing down to a crawling pace, like motorists passing the scene of an accident. Once again it is part of the whole, a rediscovered truth that needs to be made clear by the posture of the assembly and its presiding minister.

When we go even further and omit the institution narrative altogether, which is a healthy shock to the system at least now and again, we find ourselves in good company. Stuhlman points out that far from being out on a limb, the simple prayers of blessing over bread and wine found in the *Didache* are 'what we would expect if the church followed Jesus' command to do this in remembrance of him'. He goes on to say, 'There is no compelling reason to expect the prayer to include the account of the institution. The biblical account is a warrant for the Christian celebration, not the text of its prayer' (Stuhlman, 2000, pp. 6 and 7).

Perhaps fewer people would have died on the rack in the sixteenth century if the Church had maintained its earliest practice and omitted the institution narrative from its eucharistic rite. The institution narrative has served all too often as a set text for a rigorous doctrinal examination of Jesus' intentions, instead of a passage which, though of uncertain origin, continues to be for many a source of reassurance and blessing. Instead of uniting the followers of Jesus, it has at times torn us apart.

Manual acts

If the assembly has some readjustments to make in being summoned from pew-bound obscurity to stand around the altar table as co-celebrants with the presiding minister, then the presiding minister has no less a task of adjustment to change, perhaps even more so. In my year as a transitional deacon, I was grateful to be meticulously trained by my devoted parish priest in how to say Mass correctly, and put through my paces in the heart of the mystery: the manual acts. The manual acts covered all the detailed procedures as to how the priest was to handle the eucharistic species, how for example the priest, once he had touched the host, must never part his forefinger and thumb until they were washed at the ablutions after communion. It was a mystique into which one felt deeply privileged to be admitted, and I felt I had really arrived when I knew how to 'finger and thumb' with the rest of the boys.

Today, even though Rome has things fairly well squared away with a simplified ceremonial of manual acts, the things that one observes among Anglicans can sometimes be bizarre. All kinds of hangovers from English Missal days survive, with many triple crossings, bowings and genuflections and beating of the breast. No one seems quite certain what to do any more. In the light of our renewed emphasis on the eucharistic prayer understood as a single whole, is it any longer appropriate to elevate paten and chalice at the institution narrative? How can we simplify something which has got so fussy? What signs and gestures remain meaningful and useful?

If we start with recalling the *purpose* of the manual acts, we can see how necessary they were for an assembly penned into its pews at a considerable distance from the presiding minister who stood with his back to them at an altar against the east wall. It was therefore essential, given the theology of that period, to make it clear to the whole congregation at what point the elements were consecrated and transformed into the Body and Blood of Christ. The elevation of the host and then the chalice, immediately after the words of institution which referred to them, was the visual dramatic moment of the whole eucharistic action. For good measure it was accompanied by the (usually rather frenetic) ringing of a sanctuary bell, to heighten the drama of the moment and to recall to wakefulness anyone who might have dozed off.

In the post-Vatican II era, when the presiding minister usually faces the people across the altar table, presiding at a rite in which the institution narrative is seen as but one part of the whole, the need for manual acts is obviously considerably reduced. At least a good proportion of the assembly can see what is going on, and in any case the need to dramatize the 'magic moment' has passed. Nevertheless, given the number of unhelpful buildings with poor sight-lines that communities of faith find themselves required to survive in, some simplified form of manual acts within the eucharistic prayer may be helpful.

When, however, we come to our present day and age, with the opportunity for the assembly to encircle the altar table as a body of co-celebrants, we arrive at a different place. Not only are manual acts no longer necessary, they are theologically indefensible. The 1995 International Anglican Liturgical Consultation's working paper on eucharistic theology states that 'the unity of the (eucharistic) prayer is emphasized if there are no changes in posture of either congregation or presider. Gestures which draw attention to the institution narrative or any other component may undermine the essential unity of the prayer' (see Stuhlman, 2000, p. 163).

In arriving at this conclusion I am indebted to those two stalwarts of liturgical renewal in the Anglican Communion, Rick Fabian and Donald Schell, co-rectors of St Gregory's, San Francisco. By the time I was able to visit St Gregory's and take part in their Sunday Liturgy, I found that, in a quite wonderful and affirming way, much of what we in West Yorkshire had been striving to establish in terms of a participatory and processional liturgy mirrored the incredible ground-breaking work of St Gregory's.

In one particular, however, I was struck by the powerful simplicity by which St Gregory's had rewritten the rule book as far as the presiding minister's manual acts were concerned: they abolished them lock, stock and barrel.

It remains of course an entirely theological rather than practical question. If our theological position is that priesthood resides in the community of faith assembled to 'make eucharist'; if the assembly is truly the agent of transformation; if the presiding minister is the co-ordinator and enabler of the assembly, drawing forth from it its latent priestly ministry; and if therefore the circle of co-celebrants around the altar table is no mere gesture but an effectual sign of the assembly's character and calling under God; then during the eucharistic prayer the whole assembly, presider included, should act as one.

For this reason, as St Gregory's clearly showed me, the presiding minister, by the place in which he/she stands and by the posture he/she adopts, indicates to all present that the presiding minister's place is as one of the assembly. Yes, the presiding minister alone speaks the words of the prayer, for to serve as spokesperson in these encounters between God and God's people is the presbyter's joyous and privileged calling. Yes, the presiding minister may indicate the bread and wine on the altar table when the prayers refer to them. And yes, there is no reason, given time and if it seems to work when we try it (the supreme test of any suggested new liturgical practice), why the whole assembly should not, following the presiding minister's lead, also point with their hands to the sacred elements. We expect ordained con-celebrants to do so, why not therefore the co-celebrants of the assembly also?

Now this brings us immediately into conflict with the rubrics of our Churches. The *Book of Common Prayer* (1979), for example, leaves nothing to doubt, inserting into the text of the eucharistic prayer itself the rubric that 'concerning the bread, the Celebrant is to hold it, or lay a hand upon it'. Although *Common Worship* (2000) no longer specifies this, it nevertheless remains almost universal practice.

For those committed to liturgical renewal, here is one of those unavoidable

moments of choice. If we firmly believe that the theological and spiritual formation of our assembly is at stake, it will be appropriate to drop the manual acts and
wait for the warning letter from the bishop, if it ever comes. We must move on,
and liturgy is renewed at the grass roots just as much as at the level of commissions and committees. Bon courage!

The eucharistic prayer (conclusion)

Ceremonial

*At the conclusion of the eucharistic prayer the assembly sings a joyful and triumphant
response.*

*The assembly, at the direction of the presiding minister, then gives a profound bow
of reverence.*

The assembly makes a profound bow

Commentary

Even when the assembly is right there in the thick of the action, it is possible for our attention to slip as we hear the familiar words of the eucharistic prayer led by the presiding minister. At the end of the prayer therefore it is a very necessary thing for the assembly to proclaim, loud and clear, its assent to and approbation of all that has been said in its name.

This was the custom of the primitive Church, and Justin Martyr (100–165) describes in his *First Apology* (written for a pagan audience) how 'The president likewise offers up prayers and thanksgivings according to his ability, and the people assent by saying, Amen' (Thompson, 1961, p. 9). This may seem obvious enough to us today, but this is a privilege only recently restored to many of us, and we should exult at the top of our voices in this invitation to play our part in the eucharistic action.

Anglicans and Amen

Anglicans in particular have travelled a long way in this regard. The first English Prayer Book of 1549 included a people's 'Amen' at the end of the doxology at the close of the eucharistic prayer, but this was suppressed in the second book of 1552; indeed there was no doxology to which an 'Amen' could be added. This was a deliberate and highly significant attempt to send the English Church hurtling in a Protestant direction, consigning the faithful to being hustled from the recitation of the Lord's words at the Last Supper straight into the reception of bread and wine.

Some sense of decency and order was restored in the 1662 book, with the reinstatement of the people's 'Amen', though awkwardly tacked onto the institution narrative (a doxology evidently viewed as a dangerous papist notion at that time), but it took the Americans to lead us back onto the straight and narrow. In the *Book of Common Prayer* (1979), the people's 'Amen' is actually printed in large-point italic capital letters, and in the 'Rite III' eucharistic framework on p. 401, the 'Amen' is even graced with an exclamation mark.

Daniel Stevick makes this comment about the 'Amen'.

This word stands as the people's ratification of the Great Thanksgiving. It was spoken of by early Christian writers as though it was cherished by the laity and said heartily. Jerome said that the Amens of the Christian congregations

> resounded in the basilicas of Rome like peals of heavenly thunder. (Stevick, 1999, p. 201)

The great Anglican liturgist Gregory Dix, in his classic *The Shape of the Liturgy*, comments:

> What for the jew was a longing hope for the future coming of God's truth, was for the christian a triumphant proclamation that in Jesus, the Amen to the everlasting Yea of God, he had himself passed into the Messianic Kingdom and the world to come. It was the summary of his faith in Jesus his Redeemer, and in God his Father and King. As such it was the fitting conclusion to the last words of the christian scriptures; and an equally fitting response alike to the eucharistic prayer and the words of administration, where that redemption and that fatherhood and kingship find their full actuality within time.' (Dix, 1964, p. 130)

So then, our assent should raise the roof, and there are various ways of achieving this. We might sing the 'Amen' repeated several times, or an alleluia with percussion, or a short chorus of praise, or in fact (if the presiding minister slightly adapts the ending of the eucharistic prayer) the *Sanctus*. For some alternatives, see Appendix J. Whatever variation we use, it needs to be learned by heart, for the conclusion of the eucharistic prayer is not the moment to be scrabbling for bits of paper on the floor or desperately seeking a page number.

Of these alternatives, the *Sanctus* can provide a glorious conclusion to the whole shebang, and Stuhlman reminds us that this Jewish hymn of praise was beloved of the early Christians because it expressed vividly the Judaeo-Christian view of worship 'as a participation in the heavenly liturgy' (Stuhlman, 2000, p. 23). It is a hymn of ancient provenance which deserves a place of honour in a moment in the liturgical action when we can really let rip. This is it! The dramatic change in tempo between the solemn words of the presiding minister and the sudden thundering of the organ to lead the assembly into the *Sanctus* can certainly qualify as a transcendent moment.

This practice also rules out any possibility that the *Sanctus*, left in its more familiar position in the middle of the eucharistic prayer, might be hijacked by the music department and turned into a short concert. This deplorable custom destroys the unity of the Great Thanksgiving and robs the assembly of its proper role as the 'choir' for this significant paean of praise of the whole people of God.

The *Sanctus*

As we have seen, the position of the *Sanctus* deserves careful consideration. Many scholars (for example, Jardine Grisbrooke in *A New Dictionary of Liturgy and Worship*) point to the difficulty the *Sanctus* poses in all the ancient rites as an interruption which 'has done as much as anything to confuse the clarity of the structure which ought to be apparent in the anaphora' (Davies (ed.), 1986, p. 17). In other words, the *Sanctus* appears to divide the eucharistic prayer (which we now are trying so hard to express as a single unity) into two distinct halves.

In making the *Sanctus* the *coda* of the eucharistic prayer, we shall be in good company, even if we are regarded a little strangely at first. Peter Cobb, in his examination of the *Apostolic Tradition* of Hippolytus in *The Study of Liturgy*, draws attention to E. C. Ratcliff's 'disputed but not disproven hypothesis that the prayer originally culminated in the *Sanctus*' (Cobb, 1987, p. 175). The 'prayer' referred to is the eucharistic prayer composed by Hippolytus (170–236) which has been a highly influential source for new eucharistic prayers in both the Roman and Anglican traditions. Even if the composers of our contemporary prayers could not bring themselves to go the whole hog with a *Sanctus* as culmination, there is no reason why we shouldn't try it ourselves. Others have gone before us.

Having sung the final acclamation, the assembly, taking its cue from the presiding minister, makes a profound bow. The presiding minister may wish to add a word of explanation and invitation, drawing attention to the mystery that is before us on the altar table and within us as a sacred community. Something very simple will suffice:

Before the mystery of God-with-us at this table, let us give a deep bow of reverence.

Mindful of the privilege, the joy, of being God's people, of being God's friends invited to his table, we bow profoundly, from the waist. This is the moment when are at once acutely aware of both the presence among us and between us, of God-with-us, Emmanuel, and the glory and the splendour of God who is completely other, and beyond our knowing or imagining. Immanence and transcendence in one moment: that's no bad deal.

Let David Philippart again put it better:

And so . . . we bow. We bow low so that God – in the miracle that is a morsel and a sip – can raise us up, nourished, united to each other and united in Christ. We bow down because the wood of the oppressor's cross bowed down Jesus' back; we bow down so that as with Jesus, God may raise us up to a new life lived forever for others. 'I will bow and be simple, I will bow and be free' [from an old Shaker hymn]. (Philippart, 1996, p. 9)

Transcendence

One of the continual gripes that assail those concerned to redesign liturgical space or to renew liturgy is that 'you are depriving us of transcendent worship'. I can only think that these complainers have been inhabiting another planet – certainly a different worship space – from the one I know.

While writing this section of the book, I happened to pay a visit to the seasonal (Episcopal) chapel on the Atlantic shore town where I had gone to write. It was an early morning eucharist, Rite II, with an obviously kindly retired priest, but who at the offertory disappeared through an empty choir to stand with his back to us at an altar built into the east wall, about thirty yards distant. The building itself, of charming external design and proportions, had been 'Episcopalized' by the insertion of opaque stained-glass windows, alien to the architecture, which totally eliminated any glimpse of the glorious sunshine shimmering on the bay alongside. Did all this add up to transcendence? God help us if it did.

Transcendence is not defined by the degree to which we preserve, untouched, ancient monuments or perpetuate antique texts or olde worlde language. Transcendence is an acute awareness of the presence of the living God before our very eyes, nay in our very midst.

That being so, an assembly gathered in a large uncluttered beautiful space, called forth to give expression to its sacred calling as a priestly community, is likely to have a very real experience, as it comes face to face with the holy, as it takes into its hands sacred gifts, of the complete other-ness and wonder of God who in his mercy stoops down to embrace us and empower us.

5 The Lord's Prayer

Ceremonial

The presiding minister invites the assembly to join hands and to say together the Lord's Prayer.

Commentary

Since the fourth century, it has been universal practice for the Lord's Prayer to be said between the eucharistic prayer and the breaking of the bread. It is not difficult to see why. The themes of 'daily bread', which we are about to receive; of forgiveness and reconciliation, which we are about to express in our sharing of a meal; and of ushering in the kingdom, for which the eucharist will strengthen us, are all explicit in this, the only known liturgical prayer that Jesus left his followers: 'As our Saviour taught us, so we pray.'

It goes without saying that this prayer too is a prayer of the whole assembly, and the *Book of Common Prayer* (1979) does well to make it absolutely clear that presiding minister and people begin the prayer together, thus pre-empting the dreadful habit of the presiding minister prompting the people with the opening phrase, then repeated, as if they were a bunch of kids in a kindergarten.

The presiding minister introduces the prayer with a phrase such as the customary, 'As our Saviour taught us, so we pray', or (as in the English Prayer Book of 1549), 'as our saviour Christ has commanded and taught us, we are bold to say'.

In Anglican and Lutheran settings, the presiding minister will, however, need to be firm, loud and clear in taking the lead by saying in one breath the whole of the opening phrase, 'Our father in heaven', thereby making clear that the traditional (i.e. Tudor) version, with the shorter opening phrase, 'Our Father', is not being used. This is where our three liturgical traditions have come unstuck in the matter of translating the Lord's Prayer. Two moved forward, one stayed put, but then the two bolder ones looked back and lost their nerve.

Things old and new

In the wake of Vatican II the Roman Communion deserves untold praises heaped upon it for the masterly way in which it translated ancient texts into contemporary ones of great beauty, simplicity and power. In one respect only did their liturgists let us down, and badly, and that was in failing to translate the Lord's Prayer out of Reformation period English (which, when you think about it, you might imagine they would have been rather keen to do). They balked at this last fence, and as a result have left the rest of us floundering to some extent.

As a result, those Communions that have attempted a modern translation do not quite have the courage of their convictions. The new Anglican prayer books on both sides of the Atlantic hedge their bets, as does the *Lutheran Book of Worship* (1995), printing both the new and old versions of the Lord's Prayer at this point in the eucharist. *Common Worship* (2000) and the *Lutheran Book of Worship* (1995) are just a little more incisive, giving subtle precedence to the new version, in positions reversed in the *Book of Common Prayer* (1979).

Many excuses are trotted out for choosing the traditional option, the most irritating, and surely most hypocritical, being the argument that we are being missionary minded and inclusive by doing so, and this (most often) from clergy whose own liturgies are a byword for obscurantism. In reality, the continued use of the traditional Lord's Prayer, 'trespasses' and all, is *exactly* the kind of last straw which breaks the back of those thoughtful people who struggle with the anachronisms and self-deceptions of mainstream religion.

So if we believe in a holistic approach to liturgy, with a consistent language that flows through from beginning to end, then we just have to bite the bullet and adopt the contemporary version. At the end of the day, the traditional version is self-indulgence on the part of an assembly unwilling to go the second mile in changing its ways. Keep the faith, and the world will cotton on, even if it takes a generation or two. Certainly it will take quite a while for the new to replace the old if we continue to build into the texts of our prayer books our lack of consistency, purpose and direction. Let's get a grip here.

It is fitting that the assembly should join hands, as a symbol of that unity God gives us in the eucharist of Christ, and as a token that we mean what we say about mutual forgiveness in order to be equipped to carry out the work of God. This may be considered corny by some, but it works. African-Americans enjoy a sung version of the Lord's Prayer that involves raising hands, still joined, high in the air for the doxology, to end on a triumphant note (see Appendix K).

The assembly joins hands to say the Lord's Prayer

In this custom of joining hands for the Lord's Prayer we can in fact 'have our cake and eat it'. If we are Anglicans or Lutherans, having shared the Peace at the conclusion of the synaxis, we have a second 'mini Peace' at this point. We again risk bodily contact and speak of forgiveness, at almost the same point as in the Roman rite. It is the best of both worlds.

6 The breaking of the bread

The fraction

Ceremonial

The presiding minister moves forward to stand at the altar table, and takes the loaf of bread in his/her hands, breaking it in two as he/she says the fraction sentence.

The presiding minister breaks the bread

Commentary

The fraction is one of the four 'actions of the Mass' – taking, blessing, breaking, giving – identified by Gregory Dix in *The Shape of the Liturgy*. Significantly, it made such an impression on the faithful that it became an early title for the eucharist itself (Acts 2.42).

It is clear that a breaking of the bread needs to take place at this point, but how it is to be accompanied – by words or by silence – is a matter for debate. Interestingly, there is for Anglicans a choice to be made between American and English practice at this point.

The *Book of Common Prayer* (1979) has a clear preference for silence as the bread is broken, after which the presiding minister keeps a further period of silence before speaking an optional fraction sentence. This sentence, referring to Christ the Passover sacrifice, is clearly separated by the rubrics from the fraction itself. It may be 'sung or said', indicative of its purpose as a (choral) reflection after the event. Galley (1989, p. 118) suggests that the presiding minister might say a silent prayer at this point.

Such a treatment of the fraction has much in common with the Roman rite in that here, too, the presiding minister says nothing aloud during the fraction. The breaking of the bread is done as the rest of the assembly says or sings the *Agnus Dei*, while the presiding minister says quietly a prayer of his/her own.

Common Worship (2000) expects something to be said by the presiding minister as the bread is broken, and provides two scriptural sentences with responses. The first of these, familiar from the *Alternative Service Book 1980*, is:

Presiding minister: We break this bread to share in the body of Christ.

Assembly: **Though we are many, we are one body, because we all share in one bread.**

Critics complain that this is a case of stating the obvious, but I have to admit that my own liturgical instinct is that after a suitably pregnant pause, appropriate words heighten the significance of the moment. They also serve to avoid that hiatus when no one is quite sure what happens next or when the musicians should come in for the music that follows.

The fraction is also an appropriate moment to bring to mind in the assembly our broken world and the shattered company of believers and seekers after God. Christ gave himself to be broken that all of us might find reconciliation and wholeness. Grace Cathedral, San Francisco, uses some very fine words (originally harvested from England, apparently)[1] which help place our own bread-breaking in the context of the yearnings of all humanity:

The Cantor sings, and all repeat: Alleluia, Alleluia, Alleluia.

Presiding Minister: We break this bread for those who journey with us:
for those who travel the way of the Hindus,
for those who follow the path of the Buddha,
for our sisters and brothers of Islam,
for the Jewish people from whom we come,
and for all who walk the way of faith.

Cantor, then all repeat: Blessed be God for ever.

Presiding Minister: We break this bread for the earth we have wasted, for those who have no bread, and for ourselves in our brokenness.

All: Blessed be God for ever.

Although the fraction is a dramatic moment, it is not a theatrical moment, and the presiding minister should resist the temptation to break the bread with a great flourish, waving the two pieces around in the air in a radius of 360 degrees. This draws attention to the presiding minister, not to the fraction.

The filling of the vessels

Ceremonial

The presiding minister, assisted by the deacon and/or other ministers, oversees the division and distribution of the bread and wine into an appropriate number of vessels.

The filling of the vessels for communion

Commentary

Here we come to what may be described as 'part two' of the fraction, that is, the breaking down of the single loaf into fragments of suitable size for each communicant, and the decanting of consecrated wine from the single chalice into several chalices sufficient for the size of the assembly.

After the initial breaking of the bread in two, and following a short period of reflective silence, the presiding minister motions for members of the assembly to bring forward from a small credence table, conveniently situated to one side, an appropriate number, depending on the size of the assembly, of secondary patens and chalices or cups.

The presiding minister then places the two large broken pieces of the one conse-crated loaf in two of the patens brought to the table. Those members of the assembly designated to administer the bread then break the large pieces into fragments of an appropriate size. Meanwhile the presiding minister (or deacon) fills from the main chalice (or flagon if numbers require it) an appropriate number of secondary chalices or cups. Four chalices will be appropriate where the assembly is to be invited to the altar (as in the second method of communion, see p. 199).

If a deacon is available, this is a perfectly appropriate task for the deacon to over-see, and the presiding minister can stand back in the circle until this subsidiary frac-tion is completed. If there is no deacon, the presiding minister should oversee the filling of the vessels, but involve the help of those assisting. For example, whether or not there is a deacon, it is those who will be administering the bread that should break it into pieces. These members of the assembly are more than waiters; they help pre-pare that which they serve to others.

Once the secondary chalices or cups are filled, the presiding minister and/or deacon places a chalice on each corner of the altar table, together with a purificator, while those designated to administer the bread each take hold of a paten in readiness for the invitation.

While all this is continuing, the *Agnus Dei* is sung, the hymn that begins 'Lamb of God, you take away the sins of the world, have mercy on us'. Although there are plenty of contemporary communion songs one can use as alternatives at this point, it is good to use this ancient hymn which, for Anglicans at least, was previously regard-ed with a little suspicion. It has now been fully rehabilitated (see below), as well as updated in language, so let's make the most of it.

Agnus Dei

This hymn began life in the Eastern Church, probably in Syria, which was fond of using the image of the 'lamb' to designate both Jesus and the bread of the eucharist. It lifted the words from John's Gospel (John 1.29), spoken of Jesus by John the Baptist: 'Here is the Lamb of God who takes away the sin of the world' (which is a little confusing, as lambs were not used as sacrifices for sin, but never mind).

After the Muslim take-over of Syria in the seventh century, Syrian refugees (among them a future pope, Theodore I) succeeded in introducing their favourite hymn into the Roman rite, perhaps during the pontificate of Sergius I, himself of Syrian descent. Here it continued to be used in its original position covering the fraction, and the Syrians were able to enjoy a moment of nostalgia every time they celebrated the eucharist in their adopted city so far from home. After being shunted along for some reason to fill the gap between fraction and communion, where it languished for many centuries, the *Agnus Dei* was restored in the 1970s to its original position in the new rites springing from Vatican II.

As can be imagined, the Reformers got rather jumpy at all the sacrifical connotations of the *Agnus Dei*, and while the first English Prayer Book of 1549 retained it, the second Prayer Book of 1552 dropped it like a hot potato. It has taken a long time to be restored to Anglican rites, and we have the musicians to thank for it (which is appropriate after all).

Flowing from the Catholic Revival in the Anglican Church in the nineteenth century came a wealth of new liturgical music, including a myriad of settings of the *Agnus Dei*, most notably the setting by John Merbecke (d. 1585), a noble son of the English Reformation who was condemned to the stake for having compiled the first Bible concordance in English, but was rescued at the eleventh hour. This was just as well, as he went on to produce the *Book of Common Prayer Noted*, a setting of the new English Mass of 1549 to simple but haunting plainchant. Until very recently, the Merbecke setting, *Agnus Dei* and all, was the very bread and butter of any English parish that aspired to Catholic worship. And so it was that the *Agnus Dei* came back into the church through the choir room door.

Today, although the new American Prayer Book relegates the *Agnus Dei* to the *Book of Occasional Services* which serves as a supplement to the 1979 Prayer Book, it is not mentioned in the text of the eucharist. This is a surprising omission, given the generally more Catholic instincts of the American (Scottish) liturgical line.

By comparison, the English went rather wild in *Common Worship* (2000), printing the *Agnus Dei* in the eucharistic text and stipulating that it 'may be used as the bread is broken', not just after the fraction (as in previous rites such as the *Alternative Service Book 1980*). This is a significant return to primitive practice which we should welcome and make use of.

One detail is of interest, in that a one-letter difference remains in the translation between Rome and Canterbury. Whereas the traditional Roman version speaks of 'the sins of the world', the Anglican version speaks of 'sin'. I am not sure where this comes from – I guess from a subliminal fear of getting caught up in the sin-laundering business of the medieval Church – but at least the Anglican version keeps company with John the Baptist in John 1.29.

7 The invitation

Ceremonial

The presiding minister and other members of the assembly designated to administer Holy Communion hold up a paten and chalice and invite the assembly to share in the sacred meal.

Commentary

This is where the Roman rite wins hands down, because it knows what it wants to say and says it boldly, in a sentence and response which is universally used. The sentence said by the presiding minister as he holds up the host and chalice conflates John 1.29, unequivocally identifying the bread with Jesus, Lamb of God, with a slight adaptation of Revelation 19.9:

> Behold the Lamb of God,
> who takes away the sins of the world.
> Happy are those who are called to his supper.

The response is a clever adaptation to a eucharistic context of the cry of the centurion (Luke 7.6) who felt himself unworthy to receive Jesus in his home:

> Lord, I am not worthy to receive you,
> but only say the word and I shall be healed.

Perhaps there is a *slight* mismatch there, between the happiness of the celebration in the Book of Revelation, and the rather grovelling response, which has about it a touch of the later Cranmer (a wonder he didn't think of it first). Nevertheless it is a splendid example of the creative use of Scripture adapted to a liturgical context, and which has stood the test of time and doesn't have to be thought about.

Anglicans on the other hand encounter at this point a real mish-mash of possibilities, each with its nuance of theological thought. Many find the adaptation of the old Prayer Book invitation, 'Draw near with faith', vaguely unsatisfactory with its spiritualizing tendencies inherent in 'feed on him in your hearts'.

Common Worship (2000) now includes (as did the *Alternative Service Book 1980*) the Roman option, albeit with a slight variation ('Jesus is' instead of 'This is') in case we get just a bit too carried away in our sacramental theology.

The *Book of Common Prayer* (1979) has a very fine sentence in which the presiding minister announces, 'The gifts of God for the people of God', but it has no response, and I for one am always left looking for one in the back of my mind, feeling that there must be a response which I, and the whole assembly, has somehow forgotten.

Common Worship (2000) attempts to remedy this by providing a response for the people, but for some unknown reason it was felt necessary to meddle with the original, and the end result, beginning with a possessive, is somehow more pedestrian, with less of a ring about it. The response is fine in itself, but doesn't seem quite to fit – there is a touch of the non sequitur about it, as though it was picked up at a secondhand response store:

Presider: God's holy gifts
for God's holy people

Assembly: Jesus Christ is holy
Jesus Christ is Lord
to the glory of God the Father.

In summary, the Anglicans suffer from too much choice at this moment in the eucharist. A less than satisfactory Prayer Book original has been adapted and then replaced with several options, with the result that no one is quite sure what they are supposed to say at this point, not least the presiding minister.

8 The communion

Ceremonial

The consecrated bread and wine is shared among all members of the assembly, the presiding minister and other ministers receiving last.

When each member of the assembly receives the sacrament, he/she responds by saying, 'Amen!'

See photograph in colour section: 'The communion'

Commentary

This is another of those moments when the assembly will give itself away as to how it *really* thinks of itself. The method of communion is almost as significant in this regard as the assembly's configuration for the eucharistic prayer.

There is no need for the presiding minister to administer communion, and by choosing to refrain from so doing, the presiding minister can make yet another gesture in which the ministry of the whole assembly is affirmed. Here, a sacred and joyful task formerly restricted to the ordained is now shared by (lay) members of the assembly.

When he/she is not administering, the presiding minister returns to stand in the circle, and is communicated last by the assistants.

The presiding minister is the last to receive communion

The age-old custom of the presiding minister communicating him- or herself first is plainly unacceptable in a mature liturgical assembly that thinks theologically. It perpetuates an outrageous model of sacerdotal privilege, and we need to grow beyond it if we are to exalt the assembly above its individual members and servants.

The communion is by definition a dialogue, not a monologue, as otherwise no real communion of mutual love and respect is taking place. Whenever the sacrament is received by one member of the assembly from another, the recipient should declare his/her assent and joy with a loud 'Amen!' As with the 'Amen' at the end of the eucharistic prayer, so with the 'Amen' here as we receive the sacrament. We affirm this glorious gift with full hearts and loud voices.

The old tradition of receiving the sacrament directly onto one's tongue, declaring thereby our utter dependence on Mother Church before whose generous provision we were rendered speechless, will no longer suffice. It is a romantic gesture, but fails to do justice to our rediscovery of mutual love within the Body of Christ, with God and with one another.

By way of contrast, I still vividly remember – 35 years on – the experience of presiding at the eucharist at the Convent of the Sisters of the Love of God in Oxford, and at communion hearing each sister shout out the 'Amen!' with ardour and joy. They practically made me jump out of my skin.

All too often the minister of communion hears nothing at all in reply to the words of administration and the gift of the sacrament. It's enough to make you want to take the sacrament back and start again!

It is highly appropriate that music should be played and sung throughout the period when communion is being administered. If so, the musicians should receive communion last, because, firstly, they are ministers of the eucharistic celebration and should (along with the clergy) intentionally take last place as a symbol of their servanthood, and secondly, communicating musicians first creates an unfortunate hiatus for the rest of the assembly.

There is a wealth of new liturgical music written for precisely this part of the liturgy, of rare beauty and rich meaning. If musical accompaniment is limited, it will be helpful for the assembly to learn by heart a basic repertoire of refrains, chants and choruses (Taizé chants are excellent here) that can be sung unaccompanied. See Appendix M for some suggested songs and refrains.

Where eucharistic ministers are to take the sacrament to the sick directly from the Sunday Liturgy, the ideal as well as the primitive custom, then fragments of the one loaf should be used.

'After you'

The Church is little help in the matter of 'who goes first?' It has been too long at the game to see straight. While we might expect the Roman rite, despite Vatican II, to make much of the 'the priest's communion' – it even provides it with its own subheading – it is a huge disappointment to find that the *Book of Common Prayer* (1979) makes this damaging custom equally explicit: 'The ministers receive the Sacrament in both kinds, and then immediately deliver it to the people.' *Common Worship* (2000) does *slightly* better, but only just, the rubric at this point stipulating that 'the president and people receive communion'. Although it doesn't spell out the pecking order, as does the *Book of Common Prayer* (1979), you nevertheless know which way it's going to go.

William Seth Adams, in his book on the art of presiding, *Shaped by Images*, devotes a chapter to the presiding minister as 'One who Hosts' and says this about the unhelpful rubric:

> The rubrical directives of the Prayer Book remain consistent with the received tradition, a tradition seemingly rooted in the hierarchical precedence rather than hospitality. Reading this precedence this way, the rubrics seem to suggest that the communion is properly the priest's communion, into which the people are invited to join. (Adams, 1995, p. 56)

This hierarchical mindset is deeply embedded in the Church, and demands of us that when we have an opportunity to model 'a still more excellent way', as Paul used to say, we should seize it with both hands (or perhaps that's an unfortunate turn of phrase in this instance).

We need to take a huge leap into a brave new world in which the communion is understood first and foremost as the *assembly's* communion in which the presiding minister, as a member of the assembly, also takes part. As host, the presiding minister is anxious that others go first, delighting to see everyone fed and satisfied before eating anything him- or herself. For the contented host, the leftovers are just fine.

No touching!

The issue as to which lay members of the assembly shall, or shall not, assist in the administration of communion has been allowed to become a vexed question in many parishes, or at least a potentially divisive one. This is because in the Roman and Anglican Communions we have created a new pseudo-clerical species of liturgical being called a 'eucharistic minister', 'minister of communion' or even 'extraordinary minister', requiring in the Anglican case a recommendation from the parochial church council or vestry and a licence from the bishop.

As with the question of who should communicate first, we have got ourselves into this predicament because we have developed over the centuries attitudes and thought forms that take us from the top of the hierarchy down instead of from the assembly up.

A pause to consider the nature of a religious community of monks or nuns may help us take a fresh look at the nature of the assembly. In such a community, the notion of 'special people' only being authorized to give communion to the others would be absurd, and would undermine the theological understanding that all members of that community have consecrated themselves to God. (Yes, religious communities continue to live with the anomaly of the ordained priesthood which confuses the issue of monastic vocation, but in an enlightened church this would be rendered unnecessary by the bishop authorizing the 'head of the household' (male or female, ordained or lay) to preside at the eucharist. But that's another story.) It is for this reason that in many religious communities, while the bread is administered, the chalice is not. Instead members of the community come forward to take into their own hands one of several chalices set upon the altar table.

The reason why we might instinctively resist this approach in a parish setting is because at base we have no real confidence in the baptismal covenant. We talk about it a lot, we celebrate splendid Easter Vigils, in which we reiterate its centrality, but we don't actually believe that it *works*.

What we are saying in effect is, 'Oh yes, it's fine for monks and nuns; they are special people.' Then what in the world does that make us? Less than special? Not consecrated to God? But if we believed only half the things we proclaim about baptism, in which we die and rise to Christ, by which we are filled by God's Spirit, by which we are adopted by God, then we would know ourselves to be very special people indeed. More correctly we would know our *assembly* to be a very special 'religious community' indeed, for on our own we continue to struggle, while when we gather around the Lord's table we remember who we are as 'holy nation, royal priesthood, chosen people'.

So then, if we actually believe that by our baptism we are set upon a course of transformation, and if we believe that the assembly of God's people is holy, then what possible excuse can we have for making a distinction between one lay member and another in an attempt to discern who is 'worthy'? The answer is that in the assembly all are worthy, or no one is. All may handle the sacrament, or no one should be authorized.

When it comes to the designation of ministers of communion (for the bread), their selection is a tricky issue only if subjective judgements as to 'worthiness' are allowed to play a part. The way to avoid committee resolutions or bishops' licences in this matter is simply to link this ministry to other ministries within the assembly already recognized and authorized. Further discussion on the matter is thereby pre-empted.

In the Anglican tradition, for example, this would mean that the church wardens, or the lay ministry team leaders, or chair of the worship committee, would, by virtue of their office, automatically be commissioned to minister the sacrament also.

To vest or not to vest

As to whether such ministers of communion would be vested for their liturgical ministry, much depends on their precise role. Where the minister is administering communion only, it would seem appropriate for them not to vest, but simply to step forward from the circle as and when required. Where, however, the minister is acting as a liturgical assistant to the presiding minister throughout the Liturgy, rather like a 'Master of Ceremonies' in the old days, then it would be entirely appropriate for the minister to vest in an alb, identical to those worn by the other (ordained) ministers present. This blurs the edges a little between lay and ordained, and gives a sense of visual cohesion to those leading worship, irrespective of their order within the Church.

The minister vested in this way would be part of a small team of liturgical assistants (or 'deacons' as they are called at St Gregory's, San Francisco) who, in rotation, would assist the presiding minister at the Sunday Liturgy. This group would need to be well trained in liturgical matters, and able to serve as a 'liturgical think tank' when needed by the pastor of the parish.

Whose party?

Having considered 'Who administers?', it is also necessary to ask 'Who receives?' Admittance to holy communion varies enormously between ecclesial communities. The Roman Communion defends the sacrament most rigorously, as is well known, and thereby causes pain not only to her sister churches but also embarrassment to many of her own members. The Episcopal Church in its Additional Directions devotes a whole sub-section to 'Disciplinary Rubrics' surrounding the eucharist, concerned with what to do with those of a 'notorious evil life' or whose conduct makes them 'a scandal to the other members of the congregation'. These paragraphs have now a quaint and unreal air about them in today's culture, although the section dealing with 'hatred between members of the congregation' is far from out of date or academic, being the most frequent form of scandal in the Church.

Whether it is appropriate to use the eucharist as a means of discipline is, however, a tricky question. Very occasionally we will encounter individuals who come to the eucharist to disrupt and divide, but fortunately this is rare, there being better forms of entertainment to hand. But even in such a case, our best hope is to make the eucharist so dynamic, so participatory, so engaging (and thereby so excruciating for those of evil intent) that the liturgy does its own 'screening out' without recourse to canon law or the bishop's intervention.

The English Church, previously having restricted communion to its own confirmed members, now in practice tends to admit all the baptized, of whatever Christian allegiance, although the rubric quotes the canon that in theory restricts communicants from other churches to those who 'subscribe to the doctrine of the Holy Trinity and are in good standing in their own Church'. As this requirement would be totally impossible to ascertain at the time of communion, we may safely say that communion is in effect without restriction.

For many years in Anglican churches it has been customary for the presiding minister, at the time of communion, to announce that all the baptized, from any tradition, are welcome to receive. Going further, there is a discernible groundswell of opinion moving towards an open table, to communion without condition.

This has its origin in a growing awareness that the most radical thing Jesus did was to 'eat with publicans and sinners' (Matt. 9.11). He scandalized the religious authorities of his day by his outright refusal to observe the purity laws in relation to eating and drinking. He sat down to eat with all and sundry, the elite and the riffraff. As a result, it can be said that it was his open table, his policy of unconditional hospitality, as much as anything he ever said or taught, that led to his downfall.

As a result, there is an increasing uneasiness about refusing communion to anyone, either because they are too young (we have made Christianity such a cerebral thing) or because they are considered somehow beyond the pale, due to their lack of belief or the non-existence of their washing habits (we have made Christianity such a prim and proper thing).

This unease with traditional practice resonates with our own experience of everyday life in that we know how the shared meal has a power to reconcile, to heal and to unify that is almost sacramental in its power. We recall those times when we have been 'pleasantly surprised' by dining companions we would never have chosen and from whom we instinctively shrank at first sight. The eucharistic assembly, as well as being an intimate community of the like-minded, can be understood also as God's 'mess' (double entendre intended) where we are required to sit down with 'all sorts and conditions', to have the corners rubbed off us, our assumptions challenged, and to find healing and hope in the company of people radically different from ourselves, with whom we would never have chosen to break bread.

If our table is really an open one, it will be understood that the problem of children needing a blessing from (lay) ministers does not arise. All children should be offered the sacrament, if but a tiny morsel. If for any reason this is not practical or appropriate, or if an adult asks instead for a blessing, the lay minister should pray over the person, not call over a presbyter for some sacerdotal 'magic'. If it is clear that priestly counsel is required, then the presiding minister or other presbyter will talk to the person privately after the liturgy.

In these post-Christian days, when those who seek God, or truth, or meaning, or something, present themselves in our assembly, it is no time to quote rubrics or canons. We do the Benedictine thing and treat the guest as Christ come among us.

Words of communion

What do we say as we give or receive holy communion? Above all we should remember that communion (in one kind at least) is a dialogue between giver and receiver in which each plays an active role.

Words of administration will vary between traditions. Rome sticks to the stark but dramatic 'The body of Christ' and 'The blood of Christ' to which the recipient replies 'Amen'. Perhaps as a reaction against the uncompromising simplicity of these words, the Reformers seemed to go in for long-windedness in their attempt to cover all their theological bases.

Common Worship (2000) offers its usual variety of options, beginning with the 'hedging of bets' lengthy one translated from the *Book of Common Prayer* (1662), which speaks directly of the body and blood but which also includes a little exhortation about eating and drinking 'in remembrance' of Christ's death, with a reassurance to the Protestant wing that we 'feed on him in your heart by faith'. Second of the options, however, is the Roman rite plain and simple, in addition to three other simple and attractive options.

The *Book of Common Prayer* (1979) struck out on its own with a couple of options, one of which seems to have become established as the clear favourite:

The Body of Christ, the bread of heaven. **Amen.**
The Blood of Christ, the cup of salvation. **Amen.**

The contemporary Lutheran rite in *With One Voice* (Augsburg Fortress Press, 1995) likewise provides a simple expansion of the Roman version:

The Body of Christ, given for you. **Amen.**
The Blood of Christ, shed for you. **Amen.**

If in doubt, the simpler the better, and to use the words of the Roman (and now Anglican) rite seems the best way of pre-empting any theological hair-splitting. You can't get much simpler and more direct than 'The body of Christ', and each person who receives is free to make of it what they will.

If we feel in more creative mood, however, we could do worse than to sift through the writings of the Fathers of the Church to dig out a gem or two that can be adapted to contemporary use. A prime example is the phrase from the writings of Augustine of Hippo, that king of the theological sound-bite:

Receive what you are, the body of Christ. **Amen.**

Apart from the theological reasons for devising methods of communion which make 'chalice-bearers' and other specially authorized ministers redundant, there are the purely practical ones. New methods of sharing communion actually *work* better.

The 'ceremonial' part at the head of this section was light on detail quite deliberately. There are today many different methods by which the assembly can share the sacrament, and we should try them all. It is a healthy thing if we are flexible in this matter, not getting bogged down into an unchanging pattern, but free to experiment and explore what works for us and what speaks most clearly of our communal life and purpose.

Methods of communion

First method. A method which speaks most loud and clear of the nature of the assembly as a community of co-celebrants is that whereby the broken bread is circulated in baskets throughout the assembly, each person taking into his/her hand a fragment, and holding it until everyone has followed suit and the baskets have been returned to the altar table, silence being maintained throughout. The presiding minister then holds up his/her own fragment and announces, 'The Body of Christ'. The assembly responds 'Amen!' and all consume together.

This is indeed a powerful way of affirming the assembly's calling to celebrate the eucharist as a single body, powerful enough to send a shiver down one's spine, and no community should miss out on exploring its effect on its own sense of identity and purpose. For the wine, a number of chalices can then be passed through the assembly, each person communicating his/her neighbour.

Second method. A second method, one which combines the personal touch of giving and receiving on a one-to-one basis with a renewed sense of ownership, involves two quite different but complementary postures. First the bread is administered by ministers of communion to the assembly standing in the circle around the altar table, in the traditional manner. Then for the wine, members of the assembly come to the altar table to take into their own hands one of four chalices, one on each corner.

> See photograph in colour section: 'Communion administered . . . and taken'

It is deeply moving to see how reverently the sacrament is approached and consumed, and, more importantly, this reclaiming of the altar table by the people of God, as a place where they have a right to be, is highly symbolic of the baptized come of age. After at least seventeen centuries of hierarchical clerical domination, these few steps to the altar table are a giant leap for the holy people of God.

When I was a boy, I was blessed with a vivid sense of the presence of God in the medieval church building where I was raised in the faith. So acute was it, however, that I remember hesitating nervously before entering the sanctuary where I was about to be trained as a server. The sharp words of our then curate to 'pull myself together' brought me to my senses, but I have never forgotten that sense of awe.

For the faithful now to approach the altar, no longer fenced off and distant but in our midst, is also a moment full of awe. There is no less reverence or wonder – far from it – but our awe is reserved not for an altar or a thing, but for the holiness of the assembly, touched and transformed by the power of God to experience as never before the 'glorious liberty of the children of God'. Let there be no community of faith that does not at least experiment with this method, to see for themselves how potent it can be in awakening us to who we really are as the people whom Jesus no longer calls 'servants' but 'friends'.

Third method. A third method, familiar to many especially at smaller and more intimate celebrations of the eucharist, is the passing of the paten and the cup round the circle, each person ministering to his/her neighbour. This remains one of the simplest and most effective methods of communion in smallish groups, but with larger groups is either very slow or (if more than one paten or cup is passed round) can get rather confused as the circle(s) gets bent out of shape, with people not sure who has received and who hasn't.

Fourth method. For the largest gatherings, the tested and tried method of communion stations probably remains the most satisfactory. It requires very careful preparation, crystal clear instructions to the ministers, and good traffic control. It is in fact amazing how rarely it is done well. This method can also give rise to the problem (for example, at an ordination) of queues forming at some stations while business remains slack at others. We should not allow the cult of personality to rewrite the theology of communion as an encounter with the minister rather than with God. Despite opposition in some quarters to communion at stations, on the grounds it can become rather mechanical, it does at least get people off their knees and doing something they don't usually do, which in liturgy is no bad thing.

In every method of sharing communion there lurks a gremlin that needs to be named, and the name of the gremlin is intinction. This is an antisocial habit, which smacks of fear, arrogance and lack of faith, symptomatic of our not thinking what we are doing. It is a problem that needs to be addressed by the community, led by the pastor and his/her leadership team.

Intinction

Although of ancient provenance (first springing out of the woodwork in the seventh century) it has been repeatedly condemned and outlawed by the Church.

Fear of spilling the Precious Blood of Christ, or of catching the plague, may have made sense in the Middle Ages, but surely not today. It is a particularly grave misdemeanour for Anglicans and Lutherans, whose spiritual ancestors fought so hard in the Reformation period for the restoration to the people of communion in both kinds. How ironic if today we were to turn up our noses at the chalice!

Intinction poses two problems, theological and practical:

1 The common cup has always been a potent symbol of the bond between disciple and Lord. The passing of the cup is a dramatic feature of the gospel accounts of the Last Supper, and those who would be close to him are challenged, as were James and John, with the question, 'Are you able to drink the cup that I drink?' (Mark 10.38).
2 It leaves such a mess for those who come after, especially so in the era of real bread, when those who intinct reduce the contents of the chalice to a soup.

The remedy lies in a renewed education of congregations about the history of the sacrament, the privilege of the common cup, and its safety on health grounds. We also need a few more pastors who will slap wrists.

The advantage of new methods of communion, some of which are outlined above, is that they tend to put the communicant 'on the spot' to a greater degree, making much more evident the expectation that the bread will be consumed before proceeding to the chalice, and making the receiving of the chalice a moment of greater significance.

Where people have a real difficulty with sharing the common cup, they should be asked to receive in one kind only, and be reminded that this is the norm for the communion of the sick, for example. This reminder also serves to avoid ever having to consecrate additional bread and wine (a point of honour where I come from). If by mischance the chalices run out, so be it. There is usually plenty of bread.

My own experience suggests that the opposite problem is more prevalent: that far too much wine and bread are consecrated. In calculating the amounts needed, it is often the case that insufficient account is taken of the 'monstrous regiment of dippers' who as a rule consume far less wine than usual.

The fact that the Episcopal Church allows in its Additional Directions, contained in the *Book of Common Prayer* (1979) for the sacrament to be 'received in both kinds simultaneously, in a manner approved by the bishop', is neither here nor there. Whatever it takes, strenuous efforts should be made to discourage and discontinue this bad habit wherever it is encountered.

9 The ablutions

Ceremonial

When all members have received communion, the presiding minister and other ministers return the patens and chalices to the altar.

If the sacrament is to be taken to the sick, the eucharistic minister(s) comes to the altar, places a fragment of the bread in a pyx, and departs the building immediately.

The presiding minister invites the assembly to again make a profound bow of reverence, and then to return to their seats.

The presiding minister delegates to the deacon and other ministers, together with additional members of the assembly as required, the reverent consumption of the remains except the wafers to be reserved in the aumbry. The presiding minister then returns to his/her chair.

The presiding minister places the sacrament to be reserved (in one kind only) in the aumbry and consumes the wafers remaining from the previous week.

Commentary

The 'ablutions' here are used in the popular sense of the whole 'clearing-up' process, including both the reverent consumption of the remains as well as the cleansing of the vessels.

Where the sacrament is to be taken to the housebound, and where circumstances in the home or the hospital ward allow communion to be administered within an appropriate time period, those members of the assembly appointed to this ministry come forward at this point. As directed by the presiding minister or deacon, a fragment of the bread is placed in a pyx which is then put in a small bag with a cord, and placed around the neck of the eucharistic minister. The presiding minister may say a short prayer or sentence of commissioning as they prepare to depart.

When circumstances prevent communion being taken to the housebound directly from the altar table in the context of the eucharist, the pyx containing the consecrated bread is placed in the aumbry or tabernacle until such time as the eucharistic minister is able to gain access to those due to receive.

After all have received communion, and (where communion of the housebound occurs) after the eucharistic ministers have departed, the presiding minister invites the assembly once again to make a profound bow, to emphasize the transcendent nature of the ritual act in which they have just taken part and the wondrous gift received.

The presiding minister will make the invitation with a few words of explanation:

Before the mystery of what we have received at God's table, and what we have become, let us again make a deep bow of reverence.

After making the profound bow, members of the assembly are asked by the presiding minister to return to their seats. Meanwhile the deacon and/or other ministers carry out the ablutions, consuming the sacrament and cleansing the vessels.

The ablutions

Decently and in order

One of the bits of 'culture shock' that hit me on transferring to another province of the Anglican Communion was the alacrity with which many clergy would overcome the problem of over-consecration at diocesan events by pouring the surplus out in the garden. Perhaps this was untypical, as I have always explained to confirmation candidates that the careful consumption of the elements left over was a mark of the Anglican way, as opposed to the Protestant approach where anything could happen in this regard.

Those of us from the Catholic tradition of Anglicanism were trained to go further and always insist that the ablutions take place immediately after communion, which was not allowed in the *Book of Common Prayer* (1662) but was de rigueur nonetheless. Waiting until the very end was a mark of a very different eucharistic theology.

So the ablutions reverently and carefully carried out are an important sign that all things should be done 'decently and in order' (1 Cor. 14.40), and they should be completed therefore in full view of the assembly as a gentle reminder that the Sacrament is not something that can be discarded after use.

If it is the tradition of the community to reserve the sacrament permanently for the sick, the presiding minister should do so at this point, as the deacon and/or other assistants complete the ablutions. The presiding minister should place in the aumbry the sacrament to be reserved, in one kind only. This is for the practical reason that wine is difficult to store effectively and to transport easily, and for the not-so-practical reason that this is Catholic practice (and for me the only way I know). Whatever kind of bread is used within the eucharist itself, a certain number of unleavened wafers will need to be consecrated, alongside the one loaf, for the purposes of sick communions later in the week. Yes, this is a compromise with the pure gospel of real bread, but a necessary one unless the housebound are to be fed stale bread.

The place of reservation should be at some distance from the altar table, preferably in a separate space altogether or at least quite distinct from the space around the altar table. As well as facilitating the speedy communion of those critically ill or confined to hospital, the reserved sacrament is also for many a focus for private prayer, and the place of reservation should be a quiet place where silent prayer is a realistic expectation.

Once the ablutions are completed, the deacon and other ministers return to their places in the seated assembly.

10 The post communion

Ceremonial

A period of silence is announced and the assembly sits in silent reflection.

The presiding minister then leads the whole assembly in saying the post-communion prayer.

The announcements are made.

When pastoral considerations require it, the presiding minister invites the assembly to pray over those members in special need, with the laying-on of hands and anointing with oil.

Commentary

The post communion is the graveyard of many a good liturgy, the section when everything so easily unravels and falls apart. It's a bit like playing injury time in a soccer game: you may be in the lead, but you dare not drop your guard for one second.

The post communion is also a moment when something of a struggle takes place between the purist and the practical-minded. A choice has to be made.

At St Gregory's, San Francisco, the layout of the liturgical space is such that the assembly, having celebrated the synaxis in one 'room', seated antiphonally around ambo and presiding minister's chair, then moves at the offertory, dancing as it goes, to another 'room' empty of chairs, in the centre of which stands the altar table. The second room is in fact the room adjoining the main doors of the building, so that at the conclusion of the eucharistic rite – after a slimmed-down almost unnoticeable post-communion section – the dismissal is given and the assembly moves immediately *where it stands* into socializing mode. The coffee urn is brought in and placed on the altar table which now, with theological deliberation, becomes the breakfast buffet. For those who cannot stay, the dismissal leads immediately to exit through the doors adjoining.

This dynamic movement from (liturgical) communion to communion of a different kind (but also holy) has great appeal, and maintains something of the terseness and vigour of the ancient form of dismissal in the Roman rite: *Ite missa est*, or, 'Go, mass is ended', or perhaps even, 'It's all over; get out of here!' Certainly the St Gregory's pattern reconnects the liturgy with the world outside, with its expectation of re-entry into, and interaction with, the stream of humanity beyond those particular walls. It has about it a great purity and directness which is very appealing.

At Philadelphia Cathedral we experimented with this same pattern throughout the period of renovation, when for worship we camped out in our cathedral office building, using different rooms for synaxis and anaphora. Our community took to it well, and had no difficulty with eating regular food from the table at which we had just received the sacrament.

This pattern is maintained at our weekday noon eucharist when, bearing in mind the tight schedule of those working in the neighbourhood, time is of the essence. In these circumstances our cathedral practice is for the assembly to remain standing around the altar table for post-communion prayer and dismissal, from which point we disperse.

For the cathedral's Sunday Liturgy, however, now that we have returned to our renovated liturgical space, a different order has been developed. For us the problem with what might be called the 'purist model' is that it is bad for one's digestion – it allows insufficient time to digest the miracle of our transformation in the mystery of the eucharist and to reflect quietly upon who we are and what are becoming, before we hit the streets, or the streets hit us. We need a 'decompression chamber' and the post communion should supply that.

After the communion, therefore, it is good to return from the altar table to our seats where we began, and to ponder all that has happened to us since we last sat there (was it only 20 minutes ago?). A period of silence, announced by a gong or bell

A period of meditation after communion

as before, is therefore essential after communion if we are to 'digest' our holy food and grasp the wonder of what has happened to us, of the profound mystery of Christ into which God has invited us as his priestly community.

At Philadelphia, depending on the liturgical season, we often take this a step further, inviting the assembly to go from the altar table not to their seats, but to disperse throughout the cathedral, to find a corner where, sitting or standing or kneeling, one can be alone. The lights are turned down low, silence is kept, and one of the ministers offers over the microphone a few verbal pegs – perhaps a poem or brief meditation – on which we might hang some thoughts. A number of seasonal suggestions are included in Appendix L.

After the gong sounds (possibly after just four or five minutes), members of the assembly return to their seats.

If the assembly has not dispersed through the liturgical space for a meditation period, people return directly to their seats after the profound bow at the altar table, and maintain a period of silence. 'This silent time too is an expression of communion. Habits of prayer need to be formed' (Huck, 1998, p. 89). At the end of the period of silence, the musicians gently lead the assembly into a reflective liturgical song – the kind of song that British composer Bernadette Farrell excels in writing. A couple of verses of 'Bread for the World' will suffice to make the point (the first person to bleat about 'banal' modern hymnody can go and stand in the corner):

Lord Jesus Christ, you are the bread of life,
broken to reach and heal the wounds of human pain.
Where we divide your people you are waiting there
on bended knee to wash our feet with endless care.

Lord Jesus Christ, you call us to your feast,
at which the rich and powerful have become the least.
Where we survive on others in our human greed
you walk among us begging for your every need.
(in *Gather Comprehensive*, 1998)

Following the song, the assembly stands to say together the post-communion prayer. Availability of these prayers will depend on where we find ourselves ecclesiastically speaking, but Rome has always supplied these, and now the Church of England has followed suit in *Common Worship* (2000) with a post-communion prayer for every Sunday, related to the day's theme. Only the Episcopal Church restricts its members to a choice between two hardy perennials.

This arrangement may have the advantage that the assembly can learn them by heart (although you'd never guess it from the anxious flicking of the pages) but it gets awfully boring. More importantly it misses out on the opportunity to round off the theme of the day with a prayer related to the Scriptures read in the liturgy. In this technological age, however, these new and 'illegal' post-communion prayers can pop up on computer screens anywhere in the world, even the United States of America. The liturgical cat is out of the bag.

Following the post-communion prayer the announcements are made. That simple statement will immediately irritate a good many readers, because multitudinous indeed are the different views on where the announcements should be made, and passionate their champions.

A lay leader makes the announcements

The notices

The *Book of Common Prayer* (1979) offers four places where the notices or announcements may be made, two of which are non-starters.

First option. The least satisfactory of all is the position immediately after the creed, a place also suggested in *Alternative Service Book 1980* although dropped in *Common Worship* (2000) after common sense prevailed. This position is simply intrusive, guaranteed to completely disrupt the flow of the liturgy. The only point to commend it – that the notices may inform the prayers of the people that follow – is insufficient justification for throwing a wrench in the liturgical works.

Second option. In second place in the unsatisfactory stakes comes the position for the announcements before the liturgy, which is inevitably sabotaged by latecomers. Now we may want to ignore latecomers, but they are often the people we need to get through to, especially if it's an appeal about not being late. It's Murphy's Law if there is a very important announcement that everyone needs to hear, then the people that most need to hear it will stroll in two minutes later. Then we find ourselves saying, 'For those of you who were not here earlier . . .' and submit the assembly to two doses of the medicine.

Even if everyone is on time, the moments before the liturgy begins are not the time to make announcements. This is a time to be still, to stop the chatter and prepare. Announcements at this point will serve only to agitate the waters, and get the mental list-making going at full tilt – of messages to give, people to see, things to arrange – and sometimes the temptation to do those things *now* instead of waiting until after the liturgy will be too great.

Third option. In third place comes the position for the notices 'before the offertory', presumably immediately after the Peace. This has the advantage of concealing the disruptive quality of the announcements in the general mêlée of the Peace, but nevertheless remains a disruption providing details of events happening which will then threaten to give the Peace a second burst of life as those vital messages are exchanged. The announcements are not a good preparation for going to the altar of God with singleness of heart and mind.

Fourth option. For these reasons the fourth option seems the least intrusive, as it shortens to an absolute minimum the gap between the news and the chance to talk about the news. The *Book of Common Prayer* (1979) places this option 'at the end of the service' and, although it is not clear what exactly is meant, in practice a position between the post-communion prayer and the blessing and dismissal works best. This position is also recommended in the *General Instruction of the Roman Missal* (II.90). Waiting until after the liturgy will result in people 'slipping away' as the notices are given, as well as depriving the musicians of their dramatic moment in which to play the assembly out in style.

The presiding minister should always delegate the giving of the announcements to a lay leader of the assembly. In the Anglican tradition this will mean a church warden or a team leader. This sends a significant message that the pastor is a chaplain to the community, and the community has a life of its own. The pastor is not the be all and end all.

Announcements have a bad name for hijacking the liturgy, and they make the liturgical purists groan. They need to be contained, and should not repeat things already described in the news bulletin to be handed out, although special big events can be highlighted. The fact that a lay leader will be making the announcements does, however, make a huge difference. Here is a different voice from that which we have listened to for much of the liturgy, a new angle, a fresh energy. The announcements in this context can be fun, even an art form, with the assembly enjoying them and the presiding minister not having to worry about a thing. Occasionally, very occasionally, the presiding minister will need to add a word as pastor of the community, something which it is appropriate for the pastor alone to say. The presiding minister should, however, use this opportunity extremely sparingly.

One pastoral situation that does need to be met within the liturgy, perhaps fairly regularly, and which requires the presiding minister's leadership, is the need to pray over a member of the assembly, with the laying-on of hands and anointing with oil.

Anointing

Once upon a time there was a sacrament called 'Extreme Unction', in which (I seem to remember from my boyhood) anointing of the sick was delayed until the eleventh hour, until death was imminent. In this way, the gift of God for healing and wholeness (James 5.14–15) was subverted into a final pastoral act for those about to depart this world. As an example of how the Church has contrived over the centuries to undermine the purpose of the mysteries of which it is called to be steward and guardian, that surely takes the biscuit.

Thanks largely to the charismatic renewal movement which reinvigorated much of mainstream Christianity during the 1970s, ritual anointing with the laying-on of hands has been liberated from the death-bed scene into the full and vigorous life of the Church. Anointing is now an experience of life's journey familiar to a great many Christians, and is incorporated into the regular worship, at least on an occasional basis, of more and more faith communities. We are less embarrassed (and that's saying something if you are of Anglo-Saxon stock) to be around people who are surrendering themselves in God's hands, and more sure that we have a part to play in the healing and reconciliation that flows from a community's familiarity with the presence and power of God.

The assembly's need to minister sacramentally and corporately to one of its number may arise when a member is going into hospital for tests or surgery, or leaving to live in another part of the country, or beginning a pregnancy or giving thanks for a birth. Whatever the situation, if it is something where we wish to galvanize the prayers of the assembly, then it is good to invite the person(s) concerned into the midst of the assembly, to be prayed over, anointed, sent forth with love. The presiding minister will need to assess the precise need, often in that precise moment. Sometimes a 'no-fuss' solution will be appropriate, with a prayer led by the presiding minister. At other times the whole assembly should come forward to lay on hands as an act of loving solidarity.

Giving thanks for a safe delivery

As always in these situations, the mutuality of ministry is experienced afresh. It is those ministered to who often end up strengthening those who minister, while those who minister learn a new humility and wonder before the reality of God's presence at work in ordinary, and sometimes broken, human beings.

Such a ceremony of prayer, thanksgiving or blessing sits very well at this point between the announcements (where a word of explanation may be given) and the blessing and dismissal (when the whole assembly is prayed over and sent forth).

Alternatively, it may transpire during coffee hour that someone is in need for whom anointing and the laying-on of hands would be appropriate. Those with ministerial responsibility should in these circumstances alert the presiding minister, who will then gather together an appropriate number of the assembly to exercise this ministry. In these circumstances those requiring this ministry would be led back into the worship space, and anointing with oil and the laying-on of hands would be administered in a suitable place. The baptismal font is highly appropriate, for it symbolizes the waters by which grows the tree of life whose leaves are 'for the healing of the nations' (Rev. 22.2).

11   The blessing and dismissal

Ceremonial

The presiding minister raises his/her hands over the people and prays for and blesses the assembly. The assembly responds with a loud 'Amen!'
   The deacon or (if there be no deacon) a lay minister proclaims the dismissal.
   The presiding minister and other ministers process to the main doors of the space.

Commentary

The blessing and dismissal have a very interesting liturgical history, and in various periods have jockeyed for position. Galley (1989, p. 129) summarizes the history most helpfully, explaining that of these two components of the ending of the liturgy, it is the blessing that is the interloper.

For many centuries the eucharist ended with a post-communion prayer and dismissal. It was thought that the eucharist was blessing enough, and that to add a further blessing was superfluous. The blessing became customary only in the Middle Ages, and probably derived from the blessing by the bishop of his flock as he processed out. When it first appeared, it was thought of as taking place *after* the liturgy, and in fact followed the dismissal.

Strangely, the Reformers mostly copied this medieval development instead of returning to primitive practice. The first English Prayer Book of 1549 went so far as to require a blessing and to scrap the dismissal altogether, and this has remained standard Anglican practice until the revisions of the last 50 years.

The Episcopal Church led the way, in its 1967 trial use liturgy, in a movement back to primitive practice in the justifiable belief that, as the liturgical renewal drew us back to the origins of our rites, the blessing would be an early victim. Sadly, they have not been rewarded for their bold leadership, and have had the experience of looking round to find no one following them. Both the Roman and Lutheran rites have retained the final blessing as mandatory, while the Church of England in *Common Worship* (2000) has at least made a gesture towards primitive practice in making the blessing optional and the dismissal obligatory.

The final approval of the *Book of Common Prayer* (1979) saw the Americans sticking to their guns, providing no words at all for the optional blessing, but no less than four options for the obligatory dismissal.

The final blessing therefore appears to be one of those liturgical phenomena which, while departing from primitive practice and without an adequate theological basis, seem to have a life of their own.

It must be said that the blessing, or more precisely the prayer that leads into it, gives a sense of 'rounding off' the whole liturgical action in a way that the dismissal alone,

The blessing

in its urgency and brevity, fails to do. It also provides the presiding minister with yet another opportunity to weave the theme of the day or the message of the homily into the preparatory prayer. An example from *Common Worship* (2000), which contains seven different blessings plus one for each season, will indicate its potential as a summation of the whole liturgical action:

> *Blessing to be used from Ash Wednesday until the Saturday after the Fourth Sunday in Lent:*
>
> Christ give you grace to grow in holiness,
> to deny yourselves, take up your cross, and follow him;
> and the blessing . . .

In view of the undoubted usefulness of the blessing therefore, despite its doubtful pedigree, Galley's suggestion that a blessing be given except in Lent is a good one. At weekday eucharists the dismissal alone should always suffice.

Following the reflective reassurance of the blessing, the dismissal is a sharp change in tempo and import. The assembly is exhorted to 'get out there and get busy' as salt and yeast transforming the world. Another voice is required and another rhythm, and if a deacon is not available, a (lay) liturgical assistant should do the proclaiming.

The dismissal

As with the opening sentence at the very beginning of the liturgy, the dismissal should be proclaimed boldly and with a sense of expectation, as though someone will actually listen and respond. The form that seems to have gained most ground in recent years, that is the second option in the *Book of Common Prayer* (1979) and now the first in *Common Worship* (2000), is 'Go in peace to love and serve the Lord'.

This has an excellent ring to it, that links the peace known within the assembly with the service of the world, of those who are yet to find peace. The *Book of Common Prayer* (1979) is more sensible in making the response to all its options the constant 'Thanks be to God'. *Common Worship* (2000) gives a different response: 'In the name of Christ. Amen.' This is less successful, not least because I was taught never to say 'Amen' to one's own prayers. *Common Worship* (2000) also gives different responses for each of the options, a disastrous thing to do because these responses are not read but remembered, and in my experience there is invariably a split-second but noticeable delay in the response as the assembly desperately tries to remember which one is which.

At the Sunday Liturgy, where there is a final hymn during which the presiding minister and other ministers exit, the dismissal may be given after the hymn, at the main doors, thereby reducing to a minimum the gap between the assembly's dismissal and its immersion in the world.

The post liturgy

Ceremonial

The presiding minister and other ministers process to the main doors of the space.

Members of the assembly greet newcomers and other guests and guide them to the place of hospitality, where refreshments are served for all who have taken part in the liturgy.

A period of education or training may follow.

Commentary

Welcome and hospitality are included in this liturgical overview, because unless the Sunday Liturgy concludes with hospitality it would be as well to have no liturgy at all. This assertion is the logical extension of the truth, revealed by the Liturgical Movement, that the eucharist is not a personal devotion but a communal meal.

Although aspects of personal devotion will always remain, the eucharist is primarily the joyous assembly of the community of faith around the table of the Lord.

Ever since Paul chastised his baby church at Corinth for confusing the eucharist with a feast, the Church has been nervous of attempting the two together, except perhaps for some form of agape meal or seder in Holy Week (hardly a good time for a feast anyway). After nineteen centuries perhaps we can venture to reunite, to some small degree, the liturgical and the regular forms of communal meal.

Hospitality is essential, for without it we deny all that we have said and done in the previous 90 minutes celebrating the eucharist. We also abandon the open table which was the hallmark of the ministry of Jesus. The 'open table' is not just a liturgical policy worked out in the safe confines of the liturgy with the distancing our rituals provide, but a way of life which needs to be lived out the moment the liturgy is ended. Here in the place of hospitality we shall be truly vulnerable to each other and to the person who walks in off the street, as Jesus was. Here we have opportunities to show we mean what we say.

Essential hospitality

After the dismissal the presiding minister and other ministers make straight for the door, not in solemn procession, but a dignified and purposeful walk. While the doorway is no place for a self-respecting presiding minister to be seen lurking *before* the liturgy, when he/she should be totally absorbed in quiet preparation, the leaders of the assembly should be assiduous in their dedication to hospitality immediately *after* the liturgy. Although chasuble and stole should be removed, there may be no time to remove albs before there is someone who needs greeting or directing.

This work of welcoming the stranger is not of course the presiding minister's or pastor's alone, but the ministry of the whole assembly. The Churches of the West have woken from sleep to find themselves in a mission field, and learning to be good at the ministry of welcome, as a community, needs to be a top priority. Books and workshops abound on how to do it. All that needs to be said here is that it needs to be done and done as part of the liturgy, our words of warm welcome, of concern, our listening and our embrace, all flowing from the revelation made fresh to us in the eucharistic assembly that we are children of God and ambassadors of Christ.

I said 'welcoming the stranger' because that is the priority. After ensuring that all new faces are accounted for and are, if they wish to hang around, in good company, the ministers can retire to the sacristy to disrobe before rejoining the crowd. The regulars can fend for themselves for the moment, as there will be opportunity enough over refreshments to spend time with them. The newcomers are the VIPs, and befriending them (and getting those names and addresses) should take precedence over other calls on leaders' time at this point.

Sharing some birthday news

The location of hospitality needs also to be given careful consideration. For evangelistic reasons, a separate building is no good, be it ever so handsome or well equipped. The people you need to entice there will have skipped bail long before you reach there, and all we end up with is the usual crowd of 'in' people, while the 'outsider' stays well and truly 'out'.

An adjoining hall is fine, but the transition needs to be made direct and easy. Just one bend in the corridor, or a gap between buildings, and the cry will go up, 'Oh I'll leave it until next week.' For these pressing reasons, unless the hall is right next door, it may be necessary to serve refreshments in the narthex or in the liturgical space itself. At the end of the day, the solution will be 'whatever works'. Whatever it takes to make it happen, needs to happen, for the assembly has good news to share.

Following refreshments, or overlapping with them, many parishes find it a good time to invite those who have worshipped together to an 'adult forum' or period for teaching or training, when an aspect of the church's life or worship can be further explained, and questions asked. This is more often the case in parishes in the United States, but is a good model to follow especially in churches with scattered communities for whom getting together at another time in the week is difficult to arrange. A light lunch is often a good way to build up a sense of community and to cement newer members into this many faceted Sunday experience.

In this Sunday pattern incorporating the elements of worship, social gathering, sharing a meal and learning, we are beginning to experience again the pattern of the early Church as its tiny communities spent the Lord's day together and so learnt to survive and prosper in a hostile environment.

At the beginning of the third Christian millennium, we again need to learn those simple steps by which our spiritual ancestors took giant leaps. Let us begin by relearning how to 'make eucharist', and let us pray that, from our own encounter with God's transforming power in the glory and joy of the eucharistic assembly, we ourselves may become agents of transformation and reconciliation in a broken and hungry world.

Notes

1 This was supplied by Jennifer Lord, Assistant Professor of Worship and Preaching, Lancaster Theological Seminary, Pennsylvania.

Appendix A
Following the Way

A spiritual insight from the Sufi mystic tradition of Islam, courtesy of M. R. Ritley, presbyter of the parish of St Gregory of Nyssa, San Francisco.

This is a lesson on following the Way. Remember it.

How do you follow the Way?
Go where you are sent.
Wait till you are shown what to do.
Do it with the whole self.
Remain till you have done what you were sent to do.
Walk away with empty hands.

How much will it cost?
The cost is everything, for all you are and all you have
will be asked of you before the journey runs its course.

How will you know your fellow travellers?
Their faces are marked by the scars of love.

No one will ever tell you that the Way is easy: only that it is possible.
No one can tell you if the journey is worthwhile,
for your wages are concealed in the hand of God,
and will be shown you only on the last day of eternity.

But whoever chooses to follow the Way
will have the joyous company of God's beloved fools as fellow travellers,
and a resting place, at journey's end, in the Mecca of the heart.

This is the lesson on following the Way. Remember it.

Appendix B
Alternative penitential rites

Penitential rites which allow flexibility are to be preferred above those which rely on a set prayer of penitence which, however inspired in its composition, will inevitably become over-familiar and stale.

The most convenient form is the threefold Kyrie, repeated by the assembly. These can be easily adapted to fit any season or situation, drawing on scriptural themes. Three examples are included below.

I
Lord, your son Jesus is the light of the world.
Forgive us when we prefer darkness to light.
Lord have mercy.
Lord have mercy.

Lord, your son Jesus came that we may have life in all its fullness.
Forgive us when we are content with less.
Christ have mercy.
Christ have mercy.

Lord, your son Jesus shows us the way to the Father.
Forgive us when we turn aside from your path.
Lord have mercy.
Lord have mercy.

2

Lord, your servant Jesus preached good news to the poor.
Forgive us when we are blind to our own poverty.
Lord have mercy.
Lord have mercy.

Lord, your servant Jesus proclaimed liberty to captives.
Forgive us when we spurn your freedom.
Christ have mercy.
Christ have mercy.

Lord, your servant Jesus brought sight to the blind.
Forgive us when our eyes remain closed.
Lord have mercy.
Lord have mercy.

3

Lord, your son Jesus came to reconcile us to you and to each other.
Forgive us when we cling to our resentments.
Lord have mercy.
Lord have mercy.

Lord, your son Jesus emptied himself for us.
Forgive us when we are full of ourselves.
Christ have mercy.
Christ have mercy.

Lord, your son Jesus laid down his life for his friends.
Forgive us when we cannot let go.
Lord have mercy.
Lord have mercy.

Common Worship (2000) has many examples of such alternatives (pp. 123–34).
   There are in addition many musical resources to enliven the penitential rite, for example the Kyrie from Marty Haugen's *Holy Communion: Tree of Life Setting* (copyright 2000 GIA Publications, Inc.). The *Lutheran Book of Worship* (Augsburg, 2002) contains various musical settings of the eucharist, each with a sung penitential

rite, as does *Gather Comprehensive* (GIA Publications, 1998). *Wonder, Love and Praise* (New York: Church Publishing, 1997) also contains a selection of Kyries.

It is extremely effective to use periods of silence for penitential reflection, at the end of which a phrase of a well-known Kyrie is sung. The timeless and hauntingly beautiful Kyrie from the *Missa de Angelis* works very well in this way.

A further variant is to use a refrain *ostinato* – repeated softly over and over again – while the presiding minister or deacon speaks a penitential prayer(s) over it.

Appendix C
Opening prayers

Taking as an example the Third Sunday of Lent, here are some various responses made by different traditions to the need for a collect which gathers together the themes of that day. Let the fifth example speak for itself:

> Eternal Lord, your kingdom has broken into our troubled world through the life, death, and resurrection of your Son. Help us to hear your word and obey it; so that we become instruments of your redeeming love; through your Son, Jesus Christ our Lord, who lives and reigns with you and the Holy Spirit, one God, now and forever.
>
> *Lutheran Book of Worship*

> Father, you have taught us to overcome our sins by prayer, fasting and works of mercy. When we are discouraged by our weakness, give us confidence in your love.
>
> *Roman Missal*

> Almighty God, you know that we have no power in ourselves to help ourselves: Keep us both outwardly in our bodies and inwardly in our souls, that we may be defended from all adversities which may happen to the body, and from all evil thoughts which may assault and hurt the soul; through Jesus Christ our Lord, who lives and reigns with you and the Holy Spirit, one God, for ever and ever. **Amen.**
>
> *Book of Common Prayer* (1979)

> Almighty God,
> whose most dear Son went not up to joy but first he suffered pain,
> and entered not into glory before he was crucified:
> mercifully grant that we, walking in the way of the cross,
> may find it none other than the way of life and peace;
> through Jesus Christ your Son our Lord,

who is alive and reigns with you,
in the unity of the Holy Spirit,
one God, now and for ever.
> *Common Worship* (2000)

O God, living and true,
look upon your people,
whose dry and stony hearts are parched with thirst.
Unseal the living water of your Spirit;
let it become within us an ever-flowing spring,
leaping up to eternal life.
Thus may we worship you in spirit and in truth
through Christ, our deliverance and our hope,
who lives and reigns with you in the unity of the Holy Spirit,
holy and mighty God for ever and ever.
> *Opening Prayers* (International Commission on English in the Liturgy)

Appendix D
Gospel acclamations

The great thing is to put behind us for ever the custom of singing a hymn (perhaps broken up into two, before and after) to announce or frame the Gospel. The tradition of the Church is to announce the Gospel with a scriptural text from the Gospel itself, framed by joyful alleluias. In Lent, this is replaced by a gospel acclamation devoid of alleluias.

There are countless alternatives, and, once again, both *Gather Comprehensive* and the *Lutheran Book of Worship* provide many examples.

Here are a few:

Alleluias:
'Alleluia! Alleluia! Alleluia!' (*Gather Comprehensive*, 177)
'Halle, Halle, Hallelujah' (*With One Voice*, 612)
'Hallelujah! We sing your praises' (*Wonder, Love and Praise*, 784)
'Alleluia! Lord to whom shall we go?' (*With One Voice*, p. 17)

Lenten refrains:
'Praise to you, O Christ our Saviour' (*Gather Comprehensive*, 515)
'Return to the Lord' (*Lutheran Book of Worship*, p. 63)

Appendix E
Alternative affirmations of faith

The simplest way to create some variation in the assembly's corporate affirmation of faith is to recite the creed responsively, creating a dialogue between presiding minister and assembly. The *Book of Common Prayer* (1979) provides a responsive version of the Apostles' Creed (p. 293) as part of the Renewal of Baptismal Promises at the Easter Vigil, with supplementary questions and promises, while a responsive version of the Nicene Creed can be found in *Common Worship* (2000, p. 139).

If we are feeling a little more adventurous, *Common Worship* (2000) is particularly rich in the provision of alternative affirmations using passages of Scripture, of which the following are two examples.

Let us affirm our faith in Jesus Christ the Son of God.

All
Though he was divine
he did not cling to equality with God,
but made himself nothing.
Taking the form of a slave,
he was born in human likeness.
He humbled himself
and was obedient to death,
even death on the cross.
Therefore God has raised him on high,
and given him the name above every name:
that at the name of Jesus
every knee should bow,
and every voice proclaim that Jesus Christ is Lord,
to the glory of God the Father.   cf. Philippians 2.6–11
Amen.

Let us declare our faith in the resurrection of our Lord Jesus Christ.

All
Christ died for our sins
in accordance with the Scriptures;
he was buried;
he was raised to life on the third day
in accordance with the Scriptures;
afterwards he appeared to his followers,
and to all the apostles:
this we have received,
and this we believe.   cf. 1 Corinthians 15.3–7
Amen.

Threefold affirmations based on early baptismal rites are also a frequent alternative, and provide a trinitarian base to the formula. One example is a (more inclusive) variation on a format contained in *Common Worship* (2000, p. 144).

Do you believe and trust in God the Father,
source of being and life,
the one for whom we exist?
All   **We believe and trust in God.**

Do you believe and trust in God the Son,
who took our human nature,
died for us and was raised again?
All   **We believe and trust in God.**

Do you believe and trust in God the Holy Spirit,
who gives life to the people of God
and makes Christ known in the world?
All   **We believe and trust in God.**

This is the faith of the Church.
All
This is our faith.
We believe and trust in one God,
Father, Son and Holy Spirit.
Amen.

If we wish to throw caution to the winds, it is an instructive (if exhausting) experience for a community of faith to engage in the process of developing its own interpretation in contemporary language of the essentials that hold us together.

Here is one example from our own cathedral community:

We believe and trust in God
who holds in existence all that is,
and yet is father and mother to us all.

We follow Jesus, God's anointed, God's beloved,
who showed us the mind and the heart of God
and whose love is stronger than death.
Through him we have life,
life in all its abundance.

We open ourselves to the Spirit of God,
who moved over the face of the waters at the beginning of time,
and today in the waters of baptism:
the Spirit who now lives within us
and by whom we cry out to God
with sighs too deep for words,
knowing ourselves to be God's beloved children.

Appendix F
Guidelines for the prayers of the people

Once we have let go of the crutches of set prayers read from a book, we can take our first steps towards prayers emerging from and expressive of our local community of faith. These can be further enlivened by the use of more than one voice, or by the prayers being spoken over a refrain sung by the assembly *ostinato*. The Taizé chants 'O Lord hear my prayer' or 'Bless the Lord, my soul' are but two examples of the numerous chants which would fit the bill.

It is helpful to provide guidelines for those exercising the ministry of leading the assembly in prayer, and as a starter the guidelines we use at Philadelphia Cathedral are included below.

Leading the Prayers of the People:

A General
    1 Let *thanksgiving* predominate.
    2 Avoid the 'shopping list' approach to God understood as Santa Claus.
    3 Recall Archbishop Michael Ramsey's definition of intercession – 'standing before God with you in my heart'.
    4 Don't tell God what is happening in the world.
    5 Don't preach a sermon.
    6 Don't spout political propaganda.

B Procedure
    1 Explain clearly at the outset what response the assembly is called upon to make, and the cue for them to come in:
      e.g. Lord in your mercy
          Hear our prayer

or

Lord hear us
Lord graciously hear us.

2 Bear in mind the areas to be covered, without slavishly following a check-list:
the Church – at home and abroad
         – our own diocese and our companion diocese
         – our bishops and other leaders
the world
those in need (avoid long lists!)
the saints we commemorate this week
the departed.

3 Ring the changes with the order of concerns.
4 Occasionally break the mould.

C Preparation
  1 Study the scripture readings for the Sunday concerned.
  2 Read the newspapers, watch the news.
  3 Be sensitive to concerns and events within the assembly.
  4 Spend time in stillness before God.
  5 Arrive early for the Liturgy, to be available for those who wish to raise prayer concerns.
  6 Listen carefully to the homily and if possible insert into the prayers phrases which echo its themes.

Appendix G
Alternative introductions to the Peace

The Peace should always be set in a scriptural context which eliminates the element of surprise and which recalls the assembly to the primary importance within the liturgy of reconciliation and unity.

Common Worship (2000) provides no fewer than seven introductions to the Peace (p. 290), but the themes of reconciliation and peace are so widespread in the New Testament that devising even more is not a hard task. Further examples might be:

Christ came and proclaimed peace
    to you who were far off and peace to those who were near.
Let his peace be shared among us,
    that we may be built together into a dwelling place for God.   (Eph. 2.17, 22)

Jesus said 'Whatever house you enter,
    first say, "Peace to this house!"'   (Luke 10.5)

Let those who desire life,
    seek peace and pursue it.
For the eyes of the Lord are on the righteous,
    and his ears are open to their prayer.   (1 Pet. 3.10–12)

Appendix H
Alternative preliminary (offertory) prayers

The *Roman Missal* provides a prayer over the gifts particular to every Mass, of which a typical example is the following (for the Third Sunday of Easter):

> Lord, receive these gifts from your Church.
> May the great joy you give us
> Come to perfection in heaven.

Likewise the *Lutheran Book of Worship* provides two alternative prayers to be said after the gifts have been presented, the shorter of which reads:

> **Merciful God,**
> **we offer with joy and thanksgiving**
> **what you have first given us –**
> **our selves,**
> **our time,**
> **and our possessions,**
> **signs of your gracious love.**
> **Receive them for the sake of him**
> **who offered himself for us,**
> **Jesus Christ our Lord. Amen.**

Anglicans have long dragged their feet in this regard. The *Book of Common Prayer* (1979) made no provision for such a prayer, while the *Alternative Service Book 1980* contained just one option (to be said by the whole assembly):

Yours, Lord, is the greatness, the power,
the glory, the splendour, and the majesty;
for everything in heaven and on earth is yours.
All things come from you,
and of your own do we give you.

All this changed, however, with *Common Worship* (2000), which provides no fewer than twelve prayers for use 'at the Preparation of the Table' (pp. 291–3).

The selection above includes the prayers over the gifts from the *Roman Missal*, as well as a prayer based on the *Didache*, as well as some new ones of simple elegance:

Wise and gracious God,
you spread a table before us;
nourish your people with the word of life
and the bread of heaven.
Amen.

Interestingly, *Common Worship* (2000) suggests that it 'will sometimes be appropriate to ask children' to speak these prayers. If this for some seems a rather daring departure from orthodox practice, it is salutary to remember that it was in a church of the Roman tradition (in deepest Perigord Blanc) that I was privileged to witness a Sunday Mass where the parish priest invited the children to form a circle around the altar table with him to say the institution narrative. So offertory prayers are by comparison small potatoes.

When the children are involved, *Common Worship* (2000) suggests the following:

With this bread that we bring
we shall remember Jesus.

With this wine that we bring
we shall remember Jesus.

Bread for his body,
wine for his blood,
gifts from God to his table we bring.
We shall remember Jesus.

Appendix I
Alternative eucharistic prayers

As with affirmations of faith, it is a sign of a healthy and mature community of faith when the assembly can set about creating a eucharistic prayer appropriate to its own story and situation. Here is an example from our cathedral community in Philadelphia which took as its starting point the insights of Arthur Peacocke.

The Lord be with you
And also with you
Lift up your hearts
We lift them to the Lord
Let us give thanks to the Lord our God
It is right to give God thanks and praise.

Great and glorious God, Ultimate Reality, Ground of all Being,
    you penetrate all-that-is with your eternal life and unfathomable richness
    and show us through nature, through experience
    and through the sacred writings of all who have yearned for you,
    your steadfast and faithful love for all that you hold in being.

Though we can ignore the divine presence, and alienate ourselves from you,
Jesus the Anointed One, the firstborn of your new creation,
    shows us a humanity transparent with the love that is God,
    in whom we may find our full potential,
    and learn how to live, to love, and to die.

As we now gather in Jesus' name around this table,
    as did his friends on his last night on earth,
    we thank you for counting us worthy to stand before you with hands uplifted
    in praise and thanksgiving, confident in your love.

We ask you to bless these offerings of bread and wine
   as you have blessed them throughout time
   and as you blessed them at the hands of Jesus, your Beloved.

May this broken bread and wine outpoured be to us
   means of grace and tokens of the presence of Jesus, Risen Lord,
   who stands among us now, bearing the wounds of love.

Send your Spirit upon these gifts and upon us,
   that these holy things may nourish us on our way to holiness
   that, together with your servant . . .
   we may become what you long for us to be;
   your beloved and anointed ones,
   filled, in Christ, with the life of God.

To you, o great and generous God, be all glory and honor,
   thanksgiving and praise, now and for ever.

Appendix J
Alternative doxologies

Where the *Sanctus* is not used as a triumphal song of joy at the conclusion of the eucharistic prayer, there are many alternatives available to serve the same purpose.

For example, *Gather Comprehensive* contains a doxology and great Amen by Marty Haugen (no. 296), and *The Hymnal 1982* contains several Amens (S142 to S147). *Ritual Song* (GIA Publications, 1998) is the richest resource in this regard, with seven musical settings of the eucharist, each with its own doxology (nos. 308 to 376). In addition there is a section of doxologies and great Amens from composers including Dufford, Haugen, Joncas and Proulx, all of whom can be relied upon to deliver the goods.

Two of the three musical settings for the eucharist found in *With One Voice* (Augsburg Fortress Press 1995) contain a sung doxology to the eucharistic prayer.

Lambeth Praise (Morehouse Publishing, 1998) is typical of the many collections of hymns and songs that feature world music which can be used appropriately here, such as the Amen based on a Chinese folk melody (no. 224), the Hallelujah from Zimbabwe (no. 233) or the Imela ('We thank you') from Nigeria (no. 236).

In fact any good chant or chorus of praise will serve well at this point in the liturgy, and it is sometimes fun to hijack those evergreen charismatic choruses for this purpose. For example:

We see the Lord,
we see the Lord,
he is high and lifted up and his train fills the temple.
The angels cry 'holy',
the angels cry 'holy',
the angels cry 'holy' is the Lord.

or,

He is Lord,
he is Lord,
he is risen from the dead and he is Lord.
Every knee shall bow, every tongue confess,
That Jesus Christ is Lord.

Appendix K
Alternative settings of the Lord's Prayer

Singable and memorable settings of the Lord's Prayer in its contemporary form are not that easy to come by, but surprisingly *The Hymnal 1982* has one of the best: David Hurd's version from his 'Intercession Mass' (S150).

The version popular with many African-American congregations is the Albert Hay Malotte Lord's Prayer found in H. C. Boyer, *Lift Every Voice and Sing II* (New York: Church Publishing, 1993).

As with doxologies, several settings of the Lord's Prayer are to be found in *Ritual Song*: in three of the seven musical settings of the eucharist, and two more in the section headed 'Service Music' (nos. 464 and 465). Lutheran sources are, however, more scarce, although the *Lutheran Book of Worship* provides a sung Lord's Prayer in one of its three settings for the eucharist (p. 112); *With One Voice* does not.

Appendix L
Sources of readings

When it comes to using sources for reflective meditation, everything is fair game. Sometimes the Scriptures themselves will be unbeatable as a commentary on the theme of the day and on this moment in the liturgical journey, but they will need to be read as poetry rather than a 'lesson', without the paraphernalia of chapter and verse, introduction or response. Verses from Isaiah 40 in Advent, or from Lamentations in Holy Week, are obvious examples of those times when the Scriptures seem to have been written with the liturgy in mind.

When we look beyond the Scriptures, we first encounter a whole host of resources specially designed for this purpose, outstanding among which are the worship resources produced by the Iona Community, published in the UK by the Wild Goose Resource Group and in the USA by GIA Publications. *Cloth for the Cradle* (Advent, Christmas and Epiphany) or *Stages on the Way* (Lent, Holy Week and Easter) are fine examples (both published in 2000). They include group readings and meditations which can stop us in our tracks to view the events they address as if for the first time.

All too often, however, material specifically designed for religious services is too 'churchy' and too wordy, and confines us to the shallow waters close to the shore of the familiar. A far richer source is literature which, while perhaps written from within a framework of belief (though not necessarily so), was not intended for religious use. Its relocation in a meditation within an act of worship can be stunning. Such poetry or prose can, if chosen carefully, illuminate sacred events with a remarkable appropriateness which can bring a smile to one's face or a shiver down one's spine.

A couple of examples will suffice. For Epiphany, T. S. Eliot's *Journey of the Magi*, with its opening line, 'A cold coming we had of it', will always be a favourite, but is a little long for insertion into a eucharistic rite. U. A. Fanthorpe's 'BC:AD' fits the bill perfectly (*Selected Poems*, Penguin, 1986).

In Lent, my old hero Geoffrey Studdert Kennedy, in his poem 'Temptation', describes the wrestling match of life better than most, and in a very few lines:

Pray? Have I prayed! When I'm worn with all my praying!
When I've bored the blessed angels with my battery of prayer!
It's the proper thing to say – but it's only saying, saying,
And I cannot get to Jesus for the glory of her hair.

Material with no overt pretensions to spirituality can also be extremely effective. If you want to close Compline with a hymn to God's protection, try playing the track 'Where the Angels Meet' from Bar Scott's CD *Grapes and Seeds* (LMP 04, available from www.barscott.com), a song written originally to sing to sleep her son Forrest. If you turn the lights down low and allow her remarkable voice to echo through a darkened worship space, as the presiding minister sprinkles the people before we go our separate ways to rest and sleep, then the goose bumps are guaranteed:

Go to sleep now, it's time to dream
and go to where the angels meet.
They'll shower you with kisses
and shelter you from harm
and bring you safely back in to my arms.
They will feed you milk and honey
from streams that flow with love
all around you stars will shine
where the angels meet.

Appendix M
Music resources

Compiled by Robert P. Ridgell, Director of Music, Philadelphia Cathedral
(music@philadelphiacathedral.org)

Awake, O Sleeper, rise from death, and Christ shall give you light, so learn God's love – its length and breadth, its fullness, depth, and height.
F. Bland Tucker

One of the crises facing the liturgical church today is the lack of creativity and competence in church music. Part of the problem is cultural. We live in a society that is musically very intelligent. So much so that music becomes everything to our ears. The commercial, the entertainment, the icon of popularity, the technology, the industry of digital recordings have changed much of what was in the past to a completely new and vibrant world of music. Church music has maintained its change not only due to new liturgical realms, but most importantly because of the cultural changes in daily musical life. Music is essential in the liturgical life and mission of the Church, even as a sacramental sign of God's presence and action in the world.

There are many church musicians today who constantly fight against the new for various reasons. Some think 'this is bad music'. Some think 'this music is not appropriate for church'. All these opinions are important and should be respected, for it is in all opinions that musicians are given natural opportunity to enlighten, inspire, and to help create worship of the highest order. Simply said: there is a place for all kinds of music in the Church. Remember, all music was once new. When looking at the music of the fourteenth to fifteenth centuries, composers often used 'pop' tunes of the day for melodic inspiration in polyphonic Mass settings. The reality of today's problems is not always, 'What kind of music should we hear?' – but rather, 'How do we make the music, and how do we perform the music well to the glory of God?' It is important to understand that there needs to be an aesthetic beauty in all styles of church music. The focus of today is the renewal of liturgical music to an extraordinary degree. The time is now.

It is both the Church's responsibility and those to whom music is their soul, to find and maintain their competence in singing, playing, directing, conducting, composing and performing music. As the Church maintains its cause to 'foster the arts' we must realize that there are standards of excellence which need to be developed in theory and in practice. For those who work in cathedrals or parishes with greater resources, they have a special responsibility to model excellence in liturgical music performance. Even the smallest parish has an equal responsibility to maintain genuine quality. One important aspect of this is: simple can be effective.

Nonetheless, the most important skill of the church musician is the ability to make music. Thus, it is the responsibility of the Church and the personal responsibility of others to encourage good keyboard playing skills which encourage congregational singing, good vocal technique and basic musical skills which lead people to confidence in song. Just as it is also the Church's responsibility to continue the musical education of children and youth, to help foster the cause of making music well. Last but not least, it is the pastoral leadership of the parish which is the single most influential factor in the liturgical musical life of the Church. Yet, the music education of most seminarians in this area remains seriously inadequate. Ongoing education of clergy and musicians, and resources such as moral and financial support, help improve the state of church music.

It is perhaps common to recreate a 'boxed-up' version of music by using only one or two hymnals in a parish church. This is an easy and common way of musical life in the liturgical church. However, plain and simple – music in the church is not a one-way street. It requires massive amounts of creativity and passion to awaken our minds. There are many forms and genres of music that help promote congregational, choral, cantorial, diaconal and presidential singing. As well, there are many effective instrumental genres from organ and piano music to trumpet, violin, oboe and harp repertoire which help enlighten the mind. The value of the pipe organ is at times the most effective leader of congregational singing, especially in large assemblies. With its wide dynamic range, and variety of tonal colour and especially its air-supported sustained sound, the pipe organ helps communal song.

Once again, as soon as we launch out beyond the familiar configuration of our own little inlet, we shall be amazed at the rich resources out there in open water. It is important to note that there are many 'hybrid liturgy-music' programmes, but it takes far more creative outlooks to see that in the sciences of liturgy, theology, pastoral skills and music all become the boat in which we ride in the open water of musical resources. Many parishes, especially smaller ones, are limited in material and personnel resources. Today there exists a need for the development of more adequate resources which enable sung liturgy in such communities. Essential is a body of congregational music which is easily readable, easily learnt and of sufficient quality to endure across generations. Part of the development in the renewal of liturgical music is what is known as 'ritual music'. This is music that is tied to ritual forms such as music during blessings or immediately after eucharistic actions.

The Roman tradition – perhaps it had more catching up to do in the field of music for the whole assembly in the wake of Vatican II – offers the most extensive resources to complement a renewed liturgy. Primary among them are:

Gather Comprehensive (GIA Publications, 1998)

Ritual Song (GIA Publications, 1998)

Hymns for the Gospels (GIA Publications, 2001)

Lead Me Guide Me (GIA Publications, 1987)

Taizé: Songs of Prayer (GIA Publications, 1998)

African American Heritage Hymnal (GIA Publications, 1998)

Celebration Hymnal for Everyone (McCrimmons, 1994)

Be Still and Know (Kevin Mayhew, 2000)

New Hymns and Worship Songs (Kevin Mayhew, 2001)

Glory and Praise, 2nd edn (Oregon Catholic Press, 2000)

Cánticos, segunda edición (Oregon Catholic Press, 2001)

By Flowing Waters – Chant for the Liturgy (a collection of unaccompanied song for assemblies, cantors and choirs by Paul F. Ford (Collegeville, MN: The Liturgical Press, 1999)

In general, you cannot go far wrong with composers such as Christopher Walker, Bernadette Farrell, Paul Inwood, Richard Proulx, Margaret Rizza, Malcolm Archer, John Bell, Marty Haugen and the Taizé and Iona Communities who seem to have precisely caught the mood of the Church's awakening from slumber especially in the area of using Gospel acclamations, eucharistic acclamations, and other forms of ritual music. The GIA hymnal series also provides a rich collection of musical resources for the catechumenate, the ordinary of the liturgy (Kyrie, Gloria, Sanctus, Agnus Dei) and also good hymnal-like canticles for the Magnificat.

The use of percussion is very effective and quite easy for congregational participation. Shakers are highly recommended, as well as small tam-tams and, of course, the natural percussion of clapping. Most often clapping and the like is perfect for native African/Caribbean chants, and alleluias. Usually this genre is ideal for Gospel acclamations.

It is highly recommended to have an appointed percussionist for particular moments in the liturgy. For example, percussion can be used in between readings, during the exchange of the Peace, or even as a well-improvised Postlude. Rainsticks and soft percussion instruments are most effective for sprinkling songs, softer songs, but should be employed sparingly as they can lose their effect if overused.

Even with the wealth of Roman material in the English-speaking world, there is a lack of Roman and Anglican focus on 'world music'. One of the most important aspects of being creative as a church musician is not to follow the path the publishers give you. It is critical always to hunt for new songs – even secular songs that might be adapted to fit a certain liturgical need. One of the best 'world music' hymnals is Anglican. Anglicans have not been adventurous in publishing music to enrich renewed liturgy, and the main hymnals on both sides of the Atlantic have remained cautious in their selections. Interestingly, the hymn book produced especially for the 1998 Lambeth Conference, compiled by its music director Geoff Weaver, takes us further than most, with a fine worldwide selection:

Lambeth Praise (Morehouse Publishing, 1998).

Other musical resources for ethnic and multicultural possibilities are:

Songs of Zion (Abingdon Press, 1981). African-American hymnal supplement from the Methodist Church. Excellent arrangements of spirituals and some traditional evangelical and gospel hymns.

Hymns from the Four Winds (Abingdon Press, 1983). A collection of Asian-American hymns.

Sound the Bamboo, ed. I-to Loh (The Christian Conference of Asia, 2000). A pan-Asian hymnal, with more than 300 pieces from 38 original languages.

In Spirit and in Truth (World Council of Churches, 1991). This has 66 pieces, from Taizé and Mt Athos to El Salvador and the Philippines. Helpful in introducing multicultural music to a congregation.

In the USA, *Wonder, Love and Praise*, the 1997 Supplement to *The Hymnal 1982*, edges slightly out from the shore, but only just:

Wonder, Love and Praise (New York: Church Publishing, 1997).

Most of the Episcopal Church USA musical resources are excellent for a steady diet of traditional hymns and service music; however, as the Church changes, the music changes. Some of the parishes in the Episcopal Church USA are having a difficult time balancing choices and variety of music. For example, a parish might have up to three or four hymnals in a pew. That is a huge issue of books for the average member of a congregation to deal with. One should very much consider the abilities to print service music in a service leaflet rather than using hymn books. It may require extra work in the long term, but this is part of finding the creative – rather than the restrictive. It also allows for better concentration to participate in the liturgy.

The Lutheran Community (ELCA) has kept steady pace and beyond as far as venturing into new territory of liturgical music. In fact, they have recently published a very fine supplement hymnal:

Renewing Worship Songbook (Augsburg Fortress Press, 2003).

Some other good Lutheran resources are:

This Far By Faith (Augsburg Fortress Press, 1999). African-American source.
Libro de Liturgia y Cántico (Augsburg Fortress Press, 2001). Latin American source.

The use of psalm singing is perhaps the most important element in a renewed liturgy. In the early 1950s, a new method of singing the psalms was developed by the Jesuit, Joseph Gelineau. Gelineau sought to preserve the rhythmic structure inherent in Hebrew poetry. Psalm singing has been renewed in many places especially through the use of cantor/congregational interaction. Most of the Roman song books have responsorial psalms for the entire liturgical year.

This form of congregational participation is perhaps the best use of singing the psalms because the use of psalm tones distinguishes them from other forms of music sung in the congregation. They provide a musical expression that is conducive to sung prayer, and singing the psalm to psalm tones is best understood as 'sung recitation'. Responsorial psalms engage worshippers at two levels: inwardly, as they pray the psalm as the cantor or singers prayerfully sing the psalm text, and then outwardly, as they affirm the psalm by singing the refrain. Another fine form is to alternate cantor and congregation using monastic tones. St Meinrad Archabbey in Indiana has some of the most beautiful psalm tones. Below are several sources for psalm singing.

A Hymn-Tune Psalter: Gradual Psalms by Carl P. Daw, Jr. and Kevin R. Hackett (New York: Church Publishing, 1999). A collection of gradual psalms pointed to original simplified Anglican chant tunes, which may be sung by a group of singers or cantors. The unique aspect of this collection is that the tunes for the congregational antiphons are adapted from familiar, appropriate hymn tunes.

The Portland Psalter by Robert A. Hawthorne (New York: Church Publishing, 2002). They vary in difficulty and harmonic style, making effective use of the modern, using dissonance, jazz idioms and traditional harmonic progressions.

The Celebration Psalter by Betty Carr Pulkingham and Kevin Hackett (Aliquippa, PA: Celebration Community, 1991 and 1992).

A New Metrical Psalter by Christopher L. Webber (New York: Church Publishing, 1986). This metrical method fits psalms to simple hymn melodies.

The Psalter: Psalms and Canticles for Singing (Louisville, KY: Westminster John Knox Press, 1993). From the Presbyterian Church (USA). Excellent array of responsorial psalms. Highly recommended.

Respond and Acclaim by Owen Alstott (Portland, OR: Oregon Catholic Press, 2002).

Music for Liturgy from Saint Gregory of Nyssa (1999) by St. Gregory of Nyssa, California. A variety of musical resources including psalms and canticles, representing a large diversity of traditions, countries, languages and styles including historical American idioms (Billings, Shaker, Navajo and folk hymnody).

Many of the volumes from the Iona Community have some psalm settings (Glasgow: Wild Goose Publications; Chicago, IL: GIA Publications).

In being creative, it is sometimes very difficult for the volunteer church musician to know the historical and choral aspects of church music. Here are some very good educational tools:

John Bertalot, *5 Wheels to Successful Sight-Singing* (Augsburg Fortress Press, 1993).

John Bertalot's Immediately Practical Tips for Choral Directors (Augsburg Fortress Press, 1994).

Henry Eskew and Hugh T. McElrath, *Sing with Understanding* (Nashville, TN: Church Street Press, 1995).

Jan Michael Joncas, *From Sacred Song to Ritual Music* (Collegeville, MN: The Liturgical Press, 1997).

Paul Westermeyer, *Te Deum: The Church and Music* (Minneapolis: Fortress Press, 1998).

There are many American-English resources available for church musicians. However, one of the best ways to continue the growth of a parish music programme is to contact monasteries, cathedrals and churches around the world. 'No man is an island' and neither is the church musician! It is extremely important to maintain contacts with colleagues and other musicians to hunt for new liturgical music that is creative and full of renewed life. There is a great deal of liturgical music renewal in France, Germany and Italy, as well as many of the Asian countries. The growing amount of liturgical music is astounding.

However, there is much to be done to help the creative elements of music-making. Improvisation, flexibility and liturgical studies are all key ingredients into making a cosmic liturgy that beautifully expresses the joy and delight which prefigure the glory of the liturgy of the heavenly Jerusalem. There needs to be a constructive and respectful spirit to the ongoing discussion of musical issues which often remain controversial, unresolved or even divisive, and to engage the wider ecclesial community in advancing the greater good of the Church's life in the area of liturgical music. Moreover, there must continue to be musicians trained to think 'outside of the box'. There is always going to be an entertainment or therapeutic ethos in liturgical music, which might constitute a serious problem that results in consumerism, individualism, sentimentality, introversion and passivity. Thus, various musical styles and expressions must be clearly learned and understood in order to avoid these pervasive tendencies in church music. The music of the Church, like the Church itself, is the people. It is time to awaken and jolt the church with bursts of musical energy, passion and spirit, and to do it all very well.

Appendix N
Arts resources

UK

Art and Christianity Enquiry (ACE)
107 Crundale Avenue, London NW9 9PS.
E-mail: enquiries@acetrust.org

Church Building magazine
St James Buildings, Oxford Street, Manchester M1 6FP.
Telephone: +44 (0)161 236 8856

USA

Center for Liturgy and the Arts
4327 Ravensworth Road #210, Annandale, VA 22003-5632.
Telephone: +001 703 941 9422
Fax: +001 703 941 9422
E-mail: ArtWithYou@aol.com

E&A Letter
Liturgy Training Publications, 1800 North Hermitage Avenue,
Chicago, IL 60622-1101.
Telephone: +001 800 933 1800
Fax: +001 800 933 7094
E-mail: orders@ltp.org
Website: www.ltp.org

Appendix O
Liturgical resource centres

UK

St Columba's House
Maybury Hill, Woking, Surrey GU22 8AB
Telephone: +44 (0)1483 766498
Fax: 01483 740441
E-mail: retreats@stcolumbas.co.uk
Director: Fr Paul Jenkins

Sarum College
19 The Close, Salisbury, Wiltshire SP1 2EE
Telephone: +44 (0)1722 424800
E-mail: lc@sarum.ac.uk *or* admin@sarum.ac.uk

Worth Abbey
Crawley, Sussex RH10 4SB.
Website: http://www.osb.org

USA

Georgetown Institute of Liturgy
3513 N Street NW, Washington, DC 20007.
Telephone: +001 202 687 4420
E-mail: liturgy@georgetown.edu
Website: www.georgetown.edu/centers/gcl/

Philadelphia Liturgical Institute
3723 Chestnut Street, Philadelphia, PA 19104-3189.
Telephone: +001 215 386 2216
E-mail: liturgy@philadelphiacathedral.org
Website: www.philadelphiacathedral.org

Saint John's Abbey, Collegeville, Minnesota
Saint John's Abbey, Collegeville, MN 56321-2015.
Telephone: +001 320 363 2011
Fax: +001 320 363 2504
E-mail: roliver@csbsju.edu
Website: www.saintjohnsabbey.org

Saint Gregory of Nyssa Episcopal Church, San Francisco
500 DeHaro Street, San Francisco, CA 94107-2306.
Telephone: +001 415 255 8100
Fax: +001 415 255 8120
E-mail: office@saintgregorys.org

Standing Commission on Liturgy and Music
Episcopal Church Center, 815 Second Avenue, New York, NY 10017-4564.
Telephone: +001 212 716 6000 *or* +001 800 334 7626

Bibliography

Adams, W. S. 1999. *Moving the Furniture*, New York: Church Publishing.

—— 1995. *Shaped by Images*, New York: Church Publishing.

Alternative Service Book 1980, Clowes, SPCK, CUP, Hodder & Stoughton, OUP, Mowbray.

Bianchi, E. 2002. *Words of Spirituality*, London: SPCK.

Book of Common Prayer. 1979. New York: Seabury Press.

Book of Occasional Services. 1997. New York: Church Publishing.

Bradshaw, P. 1992. *The Search for the Origins of Christian Worship*, Oxford University Press.

—— 1996. *Early Christian Worship*, London: SPCK.

Bradshaw, P. (ed.). 2002. *The New Dictionary of Liturgy and Worship*, London: SCM Press.

Cobb, P. G. 1987. 'The *Apostolic Tradition* of Hippolytus'. In Jones, Wainwright and Yarnold (eds), 1987.

Common Worship: Services and Prayers for the Church of England. 2000. London: Church House Publishing.

Davies, J. G. (ed.). 1986. *A New Dictionary of Liturgy and Worship*, London: SCM Press.

Day, T. 1998. *Why Catholics Can't Sing*, New York: Crossroad.

Dillard, A. 1982. *Teaching a Stone to Talk: Expeditions and Encounters*, San Francisco: Harper & Row.

Dix, G. 1964. *The Shape of the Liturgy*, London: Adam and Charles Black.

Enriching Our Worship. 1991. New York: Church Publishing.

Evangelical Lutheran Church in America. 2002. *Principles for Worship*, Minneapolis, MN: Augsburg Fortress Press.

Fischer, B. 1981. *Signs, Words, and Gestures*, Pueblo.

Flannery, A. (ed.). 1996. *Vatican Council II: The Conciliar and Post-Conciliar Documents*, Costello Publishing/Dominican Publications.

Foley, E. 1991. *From Age to Age*, Chicago, IL: Liturgy Training Publications.

Fowler, G. 1995. *Dance of A Fallen Monk*, New York: Doubleday.

Galley, H. E. 1989. *The Ceremonies of the Eucharist*, Boston, MA: Cowley Publications.

Gibson, E. C. S. (ed.). 1964. *The First and Second Prayer Books of Edward VI*, London: J. M. Dent.

Giles, R. 1999. *Re-Pitching the Tent: Reordering the Church Building for Worship and Mission*, London: SCM Press.

Hadaway, C. K. 2001. *Behold I Do a New Thing*, New York: Pilgrim Press.

Hall, J. 1976. *The Full Stature of Christ*, Collegeville, MN: Liturgical Press.

Hatchett, M. J. n.d. 'A Manual of Ceremonial for the New Prayer Book', *St Luke's Journal of Theology*.

Hebblethwaite, P. 1993. *Paul VI*, Mahwah, NJ: Paulist Press.

Huck, G. 1998. *Liturgy with Style and Grace*, Chicago, IL: Liturgy Training Publications.

The Hymnal 1982, New York: Church Publishing.

Instruction on the Worship of the Eucharistic Liturgy. In Flannery (ed.), 1996.

Jones, Wainwright and Yarnold (eds). 1987. *The Study of Liturgy*, London: SPCK.

Kavanagh, A. 1990. *Elements of Rite*, Collegeville, MN: Liturgical Press.

Küng, H. 2002. *My Struggle for Freedom: Memoirs*, Grand Rapids: Eerdmans.

Lathrop, G. 1993. *Holy Things*, Minneapolis, MN: Fortress Press.

—— 1999. *Holy People*, Minneapolis, MN: Fortress Press.

Leonard, J. K. and Mitchell, N. D. 1994. *The Postures of the Assembly During the Eucharistic Prayer*, Chicago, IL: Liturgy Training Publications.

Lutheran Book of Worship. 2002. Minneapolis, MN: Augsburg Fortress Press.

Michno, D. G. 1998. *A Priest's Handbook*, Harrisburg, PA: Morehouse Publishing.

Middleton, A. P. 1988. *New Wine in Old Skins*, Harrisburg, PA: Morehouse-Barlow.

Nhat Hanh, T. 1995. *Living Buddha, Living Christ*, New York: Riverhead Books.

Norris, K. 1996. *The Cloister Walk*, New York: Riverhead Books.

Pagels, E. 2003. *Beyond Belief*, New York: Random House.

Peacocke, A. 2001. *Paths from Science Towards God*, Oxford: One World Publications.

Philippart, D. 1996. *Saving Signs, Wondrous Words*, Chicago, IL: Liturgy Training Publications.

Phillips, C. (ed.). 2002. *Gerard Manley Hopkins: The Major Works*, Oxford World's Classics.

The Roman Missal. The Sacramentary. Revised according to the second editio typica of the Missale Romanum (1975), March 1 1985, New York: Catholic Book Publishing Co.

Rosenthal, J. with Currie, N. 1997. *Being Anglican in the Third Millennium*, Harrisburg, PA: Morehouse Publishing.

Ryan, G. T. 1993. *The Sacristy Manual*, Chicago, IL: Liturgy Training Publications.

Saliers, D. E. 1994. *Worship as Theology*, Nashville, TN: Abingdon Press.

Saxbee, J. 1994. *Liberal Evangelism*, London: SPCK.

Stancliffe, D. 2003. *God's Pattern*, London: SPCK.

Stevenson, K. 1986. *Eucharist and Offering*, Pueblo.

Stevenson, R. L. *Travels with a Donkey*, Everyman's Library.

Stevick, D. 1987. *Baptismal Moments, Baptismal Meanings*, New York: Church Publishing.

—— 1990. *The Crafting of Liturgy*, Church Hymnal Corporation.

Stuhlman, B. D. 1987. *Prayer Book Rubrics Expanded*, Church Hymnal Corporation.

—— 1988. *Eucharistic Celebration 1789–1979*, Church Hymnal Corporation.

—— 2000. *A Good and Joyful Thing*, New York: Church Publishing.

Thompson, B. 1961. *Liturgies of the Western Church*, World Publishing.

US Conference of Catholic Bishops. 1978. *Environment and Art in Catholic Worship*.

—— 2000. *Living Stones: Art, Architecture and Worship*.

—— 2002. *General Instruction of the Roman Missal*, International Commission on English in the Liturgy Inc.

Index